Gay Relationships

Also by the author:

How to Be a Couple and Still Be Free (with Riley K. Smith)
Love Styles: How to Celebrate Your Differences

GAY RELATIONSHIPS

For Men and Women

How To Find Them
How To Improve Them
How To Make Them Last

TINA TESSINA, Ph.D.

JEREMY P. TARCHER, INC.
Los Angeles

Library of Congress Cataloging in Publication Data

Tessina, Tina B.
Gay relationships: how to find them, how to improve them, how to make them last / Tina Tessina.
p. cm.
1. Gay couples. 2. Interpersonal relations. I. Title.
HQ76.25.T37 1989 88-35956
306.7'66—dc19 CIP
ISBN 0-87477-517-5

Jeremy P. Tarcher, Inc.
9110 Sunset Blvd.
Los Angeles, CA 90069

Distributed by St. Martin's Press, New York

Manufactured in the United States of America
10 9 8 7 6 5 4 3 2 1

First Edition

To Richard, who earned it,
and who shares all my adventures,

and to all my gay and lesbian
clients and friends, who can't be named,
but who taught me what I know
and inspired this book.

Contents

Acknowledgments

Many thanks to Jeremy Tarcher, who is truly involved in the books he publishes. I have enormous respect for him and his wisdom. Thanks also go to his staff, who are relentlessly cheerful and efficient on the phone when who knows what is going on around them.

Thanks to Hank Stine, executive editor, who understood and helped conceive this project, and who supported me even when I called, in a panic, in the middle of the night.

Thanks to Janrae Frank, my agent, who made contract negotiations easy and fun.

Thanks to Rick Benzel, my editor, who went over and over every word, idea, and example, who made me be clear and concise, and who worked hard under a tight deadline to do it. He taught me a lot, and even managed to have a sense of humor about it.

Thanks to editor Mary Nadler for her expert and sensitive work.

As always, thanks to my first book "angel," Al Saunders, and my dear friend and colleague Riley K. Smith. Without them I would never have written at all.

Thanks to three accomplished and respected writers who have been very supportive and generous with their time and expertise: Dr. Warren Farrell, for his sound advice and "male nurturing"; Dr. Jeanne Segal, for her wisdom about healing and for listening, sharing, and caring; and Arno Karlen, for his excellent research on homosexuality, and for his pearls of wisdom.

Thanks to my secretary, Kathy De Mille, whose sense of loving service and cheerful cooperation always lights up my workweek.

Thanks to the Metropolitan Community Church, Long Beach, especially Reverend Dusty, Reverend Bjørn, and Reverend Frank, for inviting me to teach and do therapy there and for providing me with information, advice, and encouragement.

Thanks go, too, to AIDS Project/Los Angeles and to the Unified Community Center, Long Beach—especially to Ruby, for always having answers.

Thanks to my dear friends Ron, Maggie, Eddie, Scott, Lewis, Sylvia, Glen, Jim and Jim, Chuck, Dave, Matt, Victoria, Toni, and Barbara, for supporting me, putting up with me, giving me input, and dragging me away from the word processor when I was about to get burned out. What would I do without you?

Thanks to my messenger crew, Cheryl, Victoria, Ron, and Clay, who schlepped chapters back and forth through rain and gloom of night.

The true authors of this book are all my gay and lesbian friends and clients, including members of my Thursday evening drop-in group, whose lives were the models and whose courage and determination enabled them to make their dreams come true. I couldn't have written this book without them.

Preface

*I*f you are gay or lesbian, and you are

- not in a relationship, but wanting to be,
- about to begin a relationship,
- currently in a relationship, or
- hurting from the ending of a relationship and wondering how to make your next relationship better

this book can be your guide. It is based on a single premise that I have believed and endorsed throughout my years of helping gay and lesbian individuals and couples: *people who happen to love others of the same gender have the same needs for intimacy, comfort, and stability as the rest of the population.*

Gay men and lesbian women can fall in love. They can learn to make their relationships work, and they can build long-term partnerships. This book is dedicated to gay relationships—how to find them, how to improve them, and how to make them last.

For the past fifteen years, I have been counseling people in what I call alternative and creative relationships. About half of my clients have been gay or lesbian. I have worked with hundreds of homosexual people in individual or couple sessions, and with many more in lectures, seminars, classes, and workshops. During the same period, I have also counseled heterosexual, bisexual, and transsexual people. For *all* of my clients, I have focused on the development of healthy and fulfilling relationships, in whatever lifestyle context this happens to be.

While most relationships—whether heterosexual or homosexual—have similar dynamics and problems, people in gay and lesbian relationships can benefit from specific and specialized information. For example, you and your partner need to know how homophobia—fear of homosexuality—affects you and your relationship. You also have to deal with gender-role confusion, with where to find role models and support for your relationship, and with coming out to family. You need to know about your rights as a gay couple under the law, and about establishing relationship traditions and ceremonies. In addition, if you're closeted at work, there are special pressures on your relationship that you should understand. While there are many, many books available concerning heterosexual relationships, to date I have found few relationship-skills books on the market that meet the special needs of gay relationships, and none that are this comprehensive.

Over the years I have heard numerous fears and mistaken beliefs about relationships from my gay and lesbian clients, as exemplified in the following statements and questions:

> "Gay men are more promiscuous than anyone else. They don't have long-term relationships."
>
> "There aren't very many lesbian couples."
>
> "My parents don't believe my relationship is real, because they don't want to accept that their son loves a man."
>
> "I want to move in with David, but I'm scared. I don't know what the rules are for two *men* in love."
>
> "How can I be friends with women and not make my [lesbian] lover jealous?"
>
> "I've tried counseling before, but the counselor wouldn't help me with my relationship; he wanted to change my sexuality."
>
> "I know I don't want my relationship to be like Mom and Dad's, but what other options do I have?"

Gay Relationships is my response to such fears and doubts, which can prevent you from living and loving happily and successfully. This book addresses not only your fears and doubts but also your wants, needs, and hopes, and it gives practical, step-by-step guidelines and exercises that can help you find love and improve your relationships. It covers all aspects of gay courtship, from finding a lover, to dating, to commitment and marriage, to handling in-laws, legal matters, and joint finances. I hope you will find it a good read, a useful how-to book, and a valuable reference volume.

This book is designed to be read, reread, used by you and your partner separately and together, and referred to frequently throughout your relationship. As a self-help book, it is aimed specifically at men and women who are currently in homosexual relationships or who are actively seeking gay partners. The subjects covered are drawn from the questions asked most by my gay and lesbian clients. For reasons of privacy, all actual names and identifying details have been changed in the text.

Where appropriate, I have included as background the psychological motivations and inner reasons that lead us to behave as we do. Many of the fears and problems that come up for us in relationships are connected to our childhoods, our family dynamics, and our histories in previous unsuccessful relationships. Understanding this background can provide us with insight about the changes we may need to make in our relationships. In addition to insight, however, we need practical, how-to information. The Reverend Denton Roberts, author of *Able and Equal: A Gentle Path to Peace* (and my mentor and supervisor before I was licensed), puts it this way:

> All of us have bright, insightful, and even inspiring ideas that we'd like to adopt, but *how* to establish them is often a major obstacle for us. So, we gradually abandon the "good" ideas because we have inadequate means for establishing them in our thought. But by focusing on methods for change, I hope to get past this obstacle. Once we experience ourselves as knowing *how* to make a change, we usually address issues with enthusiasm and vigor.
>
> In my clinical practice, in my institutional life, and in my personal relationships, my most frequent block to changing from maladaptive functioning to healthy functioning is "I don't know how!" This is the major resistance to change encountered in my experience and in the experience of those I work with."

In response to this reality, *Gay Relationships* is short on background and long on specific examples, exercises, and advice.

I begin with general information about gay relationships, contrasting and comparing homosexual and heterosexual love patterns. I discuss why homosexual relationships have tried to imitate straight models, and whether or not there are better alternatives. I also examine the significant differences between male and female homosexual relationships.

The book then follows the development of gay relationships

from the search for a suitable lover, through the beginning of the romance and its development, and even to its possible end. There is considerable research showing that love relationships develop in predictable stages. I have loosely followed these developmental phases, analyzing each stage and incorporating useful information and effective techniques for success. Because my assumption is that you want to know how to handle your situation immediately and you may feel anxious and urgent, I have made the tone of my advice reassuring, confident, and matter-of-fact.

In addition, at the back of the book you will find three appendixes. These provide, respectively, a list of resources for support and legal advice; information on safe-sex practices; and information on homophobia and how to deal with it.

One caveat: While you can accomplish a vast amount of growth, learning, and problem solving on your own with the aid of books such as this, there is also great wisdom in knowing when to seek objective, professional help. Abuse (sexual, verbal, psychological or physical) and addiction are two relationship dynamics that are too complex and compelling for most people to solve using self-help techniques alone. I also recommend that a couple seek counseling if they cannot solve a problem together within a few days.

Some words on the terminology used in this book: The politically correct terminology for homosexual men and women is still in debate. Does *gay* refer only to men and *lesbian* only to women, or is it okay to use the term *gay* for both? While I know many women who strongly prefer the term *lesbian,* I know an equal number of women who prefer to be called gay. Wherever it is necessary in this book to make a distinction between men and women, I use the terms *gay men* and *lesbian women.* When there is no need to make the genders specific, I use the term *gay persons* (or *gay relationships, gay community,* and so on). In instances in which I need to be especially clear that the writing is inclusive of women, I use a phrase such as "gay and lesbian community." I also prefer the use of "gay," "lesbian," and "homosexual" as adjectives rather than nouns, because people are defined by much more than their sexual preferences. I hope you will bear with this terminology, accepting my apology for its necessity.

Another term I use here, with some reservation, is *straight* in referring to heterosexual (or undeclared) persons or groups. I dislike the implication that anyone who is not "straight" must be "crooked," but as everyone I know uses this term continuously and comfortably, I will use it here for ease of expression.

In referring to sexual/life/love partners, I generally use the terms *partner, lover,* or *spouse* throughout the book. Please take these terms to mean the significant person or persons with whom you share deep emotions, sexual play, living quarters, or any combination of these.

Some of you may also question my use of the term *we,* because I am obviously not a gay man, and I'm bisexual rather than a lesbian woman. However, I feel a strong sense of shared experience with the gay and lesbian community. My credentials include fifteen years of active participation in that community, as well as a circle of dear friends that includes people of all sexual persuasions. When I use "we" in this book, it is because I have personally experienced whatever I am referring to at the moment. Wherever your experiences differ from mine, consider the "we" rhetorical.

It is hoped that our grammar and terminology will someday catch up with our personal growth. In the meantime, we do as well as we can with what we have.

I have done my best to make *Gay Relationships* a survival manual, a guide, and a book of inspiration. Enjoy.

CHAPTER 1

Gay Relationships: What Are They?

Perhaps you, like many of my gay clients, have been going to bars searching for a companion, a long-term partner. You're discouraged and tired of this scene, and you're beginning to wonder if there are any serious homosexual people for whom you could feel love and a sense of commitment.

Perhaps you are a gay male who has had lots of sex partners, none of whom has turned out to be a lover. You're tired of this pattern and are seeking something more meaningful.

Or perhaps you are a lesbian woman, living with a lover but finding that the relationship has begun to feel tense, unsatisfying, and unstable. You're tired of struggling with partners, and you want to learn how to choose a better mate.

Or perhaps you're a gay man or lesbian woman who is in a good relationship, but you're wondering how far it can go. You want to deepen the love and intimacy you already have, and you want to avoid making mistakes that might jeopardize the bonds you've established with your partner. You're looking to achieve greater security and a more fruitful, fulfilling partnership, one that might last for many years.

No matter which of the above scenarios applies to you, the questions that brought you to this book are the same. As a gay person, you want to know the answers to these questions:

- What is healthy gay love, and can you have a successful, committed gay relationship?
- How can homosexuals love and live within an often homophobic social atmosphere?
- What relationship options do gay couples have (for example, friendship, dating, being lovers, living together, commitment, and marriage)?

- Where can you find role models that exemplify a lasting gay or lesbian relationship?
- How can you deal with being closeted, or with your lover being closeted?
- What impact does AIDS and the fear of AIDS have on your sexuality and your relationship?

As a gay man or lesbian woman, you're seeking answers to these questions because your fears and doubts about relationships undermine the quality of your life. Sometimes your frustration and confusion lead to despair, and you find yourself accepting inappropriate, uncaring, or abusive partners because you think you will never find the relationship you really want.

The good news is that you're not alone, and that this book provides you with the answers you need. Thousands of other gay men and women are confused about relationships, unable to keep them, or disillusioned when they can. Many gay and lesbian clients come to me confused and afraid about relationships, having failed at several. They want to know how to find a lover, how to date, and how to evaluate potential candidates. They're not sure if they want commitment, marriage, or monogamy. Like you, they, too, are wondering if gay relationships can succeed.

I assure you, gay and lesbian relationships can and do work. They can be as beautiful, as richly satisfying, as successful and rewarding, and as full of love as any other relationship. Let's begin now to see why gay people can feel hopeful about love, and how they can learn to find it in caring, lasting relationships.

THINKING POSITIVELY ABOUT GAY RELATIONSHIPS

I believe that now is the time for more gay and lesbian individuals to consider long-term relationships. There is currently a growing base of support, and a feeling of safety and acceptance, within the homosexual community for looking at the quality of one's life—and this includes love.

For years, being gay meant being ostracized, isolated, and condemned. Many of us were hidden, known only to a sexual partner or a lover. Because of the need for secrecy, life as a homosexual was very stressful and was focused on survival. Several factors are now converging that allow the gay and lesbian population to focus on, and to feel more positive about, entering long-term relationships that can survive openly and honestly.

Safe Sex

While new attitudes had begun to develop before AIDS appeared, this devasting disease has definitely encouraged gay people to reflect seriously about their relationships. The severity of AIDS and other sexually transmitted diseases has given all of us a new motivation to view long-term committed relationships as safer. In order to protect our health, most of us have learned to limit our sexual practices to safe-sex practices. Along with other factors, the health issue has helped to accelerate a natural growth phase in the community toward honest and caring relationships.

Media Image

Although there are still people who refuse to see it, many medical, political, and social groups have been impressed and enlightened by the heroic way in which the gay and lesbian community has responded to the AIDS problem. The story of our sexual and social responsibility—educating ourselves and caring for one another—has been told repeatedly in the media.

Our community's response to AIDS, coupled with activism, has enhanced the media image of gay and lesbian lifestyles enough to encourage many frightened and closeted gay and lesbian people to believe they can have a viable, open lifestyle and workable relationships.

Activism

Political repression and bigotry against homosexuals are now often exposed in an unfavorable light in the media. The gay population has found its voice, and through demonstrations, projects such as the AIDS memorial quilt, and books, television, and movies, the larger gay community is reaching out to the thousands of geographically and psychologically isolated gay individuals to let them know that they are not alone. With greater numbers and more status in the larger society, many gays have channeled their anger, grief, frustration, and rebellion against bigotry into political action.

There still remain important political and social issues, and the need to educate the general population has not dissipated. But the gay community now has access to the legal and political process, and it has the collective knowledge and power to assert constitutional rights. Gay men and women are asserting their freedom to share in the necessities of life and to live and love in the secure knowledge that their relationships are respected and supported by law, and they are finding legal methods through which to accomplish this.

Role Models

As the homosexual segment of society becomes more visible and vocal, the need for role models and information is more and more obvious. The media are finally beginning to give us a few examples of healthy gay individuals or gay relationships. However, we need much more information about how homosexual relationships can work, and we need guidelines for developing healthy patterns and lifestyles.

New Social Phenomena

In recent years, a new focus has emerged on the social aspects of relationships. Gay centers and churches are providing support groups specifically designed for couples. The best example I have seen is "Couples," a very successful gay organization that was started in Long Beach, California, in 1984 to provide "a social and educational outreach to persons in an alternative lifestyle relationship." The group's statement of purpose reads: "With no specific political or religious affiliation, we pledge our support to the positive aspects of a relationship and the sense of stability that they represent for our community and life style." The original organization, which was very small, has since grown into the much larger Couples National Network, a gay organization with branches in many states.

A RELATIONSHIP IS A RELATIONSHIP—OR IS IT?

You probably know at least one heterosexual person who has relationship difficulties. Everyone, regardless of sexual orientation, goes through similar problems in finding a lover and developing a successful relationship. The following are difficulties that are common to all types of relationships:

Meeting a suitable partner
Power struggles
Communication problems
Expectations
Idealistic fantasies
Fears about intimacy
Resistance to change and growth
Issues of personal space and privacy

Perhaps you have had problems in some of these areas. Everyone has expectations and fantasies about love and the ideal mate. Straight lovers get as upset and confused as gay lovers when their wishes are not met. Such issues as sex, money, equality, and power are problems that cross the boards—everyone has trouble with them. Lovers of all types jockey for position, play roles, and have family and in-law problems. All relationships change and grow, and lovers of any orientation need to learn to handle the transitions.

The therapy techniques used to solve relationship problems work whatever the sexual orientation or relationship of the people involved. Communication between two people has many consistent aspects, regardless of sex, sexual preference, or relationship status—in fact, the same interpersonal skills that work with your boss or secretary will work with your spouse.

With so many relationship dynamics common to everyone, why am I writing a book just for homosexual relationships? Why aren't all the books on heterosexual romance enough? As I noted in the preface, gay and lesbian relationships have many special issues. In our society, being gay is being *different.*

HOW GAY RELATIONSHIPS ARE DIFFERENT

As a result of the many pressures of social nonacceptance, the dynamics of gay relationships are different from those of heterosexual relationships. Gay and lesbian lovers must deal with several issues—the lack of role models and social rules, homophobia, being closeted, being denied civil rights, and the impact of AIDS—that are unknown to straight couples. Add these extra dynamics to the usual relationship difficulties of establishing trust, balancing power, and creating clear communication, and the problems are multiplied.

For example, if you are straight and you announce that you're getting married, everyone (even those who are not being honest) will say, "How wonderful!" People will give you gifts, throw parties for you, and attend your wedding. But if you're gay or lesbian and you announce that you and your lover are going to live together, you will likely get many different reactions, ranging from shock or surprise to disgust. Gay love is not commonly recognized in this country, and the confusion, guilt, anger, and fear generated by this discrimination often contribute to the lack of success of gay and lesbian relationships.

Perhaps you can relate to one or more of the following:

- You often feel that your relationships are doomed from the beginning.
- You frequently have trouble choosing an appropriate partner.
- You do not know where to look for suitable friends and lovers.
- You are often afraid to make a relationship commitment.
- You panic at the first sign of relationship trouble.
- You sometimes adopt unsuitable or rigid roles in relationships.

Let's look more closely at the issues behind such feelings.

Lack of Social Rules

From early childhood to adolescence, we get extensive—albeit confusing—information about heterosexual relationships. We read books about love, see it portrayed on television and in films, and are exposed to an overwhelming number of ads using symbols of heterosexual sex. Until very recently, most children were not at all exposed to the idea of different sexual lifestyles.

At some point, those of us who are homosexual realized that our sexual preference differed from the expected norm. This realization suddenly altered all the information we had thus far received. Because much of the heterosexual culture does not fit us, it is easy for us to feel lost and confused about relationships.

Think back to the time when you realized you were gay. In that moment of recognition:

- Did you know there were others like you?
- Were you able to picture yourself living with a lover at some future point in time?
- Did you know what sexual techniques and behavior you could use with another person of the same gender?
- How healthy were the homosexual images you had, if any?
- Did you know how to ask another gay man or lesbian woman for a date?

Chances are that you had little or no idea of what romance and love would be like for you as a homosexual, or even if that was possible. For gay people, there are no automatic, socially condoned rules about what to wear to attract another person, what to do on a date, what kind of person makes a good partner, or who is supposed to take the "lead" in a relationship.

Scott, a client of mine, relates this story:

> I kept having "friendships" with other boys, and they would casually neglect me for some girl. I was always devastated, and I didn't know why. I didn't even know that my feelings were sexual. I had never met a gay person, and I didn't know what homosexuality was. I just liked boys, and I seemed to do it wrong—I liked them way too much.
>
> When I finally got to college and out of my small town, I met some gay friends. Then I knew what I was, but I didn't like it. I had always wanted a wedding, a family, and I thought that I couldn't do this if I was gay. It took me a few years to find a counselor who said I could have what I wanted. Today, married to Lewis, I know I've come a long, long way.

Most gay men and lesbian women have experienced similar confusion, and many have spent years sorting things out. Often, gay people attempt to conform to traditional patterns of heterosexual love, which may not be the best solution for them.

In searching for ways to make their relationships work, some gays and lesbians jump into commitment and monogamy too quickly or adopt inflexible rules that inhibit personal growth within the relationship. Others go to the other extreme, and, feeling lost without social rules, fall into self-destructive relationships. Without the security of knowing what will work, homosexual men and women often have trouble in evaluating the possibilities before making a commitment. In essence, they follow no rules, and as a result they can become confused, hurt, and lost. They may become involved in one destructive relationship after another, engage in promiscuous sex without satisfaction or goals, or simply jump into relationships without first dating to become acquainted with the other person. Often, because they feel that relationships won't work anyway, gay people avoid commitment and intimacy altogether and become lonely and isolated.

Lack of Role Models

Heterosexuals have the head start of seeing the roles played by many husbands and wives, including their own parents. Although some examples are better than others, even the worst of them will at least demonstrate what *doesn't* work in relationships.

To illustrate the power of growing up surrounded by successful role models, I refer to a phenomenon I call the "Jane Fonda advantage" (there are other show-business examples I could use; I just admire Jane). Children of people who are already successful in a field become familiar with the necessary skills, contacts, attitudes for success in that field and often begin careers early. The show-business people who dandled Jane on their knee when she was three were wonderful examples of success, and they were the same people who helped her career when she was twenty. She was familiar with the language, etiquette, attitudes, and problems of movie stars throughout her life. If Jane had wanted to be a doctor, lawyer, or computer programmer, she would have had to begin at the beginning, without any role models. By contrast, there are few, if any, visible role models for gay and lesbian youth. Homosexual historical figures, such as Walt Whitman and Gertrude Stein, exist, but the facts of their sexual orientation have been hidden in most school history books. The few present-day models who are open—such as Ron Reagan, Jr., Charles Nelson Reilly, and Billie Jean King—are also not talked about, except when details of their lifestyles create some kind of news scandal. No wonder gay marriage is so hard to imagine—with few visible successful examples, people cannot believe it's possible.

Where are the gay role models, the magazine articles about gay and lesbian dating, sex, intimacy, and love? Straight people can find literally hundreds of books and thousands of articles written especially for them about how to be successful in relationships. There are friends and relatives to ask, movies and plays and TV shows to watch. Examples, ranging from great to awful, abound. For gay men and lesbian women, there are few such resources.

Recently, Oprah Winfrey had a show that included several lesbian panelists. Most of my lesbian friends were dissatisfied with the image portrayed. While one of the panelists was a positive role model—attractive, intelligent, reasonable, and convincing—several were dressed in a "punk" fashion and seemed abrasive, politically hostile, and separatist (that is, negative toward men). Although the consensus of my friends was that each of these women had a right to her style and her views, we all felt that this was not a balanced, accurate, or helpful way in which to represent lesbians on national television, and that the show had simply reinforced stereotypical images of gay women.

After further discussion, we concluded that Oprah's guests are drawn from those people who have a reason or a willingness to be open on national TV. Suddenly, a major reason for the unbalanced models in the media became plain. For schoolteachers, lawyers, doctors, secretaries, union workers, military personnel, and many others, many of whom might have more conservative appearances, it is not often wise to be open in the media.

The people who appear on shows such as "Oprah Winfrey" and "Phil Donahue" have a specific reason for doing so. They promote books or organizations, or they are active in a political cause, or they have an emotional need for the attention. At any rate, it seems that few of these people are representative of most of our community, and they do not often present useful role models from which gay couples can learn.

Confusing Behavior Codes

To add to the confusion created by the lack of role models, social and sexual behavior codes are not the same for homosexual couples as they are for straight couples. Such basic relationship elements as the roles of wife and husband no longer make sense, and many gay people are confused by the models they see idealized in the majority culture. The realistic behavior and lifestyles *we* can have are hidden; we do not see thousands of images of gay couples meeting, dating, falling in love, and living "happily ever after." We do not see examples of how two women or two men can divide up household chores, handle finances, and deal with emotional stress. We have no way of knowing who is supposed to initiate sex, who makes the financial decisions, or how these power issues are resolved. Until recently, our friends, neighbors, and family members who were gay stayed closeted, and we were not aware of their lifestyles. As a result, each of us has had to attempt to reconstruct role models and certain behavior codes from scratch, never knowing whether we're doing it "right" or not.

Julie and Joan, lesbian lovers who had lived together for five years, came to me with a sexual problem. "I always have to be the one to ask," Joan said. "I'm tired of being the aggressor all the time, so we're not having much sex at all now."

Julie remained quiet and withdrawn, looking embarrassed. After some talk and time to relax, she began to warm up. She said, "I just can't do it. I can't initiate sex." I asked her what she thought she had to do. "Well, I guess I'd have to wear something frilly, and act sexy. I just can't do it."

Joan burst into laughter. "You don't have to do that! I'd die laughing if you did that." This embarrassed Julie further. I asked Joan what she would need from Julie, and she said, "Just a wink, a pat, holding my hand, sitting close to me on the couch. I'll get the message. I just don't want to always be the one to risk being turned down. If she lets me know she's interested, I'll be fine."

What Joan and Julie lacked was a clear idea of who should initiate sex and of how this is done. Once they had some guidance, the problem was resolved simply. The lack of meaningful gay behavior codes leads to this kind of confusion and helplessness in all areas of relationships: meeting, dating, becoming intimate, and making a commitment.

Homophobia

Most of us in the gay/bisexual community are well aware of the pervasive homophobia in our society. Homophobia, for those who do not recognize the word, means fear of homosexuality. What you may not know is that homophobia is a subtype of xenophobia, which is the exaggerated fear of anything different or unusual. How does homophobia impact gay relationships?

We are all concerned about being accepted, but people who are gay often have a damaged image in the eyes of family and friends. Consequently, a gay person often experiences guilt and self-hatred about being homosexual, and can cave in to the social pressure by internally condemning his or her own sexual preference. This can make a gay person phobic about his or her own homosexuality.

Not surprisingly, being fearful of your own sexual preference can be severely damaging to your relationships. I have seen self-directed homophobia express itself in even the most mundane of issues. In attempting to compensate for their fear of being different, some gay men and lesbian women become fanatic about making their relationships match the "traditional" model, with rigid role-playing. They may also frequently become upset about a partner's behavior in public, since they consider certain behaviors to be inappropriate or too obvious. A relationship built on a foundation of homophobia can become ruled by "what the neighbors think"; such a relationship is very restrictive and uncomfortable.

Self-directed homophobia can also result in a gay couple's feeling stuck—that is, not knowing how to carry their relationship past the early phases of dating. They feel they cannot go further because, in their opinion, commitment and marriage are not a possibility. Some may feel that in having stepped outside the "norm" to fulfill their sexual orientation, they have forfeited the right to declare a permanent commitment.

One lesbian couple I worked with had this problem. Dina is a divorcée with two children in their twenties. Peggy, Dina's lover, has been "out" for years in all aspects of her life—at work, with her family, with friends. Dina has never had a relationship with a woman before. She says, "I care for Peggy, but I don't really think I'm gay. I still like men. I don't want my children to know what I'm doing, and when they come over, I want Peggy to be nice to them but not be too close to me. Also, I feel bad after we have sex. I enjoy it, but I feel wrong about it. If my family ever knew, they'd probably never want to see me again.

Peggy says, "I feel awful when Dina's family is around. She treats me like a stranger. Actually, she's nicer to strangers. We have great sex, but I want more. I want a real relationship, where Dina treats me like a lover, like a partner, like family.

Before Peggy and Dina can go any further in their relationship, Dina must deal with her internal homophobic struggle. She must either accept her feelings for Peggy and acknowledge her homosexuality or bisexuality, or she must choose to continue to live a heterosexual lifestyle. Either way, there is nothing much Peggy can do until Dina decides, except to realize that homophobia is at work here and protect herself from being hurt.

Another gay couple I worked with was successful in overcoming self-directed homophobia. Phil and Harry are well established in their relationship, and for the most part they have felt comfortable with themselves and with each other. Last New Year's Eve, they attended a dance for which Phil, a photographer, had been hired to take pictures. After the work was done, Phil wanted to dance with Harry. Harry objected, and they had an argument about it. Here's what they said in a group session a few days later:

Phil: I never thought about it. I'm so open that people sometimes call me "the little faggot photographer," and it's okay with me, if they keep doing business with me. I don't care. I just didn't realize Harry would be upset.

Harry: I'm okay if we're in gay places. But I was in the navy, and I'm used to hiding my orientation in public. That dance was all straight couples, lots of them were drinking, and I was afraid we might get beaten up. I didn't want to take the risk.

Phil: I guess I just have to realize that we're different, and that Harry doesn't feel the same as I do about it. We stay mostly in gay or mixed company, where we're accepted, so it doesn't come up too often. Our friends, of whatever sexual orientation, all accept us. I am willing to be more conscious when we're together in unfriendly places. I think it's safer, too. Next time I'll ask Harry what he thinks, and not just assume it's okay.

Harry: Phil's lucky. His family loves him anyway. Mine have rejected me. I think it makes a difference. I really appreciate how Phil has helped me to be more open, but there are times when I still get scared. Phil, thanks for being understanding. I love you.

Phil: I love you, too. You're much more important to me than some silly dance. Let's not fight about it anymore. But I want to go dancing this weekend to make up for it.

Harry: You have a date.

Phil and Harry learned not to blame each other for homophobia problems. They came to respect and understand each other's different experiences, wants, and needs. Although the issue of homophobia still comes up for them, it's not a major problem.

Because homophobia is a reality of homosexual life within our social atmosphere, all gay and lesbian couples need to understand the problems it can cause and learn how to deal with them. I will, therefore, be addressing issues of homophobia throughout this book, at discussions of every stage of a relationship. I have also included an appendix on homophobia.

Love in the Closet

In an environment that is neither open nor realistic concerning sexuality, homosexuals often feel they must hide their sexual preference, remaining "in the closet."

For example, while gay men and lesbian women make up a significant portion of our military forces, the military summarily dismisses anyone found to be homosexual. As a result, gay people desiring military careers must keep their sexual preference a secret. This is also true of many teachers and of people in certain other careers.

When such pressure exists for one or both partners, a gay relationship can become very complex and stressful. Sneaking, hiding, and living in constant fear makes relaxed, secure intimacy nearly impossible. If one partner is reluctant to be closeted while the other feels it is important, the issue can become critical to the survival of the relationship.

Susie and Teddie, a committed lesbian couple I counseled, were obliged to separate for two years when the army sent Susie to Japan but kept Teddie here. As lesbians, they had no recourse and could not request that they be kept together. That period really tested their commitment. They were also kept on edge by frequent investigations into their personal lives. When they were reunited, they sought counseling to help them reestablish their former connection. A subsequent separation, in which Teddie was sent to Italy for two years, strained the relationship so much that it finally ended. Susie and Teddie's relationship was thus destroyed by the conflict between their desire to have their careers and the necessity of being both closeted and separated.

One difficult situation that can arise when one partner is closeted is that person's having to take a friend of the opposite sex to business functions, while the spouse must sit at home. Sheila, a very successful saleswoman, was distraught when she came to see me. She said,

> I'm looking for a gay man to accompany me to Bermuda on a trip I won for top sales. My lover, Carol, can't go and share the triumph. We had a big fight about it, but I *know* I'd lose my job if the company found out. It's hard on the relationship. I tend to hide things from her, and we fight when she finds out. I hate to hurt her feelings, but I also love everything else about my job, and I couldn't make this kind of money anywhere else.

Having a deep, long-term commitment and not being able to share that wonderful fact with business associates, friends, and family is a sorrow specific to gays and lesbians. It takes sensitivity and cooperation to handle these closet issues.

Although certain portions of society are becoming more informed about homosexuality, gay and lesbian people in America still encounter a range of environments: accepting, neutral, and downright hostile. In each of these three environments, there are different choices and needs for closeted people. With an accepting family, for example, a couple feels more supported and so might be open about their relationship. Their need for a network of supportive friends is less intense. When the extended family or community is neutral, the need for support increases. And in the face of a hostile family or community, support becomes crucial.

While I strongly believe that it is important for each of us to come out when we can, I also recognize that it is not prudent for many gay men and women to do so today. The fears of losing one's career, family respect and acceptance, and good friends are very difficult to overcome. Although many times the reactions of friends and families are far better than we had expected, there is no guarantee that this will be so. For some gay persons, the risk is too great to take.

Coming out is a very personal decision and must be made carefully. If you or your lover is closeted, use the suggestions in chapter 8 to work on the problem with your partner. Be gentle with each other, and don't push your lover to come out.

Differences under the Law

Recently, the gay community has achieved some modest gains in legal protection on an individual basis through challenges and suits involving discrimination and injustice. Nevertheless, many issues surrounding gay relationships are still treated differently under the laws of our government at the city, county, state, and federal levels. This legal atmosphere has a profound influence on our lifestyles and partnerships.

Specifically, it is difficult or actually illegal in some or most states for gay and lesbian couples to

- dance, hold hands, or kiss in public
- visit each other in intensive care
- inherit community property
- have sex
- marry
- name each other as insurance beneficiaries
- make medical decisions or arrange a funeral for a "spouse"

Such discriminatory conditions are upsetting and frustrating, and they affect our lives and our relationships. In my practice, I have seen how these legal issues discourage gay men and lesbian women from believing that their relationships are viable and worthwhile. When this belief is lacking, it becomes much harder for a couple to go the distance, sustaining a committed, long-term relationship.

One example is Fred and Paul, who came to me because while their relationship was going well, they felt that the future was uncertain. Paul said, "Our jobs, our lives, and our love are all going well, and we'd like to make more of a commitment, but we're afraid. Being committed means coming out in ways we never have before. People will know, and we'll be obvious. Is it legal for us to live together? Can we go to jail?"

Paul's question was serious, though not surprising to me. Fred expressed further concerns: "We'd like to buy a house together, have a joint checking account, and I'd like to make Paul my insurance beneficiary—but how can we do these kinds of things?"

Paul and Fred took my suggestion that they learn all they could about protecting themselves financially and legally (with contracts, powers of attorney, and joint-tenancy agreements) and that they seek professional legal advice to find out exactly how they

were vulnerable according to the law. Once they learned that they could make a legal, financially clear agreement and commitment, they were able to move in together and get on to the deeper development of their love.

Because of our society's discrimination and homophobia, finding competent, informed, aware lawyers to handle such legal issues as domestic problems, false arrests, property settlements, medical rights, and estate and inheritance settlements can be especially difficult for gays.

AIDS

The issue of AIDS is ever present in the gay community. You may be groaning inwardly as you read this, since it may seem that everything you have picked up to read in the last few years has been about AIDS. Because the heterosexual community has not yet fully grappled with this issue, for now it remains another factor separating gay relationships from heterosexual ones.

While lesbian women have not had to worry about AIDS as much as gay men have, those I know are very aware of the problems of AIDS and of what constitutes safe sex. Many are also working hard to combat the disease through programs such as the AIDS Project in Los Angeles. This leads me to believe that most lesbian women have accepted AIDS as their issue, too.

Gay men, generally, are even more aware. Most of them have lost friends, and many have lost lovers and relatives. As a community, gay men and lesbian women have a right to be very proud, even as we grieve. We have reduced the spread of this devastating disease through education and safe practices.

Even with all that has been done, AIDS and the fear of it have a powerful impact on gay relationships. There is a loss of support as families reject their homosexual sons and daughters for fear of AIDS. There is hesitation and fear among gays, especially among male couples who had developed open sexual arrangements during their years together, but who are now afraid that such arrangements may have endangered the lives of both partners.

There is also a greater openness, as lovers are being forced to talk candidly about their sexual wants and practices. This openness can be difficult for people who find it extremely uncomfortable to talk about sex and sexuality, yet the importance of the AIDS issues makes such discussion vital.

In all, because of AIDS, relationships are being seen as more valuable, and casual sex as too risky. As a result, more gay men and lesbian women are working on their relationship skills. Every gay couple is finding it worthwhile to create more open and honest, as well as safer, agreements.

DIFFERENCE WITHIN DIFFERENCE: SAME-SEX PAIRINGS

All of the factors discussed above—lack of social rules and role models, confusing behavior codes, homophobia, the issue of being closeted, treatment under the law, and AIDS—account for the need that gay couples have for special information on making their relationships work. In addition to the differences between homosexual and heterosexual relationships, there are significant differences between gay male relationships and lesbian relationships.

Lessons about social roles are different for boys and girls. Although researchers are still in debate over how much of our behavior reflects genetic and hormonal factors, most agree that a certain amount is learned through conditioning. Studies have shown that in our society, everyone—from delivery-room staff, to parents, to teachers—unconsciously and consciously treats girls and boys differently. For the two sexes, dress is different, toys are different, adults' expectations are different, and communication and affection are different. Although the roles today are changing, many of the traditional sexual stereotypes we grew up with are still an influence. No clear role models for a new way of living have yet emerged. When they are grown, men are expected to "play the field," "sow wild oats," and resist being "trapped" in committed relationships. Women, however, have been conditioned to value monogamy, adaptation, cooperation, and sexual restraint. They are taught to feel responsible for sex and birth control and to feel incompetent about money and mechanics. They are encouraged to make sure that their relationships develop, moving toward greater commitment.

The unequal, sexually segregated training we receive as children prepares us for heterosexual relationships based on traditional roles. It also maintains a kind of stable imbalance of responsibilities and power between men and women. Often, in heterosexual pairings, the woman's drive toward commitment and monogamy comes into conflict with the man's drive for variety.

In lesbian and gay relationships, however, this cultural conditioning is exaggerated by the same-sex pairing and can frequently be destructive. It is often difficult for gay men—even those who strongly desire a close relationship—to reach a solid commitment together. As a result, long-term relationships between men often include some spoken or unspoken agreement to be nonmonogamous. From my experience in couple counseling, I have noticed other issues that frequently arise for gay men: reluctance to commit, confusion about how to enhance intimacy, a need to have sufficient sexual excitement and variety to keep their interest, and, often, difficulty with simple negotiations about domestic chores.

In contrast, lesbian women tend to reach the commitment stage too early, becoming quickly involved—and often moving in together—within a few weeks or even days, and then having trouble maintaining the relationship. Rather than having affairs, as men often do, gay women tend to break up their relationships when they become attracted to someone else.

Common counseling issues for lesbian couples include creating personal space within the relationship, resolving financial responsibility, developing self-esteem, parenting children (often, one or both members of a lesbian couple are divorced mothers), and reviving sexual desire.

There are always individual men and women who do not follow the patterns that have been described here. There are gay men who are entirely focused on commitment and who wouldn't dream of having an affair or nonmonogamous relationship, and there are lesbian women who are sexually experimental and free. However, while I deeply dislike labels and rigid generalizations, in my practice I have seen the above differences between gay men and lesbian women often enough to detect significant patterns.

Gender-specific problems add one more level of uniqueness and complexity to gay and lesbian relationships, and they make it even more important for same-sex lovers to obtain information that pertains to their specific relationship needs.

SO WHAT ARE GAY PEOPLE TO DO?

In spite of the difficulties and obstacles I have just presented, with good information and appropriate techniques, gay and lesbian lovers can overcome problems and find meaningful, lasting relationships. Further, I believe that gay men and women in fact have several advantages that heterosexuals do not.

Recognizing Gay Strengths

When I began to learn about homosexuality—my own and my clients'—and grew to know some gay and lesbian friends and teachers, I was impressed by what I saw as a subtle, yet important, benefit of being gay. What I noticed was that gay people, in having been forced by their circumstances to consider the meaning and import of their lives, have often developed great wisdom and depth of character.

Making the decision to come out (even if only to oneself) is tantamount to deciding to be rejected by a good portion of society—perhaps even by the people one loves and needs most. It is a profound life decision, and anyone who makes it is moved to reflect on a philosophy of life. Like all rites of passage, it is a hard-won experience. Those who have fought the coming-out battle become survivors, and survivors are interesting.

Another advantage of being gay is the marvelously close-knit and politically active community. Tremendous support for gay couples is available, including legal, psychological, medical, and other kinds of professional help. This is especially true in large urban areas, particularly on both coasts.

Politically, I know of few other groups who can count on having their issues expressed and fought for with the power, clarity, and humanitarian consciousness that the gay community has brought to bear. I have witnessed much less infighting here than within any other political-action group I have seen.

We have supportive newspapers and magazines. Gay- and lesbian-owned businesses are notable for their community involvement. Anyone who is gay or lesbian and feels alone has only to contact a gay/lesbian community center, newspaper, magazine, or professional group (such as the Lambda Democratic Club) to be connected with appropriate people. This support in some ways serves to replace the family and community support that many gay and lesbian people have lost. All relationships need outside support to survive, and such support is available for us in ways the straight world does not yet have access to.

Getting Unstuck

Gay people can draw power from their strengths and learn how to handle their special problems. We do not need to be stuck in traditional heterosexual patterns of relationships and commitment. I believe that gay couples need to talk about and create new rules for love, rules that truly apply to homosexual relationships. This means not only relearning some rules that apply to any couple, but also discovering new rules that fit our own special needs. This is the dawning of a time to forge new paths and explore new ways for gay and lesbian couples to live and love.

Our reeducation process may be difficult. In some ways, relearning rules and creating new models is similar to the process a divorced heterosexual person goes through when he or she is thrust back into the dating scene after years of marriage. The hardest part about it is that it feels uncomfortable. A person in this position can feel awkward or "stupid," as though he or she should know more.

It's important to recognize that this awkwardness is only temporary. As you learn to trust yourself and think clearly about your needs and responsibilities in a relationship, you will grow to accept the challenge of designing your relationships as a normal and meaningful part of being human.

This book is devoted to helping you think about love, pursue relationships, and make your life as complete as you want it to be. You have already made a start. The remaining chapters will cover all of the major issues gay couples face in long-term relationships. In them, you will discover:

- how to find the right partner
- how to date successfully
- how to know when you're ready for deeper commitment
- how to live together successfully
- how to improve communication
- how to handle universal relationship problems
- how to handle the problems that are specific to gay and lesbian relationships
- how to discuss sex and sexual contracts, monogamous or open
- how to come out to family, friends, and work associates
- how to survive being closeted
- how to marry and legalize your relationship
- how to build a support network for your relationship
- how to deal with serious illness or death

- how to handle common homosexual legal problems
- how to grow old together happily

Finding Role Models

The first effective thing you can do to begin creating a new, healthier lifestyle, including getting ample support for and approval of your gay or lesbian relationship, is to find positive role models. Having role models is basic to being successful in a gay or lesbian lifestyle. Knowing that other homosexual individuals and couples are successful will provide you with hope and motivation. Having positive role models will help you to define what you want and will encourage you to achieve it. As examples of healthy relationships and lifestyles, role models help you to

- evaluate potential lovers
- relate more successfully to other gay and lesbian people
- understand commitment: what it is and when to make one
- understand marriage: what it takes to spend your lives together
- handle stress and problems in better ways
- understand new relationship options

If you live near an active gay community, get to know the community leaders and observe the homosexual people you meet to find relationship patterns that appear healthy and effective to you. Ask questions, attend workshops, read books, and take classes. It is vital that you replace the information you would receive naturally in a more open culture.

Attend cultural events—gay and lesbian plays, art exhibits, poetry readings, and movies. If you're not fond of art for art's sake, go anyway, to observe role models! Read biographies of gay and lesbian people—for example, Gertrude Lawrence, Alice B. Toklas, and Harvey Fierstein. There are also certain positive dynamics in heterosexual relationships—communication and mutual support, for instance—that gay and lesbian couples can modify and adapt without buying the entire model.

Living in San Francisco, New York, or Los Angeles provides the most options, because these communities are highly supportive. Also, the larger population of cities means a larger number of gay and lesbian people. However, since we are spread widely through the general population, you can make connections wherever you are.

While it can be much more difficult to find role models in smaller communities, statistics say that of every ten people you meet, one will be gay. If you search, you will find. Subscribe to magazines (they come in plain wrappers, and you can get a post-office box, if necessary); look for hot lines, local centers, and lesbian and gay organizations at colleges. Use the resources at the back of this book. Get on the mailing lists of gay or lesbian organizations in cities and of distributors of gay and lesbian books.

Use your telephone or even your computer modem to connect you with areas and networks of like-minded people. Watch for gay and lesbian presentations in the media, especially on public-access or public-broadcasting stations. Spend vacations in cities with large gay or lesbian populations, and become connected with their community centers. Gay publications, such as those listed in Appendix A at the back of this book, will direct you to other available resources.

Now that we've explored the issues that are unique to members of the gay community and have seen how dealing with these issues is critical to the development of a healthy gay lifestyle, we can move on to what you really want to know about gay relationships—how to find them, how to improve them, and how to make them last.

CHAPTER

2

How (and Where) to Find Relationships

Not surprisingly, the first step in having a healthy relationship is finding a partner. It may also seem to be the hardest step. It is in this first step that many gay people make the mistakes that set them up for future failure. I have had many gay clients who cannot find suitable partners because they do not know how to meet the right people, or because they are locked into destructive patterns of repeatedly becoming attached to the wrong people.

The factors that cause these problems include the following:

- not knowing how to evaluate and screen candidates
- not knowing what one wants in a lover
- having no clear idea of what kind of relationship to look for
- not being prepared for a significant relationship
- only going to bars to meet potential partners
- using sex as the entry point into relationships
- having negative opinions of other gay and lesbian people (homophobia)

It's actually quite ironic to find that meeting other gay people is so hard, because we're everywhere. Although there is no absolutely reliable way to determine the actual number of gay and lesbian people in America, most experts believe that 10 percent of our total population is same-sex oriented, as noted in chapter 1. That's more than 23 million gay and lesbian Americans—and I think this estimate is too low.

The Kinsey research findings of 1948, still recognized as the most (and some say the only) thorough and reliable research into sexual-behavior patterns, generalized that "37 percent of the total male population has at least some overt homosexual experience to the point of orgasm between adolescence and old age. This accounts for nearly 2 out of every 5 [men] that one may meet."

Suffice it to say that there are significant numbers of us. However, how prevalent we are in society has not quite fully registered. The light is only beginning to dawn. Those of us who are active in gay and lesbian communities are aware of how many of "us" there are, and how many of us appear straight to the general population.

I believe that as human sexual behavior becomes more understood, more people will come out, and the generally accepted estimated percentage will rise. Even before that happens, there are plenty of people out there for you to meet, wherever you are. This chapter will give you the information you need to meet your ideal lover, and to make some very good friends at the same time.

Those of you who already have partners may want to move ahead in the book. Or, you could create a little fresh excitement with your lover by pretending to be strangers, reenacting your first meeting and the "getting-to-know-you" stage. It's amazing how exciting and intriguing your familiar lover can seem when you look at him or her the way you would look at a stranger.

MASTERING MATCHMAKING

Looking for a partner is a process of making a match. The first step a matchmaker takes is finding out what the client is like—and in your case, the "client" is you.

Most of us haven't stopped to take inventory of who we are as lovers, except perhaps in a negative and self-deprecating way. When I first ask most of my gay and lesbian clients to tell me about themselves, they give me a long list of what they don't like (too fat, too shy, and so on). When I ask them to tell me what they *do* like, they're lost.

So the search begins here: knowing yourself is the prerequisite for understanding what kind of person would be most compatible with you—with your personality, your interests, your feelings, your habits, your pastimes and hobbies. A relationship is a partnership, and *you* are going to be one of the primary partners. It's time to take stock of what you have to offer.

Are You Ready for a Relationship?

Is this the right time in your life for a relationship? Are you prepared to open up to someone else? Believe it or not, one reason gay people often have trouble finding lovers is that, even though they're looking, they're not ready. Although you may feel eager, even desperate, to bring a new lover into your life, you may not actually be in an appropriate condition for intimacy.

You are not ready if one or more of the following is true:

- You have recently broken up with someone, and you haven't completely let go or finished mourning. While you don't need to erase your previous relationship from your memory, it is vital that you regain your balance before moving on to a new relationship.
- You're not yet comfortable with your homosexuality. You don't have to have come out completely to the world, but if you're sure you're homosexual and are still having trouble accepting your sexual orientation, your own homophobia will prevent you from having a healthy relationship.

  Look for gay or lesbian role models, make gay and lesbian friends, attend coming-out discussion groups, and go to your nearest gay community center. In short, reeducate yourself with good information and examples of homosexual lifestyles. Only then will you be ready for a serious relationship.
- You have addiction or sexual-abuse problems. If you have abused alcohol or drugs, are an incest survivor, or have a history of domestic violence, get into a Twelve-Step program such as Alcoholics Anonymous, Cocaine Anonymous, Adult Children of Alcoholics, or Al-Anon. Destructive patterns usually repeat themselves unless something is done to change them. Learn to handle these issues now to keep them from reappearing again and again in your relationships.

Help and information concerning the above issues are available everywhere; telephone numbers of organizations that can be of assistance are listed in Appendix A.

Getting to Know Yourself

What do you want? While this may seem at first to be a simple question, of all the gay and lesbian clients I see who want a lover, the vast majority can't answer it. "I want a lover," a gay client says. I ask, "What kind of person are you looking for?" Answer: "I don't know . . . someone nice." That kind of description is obviously too vague to be of help in identifying a compatible lover.

There isn't one of you who'd buy a car or a truck, a new outfit, or even a head of cabbage with such vagueness. Yet I see gay men and women choosing lovers with a lot less thought than they'd put into selecting a turkey for Thanksgiving dinner. At least in the latter case, you *know* you're getting a turkey!

Being gay or lesbian, you may tend to think that a similar sexual orientation is the only important qualification for a lover. But being gay is a lifestyle, not just a sexual orientation. Building a successful homosexual relationship requires many compatible factors. You are not just going to have sex with your partner; you're going to share every aspect of yourself. For example, how you get up in the morning, how you spend your free time, and what kind of work you do all account for a far larger percentage of your lifestyle than your sexual preference.

Many of the gay couples who come to me for counseling are having problems because they didn't realize how important these factors were. They often thought that differences in lifestyle would disappear when they got together. I have witnessed major struggles over smoking, eating habits, sleeping schedules, religious differences, pets, holiday and family traditions, and parenting of children from previous relationships. The details of your lifestyle are not easily changed; they're part of your personality. Learning to blend your lifestyle traits with your lover's is a crucial part of creating a successful gay relationship.

First of all, it's essential for you to know what your own style is. You need this information to help you find a lover, to help your lover get to know you better, and to negotiate a new lifestyle between you.

"Know-Yourself" Exercise

Mentally step back from your life for a moment, and look at yourself as objectively as you can. Keep in mind that this is a fact-finding, not a fault-finding, mission. Imagine a typical day in your life, and think about what you do: your morning/evening routines, your meals, your work, your play, and your general lifestyle. Answer the following questions as though they were interview questions that Barbara Walters might ask!

Waking Up

What are you like when you wake up in the morning? Are you slow and groggy, cheerful or quiet? Are you organized or haphazard? Do you have a regular routine that never varies, or do you get yourself ready differently each day?

Are your clothes laid out the night before, or do you have a sleepy interlude at the closet deciding what to wear?

While you're getting ready, are you relaxed or tense? Are you slow or fast?

Do you exercise in the morning?

Do you meditate?

Do you give yourself extra time to read the paper, or do you cut morning preparation time down to the bare minimum?

Do you eat breakfast at home, on the run, or not at all?

Mornings are an important time in relationships. We are usually more natural and less rational first thing in the morning. How you set up your morning routine says a lot about your personality, and it's vital information for your potential lover to have. Couples who start off mornings in harmony have a better chance of continuing to enjoy each other throughout the day.

Work

What kind of work do you do? Is it creative, challenging, detail oriented, or technical?

Do you work with the public, with coworkers, or alone? Is teamwork required? Do you supervise anyone?

Do you work with other gay people?

Do you like your job or profession? If not, what would you rather do? If you do like your work, what do you like best about it?

The type of work you do and whether or not you like your job say a lot about your likes and dislikes, your strengths and weaknesses. For example, if you are in a people-oriented service job, you might be very outgoing and want to have many people in your private life. Or, if contact with the public is stressful, you may need lots of time alone, away from work.

After Work

What do you usually do after work? Do you come right home and relax?

Do you take a nap so you'll have energy for the evening?

For dinner, do you cook a special meal or microwave a frozen dinner?

Are you active—that is, do you run off to classes, meetings, or workshops? Or are you quiet, preferring to spend your evenings watching television or reading, then maybe taking a bubble bath?

Do you like to spend your evenings doing creative activities or hobbies, such as writing, building things in a workshop, or playing an instrument?

Do you work out at the gym or do some other type of exercise after work?

Do you like to go out with friends on weeknights?

Weekends

When do you get up on weekends? What is your weekend morning routine like?

Do you eat differently on weekends? For example, do you eat out more, or do you cook more?

Are you involved in organized activities, like sports, or is your activity more spontaneous?

Do you go to church?

Do you participate in gay clubs or events?

Like evenings, weekends are usually considered "couple time." Look at your current weekend lifestyle to see what activities you will be sharing when you find your lover.

Your General Lifestyle

The following questions can help you to develop an overall picture of who you are—and thus of what your wants and needs are in a relationship.

Are you more organized or more freestyle?

Are you around people a lot by choice?

Do you spend time with other gay people?

Do you spend much time alone? Do you like it?

Do you have pets? How much of your time do you spend with them? Will a lover have to like your dog?

Do you have children? Do they live with you, either permanently or part-time? Are they grown? How often are they a part of your life? How close is your relationship with them?

Are you artistic? Do you often have a creative project going?

Do you have a sport or hobby that consumes lots of time, energy, and/or money?

Is food important to you? Do you like to cook? Dine out? Do you follow a special or vegetarian diet?

Are you tolerant or critical?

Are you precise or haphazard?

Are you very physical? Do you spend lots of time playing sports, working out at the gym, or dancing?

Do you like to talk? If so, what about?

Are you careful or casual about your appearance?

Are you spiritual or religious? Do you meditate or go to church?

The Selective-Attention Trap

Many of my gay and lesbian clients who think they do know what they want somehow keep getting stuck in unhealthy and short-term relationships. There are several reasons for this, but primary among them is a perceptual trait we human beings have that is called "selective attention." In simple terms, it means we only see what we need to see or what we wish to see. An example of selective attention is a phenomenon that happens when you contemplate buying a new car. If you're considering a Jeep Cherokee, for example, the road suddenly seems crowded with them. There they are all around you, in every color! Obviously, the number of Cherokees on the road hasn't actually increased; you're just more *aware* of them.

Selective attention can cause us to keep falling in love with the same type of problem person. We may unconsciously seek out lovers who are addictive or abusive, who can't hold jobs, who squander money, who "con" their partners and don't tell the truth, or who are otherwise poorly functioning people. Selective attention causes us to notice people who feel familiar to us, who remind us of our family members and who have patterns of behavior that are similar to theirs—even if our parents, siblings, or other relatives were not particularly good to us or for us.

What we are doing in such cases is continuously searching for a resolution to past problems. Those who felt unloved search for love; those who felt unheard seek lovers who will listen to them; those who felt unappreciated search for appreciation; those who felt smothered search for lovers who will give them lots of space and freedom. By fixating on early sources of frustration and hurt, we keep attempting to relate to the same toxic personality types.

Our search is a natural healing process, a chance to correct what was misunderstood, mishandled, or deficient in our past. However, the dilemma inherent in this search is that as long as we're subconsciously fixed on the type of person with whom we had a problem in the past, we will keep repeating the struggle rather than resolving it. Psychologists call this kind of phenomenon *projection* (a Freudian definition), which means that we project onto someone else the persona of a parent with whom we have unresolved issues.

Rod, a handsome and talented young man of thirty-five, is a professional artist. He had just begun to understand the patterns he follows when he found himself with yet another problem lover. Rod said to me,

> How could I do it again? There we were, two weeks into the relationship, and he was drunk. I'd had no idea that he had an alcohol problem—I thought I had sworn off this kind of person after the first two relationships! Is it that all gay men

> have drinking problems, or am I just this unlucky? Is there anyone out there who doesn't drink?

I asked Rod to examine the clues he had had about this lover's drinking when they first met. He realized that there had been plenty, but that he had chosen to ignore them. I asked him to look at where he found potential partners. Rod realized that he was finding people in bars, which increased his chances of getting a drinker. He also recognized that he kept finding men who reminded him of his father. He was comfortable with them; he felt he knew what they were thinking, and he knew what to say.

As Rod began to recognize this pattern and figure out what he wanted, he found other places to look, and he started to notice a different kind of man. He took some "risks," such as talking to unfamiliar types of gay men and trying new, unfamiliar places to meet gay people. When he didn't say exactly the right thing in the new environment or when he misread the cues these unfamiliar, nondrinking gay men were giving him, Rod had some uncomfortable moments, some minor embarrassments, and even some rejections. But gradually, he began to make new friends.

Today, he says, "Now my gay friends are people who like me, who live their lives the way I do. They don't lie to me or cheat me, and most of them don't drink at all. I never realized what good friends were supposed to be. I thought I had to take whoever came along. I'm really glad I figured it out."

Cathleen, an athletic woman of twenty-nine, was repeatedly attracted to pretty, delicate, feminine-looking lesbian women who would eventually turn cold and rejecting. She finally came in to see me after a relationship she was in had escalated into violence.

"I couldn't help it, I just lost control—anyway, she slapped me first," she said when I asked her how the violence had begun. After several weeks of intensive self-examination in therapy, Cathleen had this to say:

> I realize now that I never got over the way my mother rejected me, and I kept finding other cold, rejecting women to try to resolve the old hurt. I now know I have to resolve this inner hurt in other ways—a lover can't do that for me, and no lover can be the mother I wanted to have. Now I'm finding that I really prefer open, outgoing athletic women like me. I'm learning to be an equal partner instead of a rejected little girl.

Although our selective attention is "programmed" during childhood, it *can* be changed. To do so, it is necessary to let go of the familiar as a criterion and to develop a new awareness of what really works for you.

If you have had a series of relationships that have all resulted in similar problems, or that have just not made you happy, then you're probably operating on old programming. You've never taken stock of what healthy gay partners are; you've just been blindly looking for someone who would love you.

In working with my gay and lesbian clients, I have found that carefully examining the kind of lover one is looking for is a powerful way to confront and reprogram selective attention. Many of us have an unconscious taboo about thinking logically about love and relationships; we may feel it is wrong, cold, or calculating. It is none of these. If you involve your conscious thought and judgment in your search for a lover, you will find amazing changes in the types of people to whom you are attracted. This concept is so simple that it may at first be hard to believe—but when you try it, you'll see that it really works.

The following section is designed to help you confront and reprogram your unconscious selective attention. Some of the steps may seem to you to be silly, unnecessary, or time consuming—but do them anyway! As you work through these exercises, you will become more and more aware of your unconscious programming, of how you've been choosing inappropriate places to meet people and allowing yourself to spend your time with people who are not really what you want. You will also be confronted with the fact that you have many choices, and that you don't simply have to "take what you can get."

Identifying a Potential Mate

In this two-part exercise you will be looking at what kind of gay or lesbian lover you really want, as opposed to what you may have been settling for. The clearer you are about your needs and wants in another person, the more you'll know where and how to look, and the more easily you'll recognize a good match when you see it. Although physical attraction is, of course, a factor, you should not restrict your selection to looks alone, because it's easy to be misled.

Ideal-Lover Exercise: Love at First Sight?

Indulge your fantasies. Ask yourself these questions: Whom do you notice when you walk into a crowded room? Is it a smile that grabs your attention? Are you more attracted to someone who is in a group, or who is sitting alone? What type of dress do you like? Do you prefer a professional, athletic, fashionable, or casual look? What body type attracts you—tall and thin, chubby or petite, wiry or muscular? Do you like a sophisticated and experienced look, or a fresh and innocent look?

Frequently, a physical type goes with a particular lifestyle. I've known lesbian women who were very athletic and who loved hiking and camping, but who would find themselves continually attracted to women with a dainty, "femme" look. This often got them attached to lovers who hated physical exertion and "roughing it."

Dainty women often look that way because they spend a great deal of time on their appearance; manicures, hairstyles, facials, and so on are probably very important to them. They may want to be wined and dined, and attending plays and museums may be more to their liking than attending outdoor events. An athletic woman who scorns beauty regimes and abhors theater and art could be a difficult match.

Conversely, I've known gay men who were thoughtful and loved verbal sparring, reading, and discussion, and who chose lovers who were muscular and athletic. Again, this is not automatically an easy combination.

Consider whether your wishes for a particular physical "type" make sense in terms of your activities and your lifestyle. For example, if you're a male intellectual whose main physical exercise is preparing gourmet meals, but you like bodybuilder types, make sure you are prepared to do at least some physical, athletic activities with your lover. Equally important, find out whether he is willing to do some of your favorite things, too. If not, your "ideal" type may be rooted too much in fantasy and may need some reevaluation.

For gay and lesbian people, the quest to accept our own sexuality in the face of opposition and disapproval often causes us to place a high priority on sexuality and physical issues. It's also the first clue we usually have about the person we've just met. But to avoid selective attention, you must look beyond your physical-type fantasies and make sure that other traits you really want are also there. Note, too, that your attraction to a particular physical type can "trigger" your programming and thereby cause you to ignore or deny warning signals.

Another reason to consider other qualities is that our objective sense of a partner's physical looks fades with familiarity. What outlasts the initial physical attraction are the mental/emotional and spiritual connections we make with that person.

Think about the issues of longer-term commitment and how these impact on your choice of a lover. You will need to look at such issues as stability, lifestyle, morals, and maturity. If you're a gay parent, or want to be, your partner's attitudes about children and his or her parenting skills are also important. Such attitudes and attributes show up during the activities and interactions of everyday life. The next exercise will help you to determine what values and interests you would like your partner to have.

Ideal-Lover Exercise: Values and Interests

Answer the following questions, in much the same way you did for the review of your own lifestyle.

Hobbies, Interests, Lifestyle

What interests would you like your lover to have? Would you enjoy a homebody? An outdoors person? A very verbal person? An affectionate type, a cuddler? Why?

Do you want a mate who can cook and entertain? What kind of entertaining do you want to do?

Would you like your lover to be very involved in church or political organizations?

Do you want someone who's highly educated, loves to travel, or has artistic talent?

Should your lover be a computer buff? A collector of comic books? A vegetarian? A gun enthusiast or hunter? What hobbies would your ideal mate have? Do you want to have similar or different hobbies?

Would you like your partner to be someone who enjoys dancing? Opera? Poetry readings? Sports? Singing? Reading?

How many of your favorite activities do you want your lover to share? What kinds of activities do you want your lover to have that you don't share?

Spending Time Together

Do you like time alone in the morning, or do you prefer lots of snuggling? Do you want a cheerful, talkative morning companion, or someone who leaves you alone?

When you come home from work, do you prefer a busy, social evening, or quiet privacy together?

When you have a lover, how much time will you need to be: by yourself? with your lover, alone together? with friends? How will you work this out?

What kind of playtime do you want to have together—quiet, relaxed times, or energetic, athletic ones? Do you want to travel, sail, ride horses, garden, go to plays and fine restaurants?

Would you like to spend a lot of your spare time working together for political causes, charity, church, or other causes?

An issue that's unique to gay and lesbian relationships is coming out. Do you want someone who's out and open about his or her lifestyle? If subtlety and discretion are not your style, hooking up with someone who is closeted could be too big a problem to handle. Also, be aware that if you have a closeted mate, you'll automatically be left out of certain events, since your lover may not feel comfortable inviting you. On the other hand, if you yourself are closeted to some degree, a lover with a similar lifestyle would likely be very understanding.

Now compare what you've learned so far from the exercises in this chapter about who you are, what kind of person you want for a lover, and what kinds of activities you want to be able to enjoy with her or him. Make note of where your answers correspond and where they seem to conflict. Are any the conflicts related to relationship problems you've had in the past? For example, perhaps you said you were slow and quiet in the morning, but later you said you wanted a cheerful, active lover and that you wanted to talk, cuddle, and spend time together in the morning. You may want to reconsider the last answer, based on how you *actually* behave and feel in the morning! Perhaps for you it would be better to have some quiet, alone time in the morning and to get in your cuddling after work. Or perhaps you need to reevaluate the type of lover you want—it might be that you'd do better with someone who's relaxed and quiet.

Comparing and evaluating your answers can help you to develop a clear picture of the differences between what you think you want and what would truly work in your life. Take your time with the comparison. You may want to go back and answer some of the questions again. If you let yourself dwell on these things for a few days or a week, your subconscious fantasies will emerge from where they may have been suppressed. This is a good way to find out the secret wishes you may have been hiding from yourself!

All of the foregoing emphasis on similarities may have given you the idea that all successful relationships must be between people who think exactly alike and like all of the same things. Not true. *In successful relationships, comfort and security arise from the couple's similarities, but excitement and growth arise from their differences.* Being truly compatible means having both similarities and differences, so that you and your partner can create a balance between security and excitement—and a fulfilling relationship that will last over an extended period of time.

THE FINE ART OF "SQUIRREL HUNTING"

The most frequent problem I hear from single gay and lesbian clients is that of how and where to search for a lover. Many of them have been searching for a long time, without success; others have been afraid to go out and search at all. To answer this need, I have devised a system I call "squirrel hunting."

There are two ways to catch squirrels. One way is to run around and try to grab them or pounce on them—but in so doing you'll only scare them away, and they'll run faster than you do every time. In the end, you'll be very frustrated and exhausted, and you'll have no squirrels.

Or, you can go to where the squirrels are, offer them something attractive, like walnuts, and wait quietly, just enjoying the day and the place. It will take a while, but if you are very relaxed and quiet, they will begin to get curious, and soon they will begin to check you out. If you stay relaxed and let them get to know that you are safe and have goodies, before too long they'll be eating out of your hand. Then you'll have your choice of several squirrels. Success is guaranteed, if you have a little patience.

Finding a lover really isn't much different. Success depends more on how you feel about yourself and your own life than on how rich or physically attractive you are. As I said earlier, looks and outer attributes fade in importance very quickly; your personality and self-esteem are what your lover really values. Like the successful squirrel hunter, you need to be able to relax and enjoy the day and place. Patience and a calm attitude not only are very attractive, but they also keep you in a frame of mind in which you can think clearly and make good choices.

Following is a step-by-step guide to squirrel hunting.

Preparing Yourself

To be a successful "squirrel hunter," you first need to have your life together as much as possible. Start with your body and your health. While you don't have to be physically gorgeous or have a perfect body to find love, you do need to be healthy in order to have the energy and motivation to go out and look for love. Make sure that you get ample sleep and that your diet is healthful. Is there an exercise program you've been meaning to start? Motivate yourself by understanding that the healthier you are, the more attractive you'll be. There's something irresistible about healthy, glowing eyes and skin and the energy that comes from feeling good. Make yourself into the kind of lover you'd like to have.

Learn the guidelines on safe sex (see Appendix B) and follow them, and go to your local gay and lesbian center to get information about AIDS and VD prevention. There's a lot you can do to keep your resistance high and play safely.

When you feel good about yourself and your life, your anxiety about finding a partner will fade, and you'll soon have your choice of a number of potential partners.

Dressing for the hunt. Every savvy hunter knows the importance of dressing for the hunt. While you don't have to look as though you've stepped out of a fashion magazine, it obviously helps to be well groomed. Your clothing will be most effective if it reflects who you are. If you're comfortable about how you look and know that you look your best, you'll be more open to meeting new people.

When you go out, do you dress appropriately for where you're going? If you're not sure what will be appropriate, get some advice from a friend who knows what most people will be wearing. If you're going to a party, don't hesitate to call and ask your host or hostess what the dress will be. Doing so will save you the embarrassment of being the only one in jeans when everyone else is dressed up, or the discomfort of being the only one formally dressed when everyone else is sitting on the floor in jeans.

If there's a secret gay or lesbian dress code in your area, do you know it? Dress codes vary from time to time and place to place. Keys, handkerchiefs, broaches, and scarves can all send messages you may not intend to send. If you see a certain accessory used a lot, ask some friends what it means before you copy it. Once you understand them, the codes can really help you to communicate.

If you wear very revealing or suggestive clothing, you're advertising for sex, not for a relationship. On the other hand, if you're too conservative, you'll discourage people. Find a middle ground between street hustler and undertaker. Leather, rubber, or vinyl says bondage to some people. Too much high fashion can be intimidating. Wearing pleasant color combinations and comfortable clothes and shoes is more middle-of-the-road and leaves room for relating.

Do wear one special accessory that can provide a clue as to who you are—perhaps a special earring or pair of earrings, a one-of-a-kind jewelry item, a badge or button, a T-shirt with a funny message, or a knockout pair of boots.

Preparing Your Lair

Your home can help you tell a new or potential lover who you are. Does your home look like you live there, or does it feel impersonal, cold, or anonymous? Would a special guest be curious to learn more about you? If your house or apartment is really a home, it will be a representation of who you are and what you like, and a new guest will sense this immediately.

In my practice, one of the first things I ask lonely people to do is to take a good look at their surroundings. The following exercise will help you to see your home through the eyes of a special guest.

Evaluating Your Home

Go outside and reenter your house or apartment as if you were a stranger. Whether or not your home is luxurious is unimportant; you are simply to observe what it says about who you are and what kind of life you lead.

As you walk through your home, answer the following questions:

- Does your living room invite a guest to feel comfortable? Is there a space that makes conversation easy and natural?
- If your fantasy of a new relationship includes making romantic dinners at home, is your house prepared? Can you create an atmosphere of low, soothing light and soft music? Is there a pleasant place to eat?
- If gourmet cooking is a hobby of yours, as it is for many of my clients, is there room in your kitchen for two? Are there cooking utensils that are fun and interesting to use? Have you used your gourmet magazines or cookbooks for decor?
- Is your bedroom a wonderful, sensual, "to-die-for" place? Or are rumpled clothes and messy papers lying all over? The lighting, the colors, and the pictures on the wall can all give an invitation. If your apartment is just one room and your bed is a convertible sofa or a futon, have you made that area of the room inviting and cozy?
- Is your bathroom clean and neat? Are there extra towels for a special guest? Do you have such inviting touches as candles, sensual bubble bath, and tub toys?

Think of your home as a showcase for your personality. Imagine what a new friend would learn about you if there were pictures around of you and your friends doing the things you love. If you're a theater buff, you could put up theater posters. If you love sailing, pictures of the sea and sailboats would help let a visitor know this about you. Lots of books, an easel and painting equipment, a display of prize ribbons or awards, or a roomful of plants would all tell a guest something about who you are and provide clues for conversation.

This type of decor does not have to be expensive. Many stores carry inexpensive prints and posters that you can use to make your home express who you are. Also, since the setting is to reflect the true you, many of the objects and accessories there can be those that you already own for your interests, hobbies, and career.

If you've come out completely, does your home reflect this? Do you display gay-pride symbols or posters, sensual pictures of men or women, books like this one, gay or lesbian newspapers and magazines, or perhaps a picture of the panel you made for the AIDS quilt? If you're closeted or need to be discreet, you can still get your message across. For example, Martha, a young tennis player, has an action picture of Martina Navratilova on her living-room wall, along with pictures of herself and her ribbons and trophies. To straight friends or coworkers, the room says "tennis," but to lesbian friends, Martina's picture says more.

Set your home up to encourage the natural, slow development of a relationship. Make your living room livable. Set up a cozy place in your living room or kitchen for conversation and relaxing. Move furniture around, reorganize, and prepare your home so that it is comfortable and reflects who you are (for example, because scents are important to me, I like to use potpourri or incense often).

Note that the bedroom should definitely not be the only place of interest. It can, however, be the "pièce de resistance." Unless you have reason to be discreet, you can go all out here. Use warm, exciting color combinations, sensual nude pictures, and lots of mirrors; you can even display your favorite sex toys. If you're male, a safe-sex poster (there are some wonderfully sensual ones) or a crystal candy dish full of condoms near the bed gives a clear message about your attitudes and will make your safe-sex discussion easier.

Make your home a place you really care about, a safe haven that soothes *you,* as well as guests, the moment you walk in the door. Author and AIDS worker Louise Hay expresses the idea of a comforting home wonderfully: "I love myself—therefore, I provide myself with a comfortable home, one that fills all my needs and is a pleasure to be in. I fill the rooms with the vibrations of love, so that all who enter, myself included, will feel this love and be nourished by it."

Dan quiet and shy, is a gay schoolteacher around thirty-five years old. He came to me in despair about finding a lover. After some discussion of his likes and dislikes and of what he wanted in a lover, I sent Dan home to do the preceding exercise. He came back the next week, astonished:

> My home doesn't look like anyone lives there! It's like a museum. It's got things on the walls from my travels, but nothing about me, nothing personal. It looks dead, boring. Every place to sit is isolated from every other chair in the room. My favorite window seat is only wide enough for me. Even *I* don't like my house when I really look at it.

We discussed what he wanted his home to say about him and made some plans, and he went home to do the work. When he came back two weeks later, he said,

> I went through my travel stuff, and instead of choosing arty, impressive things, I chose the ones I like best—a little hand-carved elephant from Africa that I watched being carved, a hat I wore, a piece of hand-woven cloth. I moved my furniture, and I put up a group of photos of me on my trips. I don't have a couch, so I put some pillows in a pile on the floor, and I put a photo album nearby.
>
> Last night, at a gay teachers' meeting, I met Al. All this stuff about my travels was on my mind, so we began talking about it, and I wound up inviting him home to see my pictures. It was great, sprawled out on the pillows, looking at the album. We talked a long time. It was so easy! We decided not to have sex yet, but I know we will. He's traveled, too—I guess lots of teachers travel in the summer. And he's invited me over this weekend to see his travel pictures.

Finding the Right Hunting Grounds

I have a saying: "Where you go is what you get." Often, when I ask despairing gay and lesbian clients where they've been finding lovers, they answer "I go to the bars." In general, bars are inappropriate places to meet potential lovers. The exceptions are bars where gay people come to dance, or gay piano bars with good entertainment. In these places, which have a reason for being other than alcohol, you have a greater chance of meeting people who lead stable lives.

Otherwise, gay and lesbian bars tend to be gathering places for two kinds of people: those who have made alcohol important in their lives and possibly have addiction problems, and those who have nothing better to do. Do these sound like the types people you want to be with? Obviously, healthy people occasionally go to bars for a night out—but they're usually with friends (and therefore harder to meet) or with dates.

Sarah, a forty-year-old accountant, is attractive, pleasant, and successful. In general, she's a "good catch." She had searched for a lover for two years in bars and lesbian singles groups before finally coming to me in despair. She told me,

> All the lesbians I meet have big problems. They're desperate or miserable, or they're so isolated that they'll only talk to other lesbians. I want someone who mixes in everywhere. In my profession, I can't afford to be too obvious, although my partners, my parents, and my friends know I'm gay. I have a mixed group of friends. I have to have a life partner who can relate to straight men, "pass" in a business setting, and handle herself well.

Sarah and I discussed the problem of where she was going to meet people, and I suggested that she try some new places. At first she said she was too busy, but after a while she decided to take some weekend classes. She had always been interested in psychology and thought it might help her in her work, so she enrolled in several business psychology courses at a local university.

Several weeks later, she came in smiling:

> I met Blythe at one of my classes two weeks ago. I never thought I'd be able to connect with another lesbian there, but I spotted her right off, although no one else seemed to know. In fact, I met several nice sisters there, but no one who'd seemed exciting until Blythe. I edged over to her at the coffee break and dropped a hint about the Sisterhood Bookstore into the conversation, and she responded right away. We've been dating a lot, and I think it's going to be serious. She's a businesswoman, too. She's so together, and she looks great, and she's a lot like me. She understands the demands of my work, and I understand hers.

Six months later, Sarah and Blythe moved in together, and they've been doing well for a year now.

The next exercise will help you to find your own hunting grounds.

Search-and-Find Exercise

In a small notebook, make a list of things you'd like to learn to do. Windsurfing, skiing, hiking, needlepoint, camping, gourmet cooking, wine tasting, dancing, writing poetry—anything you've been curious about trying goes on the list. Next, list all the places you'd like to see, including any local tourist spots you've missed but are curious about. You will be referring to these lists each time you want to go on a search.

Look at your first list, and then get out around other people who are doing the activities you want to do. Take a class, join a special-interest group (such as a Windsurfing club, a folk-dance group, a ski club, a literary club, a gourmet society, a gay Bible-study group, the National Organization for Women, or the Lambda Democratic Club). These groups can be gay or straight. Obviously, if they're gay groups, you won't have to sort out the gay people from the straight people, but don't worry too much about this; it's better to be in a mixed group of people who are doing what you love than in a gay group that is doing something you don't care about.

Don't worry if you don't find a friend or lover at your first outing or two. Be patient, and success will come over time. Remember, the more people you know, the bigger your network—and the bigger your network, the better your chance of meeting Mr./Ms. Right.

One final note about meeting other gay or lesbian people: I do not recommend therapy groups (workshops, weekends, or retreats), Alcoholics Anonymous or other Twelve-Step meetings, or even gay singles events as places to meet potential lovers. While the odds may be better here than in bars, all that the participants in such groups initially have in common are their problems or their state of being single. By all means, go to therapeutic groups to improve your relationship with yourself—but don't confuse your agenda by going there to find someone else.

Meeting and Interviewing Potential Lovers

Okay, so you've figured out where to go to find an appropriate choice of new partners, and here you are, out among strangers.

Now what? How do you go about narrowing the field to find that special person?

Pick someone! At first, it doesn't really matter who you pick, or how. Taking a bit of time to observe the people you're near will probably give you some good clues. After choosing someone, pause a moment and think about why you picked this person—what caught your attention? That's usually a good place to start when you initiate a conversation. For example: "I was surprised to find this window seat empty—do you prefer the aisle?" "I couldn't help noticing your red hair (or your unusual sweater or earring). Do you get lots of compliments on it?"

Always end your comment with a question. This is known as putting the ball in the other court—it means the other person must respond. If the response is monosyllabic and grudging, you've probably found someone who's not open to meeting you. Let the ball lie, lapse into a relaxed silence, and give it a minute. The person might have a change of mind. If not, look around again. Don't waste time and energy on uninterested people; there are plenty of interested ones out there. When you get a lively, interested, open response to your first statement, you can move on to the next step: interviewing and screening.

If you're in a mixed crowd, it would clearly be useful to find out if the person is gay or straight, but this can be awkward. If you're focusing on friendship, you can wait a while to see whether it comes out in conversation. Recently, I was talking to a stranger at a wedding about one of my books, and he asked me if the book was available at A Different Light (a local gay bookstore)—a wonderful clue, recognizable only to someone "in the know," that he was gay. Drop a hint about your Holly Near records, or say, "I just came from the Rodeo in San Francisco." If you get a knowing response, it's likely that the person is gay. If you get a naive response, such as "Oh, who is that?" or "Are you a cowboy?", you can easily step back. Go slowly—what you need to know will find its way into the conversation before too long.

If you're in a gay or lesbian group, don't take it for granted that everyone there is gay. In this type of setting, you don't need to drop hints. You can simply ask, "Are you gay?"

Whether or not you find out your candidate's sexual preference right away, you still need to "screen" the person to get some idea of your compatibility and shared values. So much heartache and frustration can be avoided by doing one thing—paying attention! People reveal themselves constantly through what they say, what they don't say, and, especially, through their behavior. It is usually simple to find out nearly everything you want to know—and if you can't, that's important information, too.

Interview Exercise

I often lead this exercise in workshops, and I'm always amazed by how much people can learn about one another in an artificial setting within a five-minute time limit!

Find a partner for this exercise. Your job is to interview the person, finding out as much as you can about his or her lifestyle and potential as a friend or partner for you. The only catch is that you can't let the interviewee know that he or she is being interviewed.

Remember that you can also learn a great deal from nonverbal clues. For instance, you can observe whether the person seems to care about his or her appearance, is assertive or passive in conversation, remains stiff or laughs a lot, is reserved or open, and so on.

A good way to begin the conversation is to remark on how you're feeling at the moment. Try something simple, such as "The music sounds terrific tonight! I love jazz, don't you?" or "You look so calm and relaxed while all this activity is going on—how do you do it?" Or mention something you found interesting: "I just saw an old Bogart movie at the Art Theatre. It was great. I usually like his earlier movies better than his later ones."

To conduct an interview without giving yourself away, offer information about yourself and invite a response. Mention things you're interested in—for example, sports, a recent political event, a new movie, hiking, biking, cooking. (Pre-preparation hint: Reading that day's newspaper or a recent issue of a weekly newsmagazine can help you to be prepared with topics for discussion.)

After each comment you make, give the other person time to come up with a response; don't rush it. Then follow up on the response: "Oh, you like Bogart, too? Which of his movies do you like best?" By showing interest in the response, you'll help the conversation flow. Don't worry about your next line. When you pause a little to think of one, that makes a handy space for your partner to come up with something to say.

Pay attention to all of the person's responses. Pretend that you'll be quizzed later, and gather as much information as you can. If you're concentrating on doing this, you won't have time to feel nervous or awkward.

When interviewing someone, avoid running a commentary in your own mind in an attempt to get inside the other person's head to see how you come across (for example: "I'll bet he doesn't like how I look. And what a dumb thing I just said! He probably thinks I'm a loser. I never should have worn this purple shirt. He probably thinks it's nelly. Should I buy him a beer, or will he think I'm too pushy?"). Don't try to guess his or her thoughts. He (or she) can think just fine by himself.

Instead, focus your attention on what you think of this person. What interests you? Don't be afraid to ask questions. Show your interest, and get your new acquaintance to talk about himself or herself. If you begin simply by finding out who this new person is and sharing some of yourself, you'll be off to a fine start.

Evaluating the Hunt

After trying the above technique with someone new, think about what you've learned about this person. Write it down if you like. Then compare this information with your answers to the ideal-lover exercises you did earlier.

To evaluate the success of your hunt, ask yourself whether the other person related to you and paid attention to you, or whether he or she often glanced past you, casing the room. Unless this new acquaintance was looking for a waiter or making sure a coat was not being stolen, this is an important sign. The person you chose was either uncomfortable with the conversation or simply unable to make a connection with you.

On the other hand, if you find that other people's attention often wanders when you are talking to them, then perhaps the problem may be yours. Many of us, because we're anxious about meeting someone new, tend to "run off at the mouth"; we wind up being overwhelming and boring. Keep in mind that trying to make an impression usually backfires, because the intensity of this usually scares people off.

ETIQUETTE FOR GAY DATING

Dating is a terrifying word! It's also a grueling ritual in our society. The setup is this: you're supposed to go out with someone you hardly know, usually pay an expensive tab, have a wonderful time, and fall in love forever.

Does this sound realistic to you? It doesn't to me, either.

Actually, I don't believe in dating strangers. Why waste all that time, money, and energy on someone you may not even enjoy being with? Like it or not, inviting someone on a date is usually interpreted as a statement of intention, and expectations tend to rise. Therefore, dating should be done selectively, with forethought.

Before you go on a date, spend a little casual time together. Invite your new friend out for coffee, to lunch, to a group activity, or to some event where you go dutch. This keeps the expectations, and therefore the pressure, lower.

Dating in gay relationships is

- for people who already have established a good reason to get to know each other better,
- for established lovers who want to spice up their lives with some romance or celebrate a special occasion, and
- something you can do with old friends when you want to show them you think they're special.

What's Different about Gay Dating?

Dating is a ritual and so follows certain social rules. In chapter 1, we saw that gay men and lesbian women lack social rules in certain situations and often end up imitating inadequate heterosexual models. Dating is one of those situations.

One difference that shows up immediately in gay dating is confusion about who leads and who follows. Since the traditional heterosexual dating ritual assigns these roles by gender (the man leads, and the woman follows), the roles obviously lose their meaning in gay or lesbian dating. For us, it's a question of preference or personality. That is, the person with the more assertive personality leads.

If you are in the position of leading, don't worry about what to do. Remember that the rules are vague in gay and lesbian relationships, and that you and your partner can choose to switch roles.

When you're following, you need to be honest about what you want. If you tell your friend that you like him or her and want to take things slowly, you will not likely encounter resistance. If the other person applies pressure, be aware that this will probably get worse as the relationship goes on. Stand your ground now, or it will be a lot harder to do so later.

A second difference between gay and straight dating is the confusion over whether your new acquaintance is a potential lover or a friend. (Actually, the same question does exist to some degree for straight people, although in my experience straight singles are not as aware of it.) Spending casual time together usually eliminates much of the confusion. Sometimes, however, asking for a date is what clarifies the situation.

The First Date: A How-To Guide

You've met, talked, and gotten to know each other. Your friend hasn't made the first move, so it's up to you. What do you do?

By this time, you should have some idea of what the other person likes to do. For your first date, plan to do something he or she is interested in. Make your invitation specific: "I've got tickets for . . . "; "The gay center is having a dance this Saturday"; "I know a great restaurant." Don't ask, "What are you doing this weekend?"—this is too open-ended and vague.

Using such phrases as "I'd like to take you to . . ." or "Be my guest at . . ." will let the other person know that you're paying. This makes it a date, with the implication that you are very interested. If you do want to go dutch, or if tickets and dinner are more than your budget will take, say so. Offer to buy the tickets and split the dinner. But let your partner know this before you ask for his or her agreement to go.

First dates should not be too pressured. Don't plan only to sit and talk to each other for four hours over dinner; that can feel very intense. Rather, plan to attend some event or entertainment you can watch—for example, a movie, concert, or sports event—and go out for coffee afterward. Or make it a group event, such as a party, dance, or excursion. This way, you can have a little time to yourselves, but there will be other people around to lighten the atmosphere. Remember, there will be plenty of time for intense romance later on.

Be careful not to place too much significance on a first date; one date does not a commitment make. It's just one more step in the process of getting to know each other.

Do's and Don'ts for Gay Dating

Following are some guidelines to help you make your dating situations as smooth—and as fun—as possible.

Do's:

- *Do listen.* Don't monopolize the conversation. You'll learn even more about your friend, and it will be much more relaxing for you.
- *Do focus on the friendship.* At this stage of a relationship, there's no way of knowing where it might go, so concentrate on simply developing the friendship aspect.
- *Do get feedback.* Find out whether your date enjoyed the time. For example, offer your comments on the event or the restaurant, and ask your date what he or she thought of it.
- *Do let your date know it if you enjoyed his/her company.* When the evening ends, say you'd like to do it again, if that's true. If you make any promises about calling, keep them. If you've decided not to continue the relationship but feel you can't say so, at least don't make any empty promises.

Don'ts:

- *Don't be afraid of a little silence.* In most cases, it's the occasional silences that allow a conversation to feel natural and unforced.
- *Don't make sex the main goal.* In addition to the current concern about sexually transmitted diseases and AIDS (see Appendix B for safe-sex information), there are other good reasons for not pushing for sexual activity too quickly: you won't be left in that awkward phase of being intimate with a total stranger; you won't be as likely to obsess about someone when you've gone slowly; and you'll have sex to look forward to. If and when sex is right, it will happen—and if you're relaxed, you'll be able to think clearly and be careful.
- *Don't get caught in a cycle of expensive dates you can't afford.* It doesn't work to go over your budget to impress your date—in the long run, you'll just have to make an embarrassing confession. Furthermore, it never works to "bribe" someone to spend time with you. If there's a difference in your financial status, that's a matter for frank discussion early on. If your date takes you out and spends a lot, you may find that reciprocating with a home-cooked meal, a hand-made

gift, or repair work on your date's ailing car will even the tally just fine.

Taking the Relationship Deeper

After several successful dates with the same person, you may be feeling very enthusiastic and have a sense of whether the attraction is mutual. You may even be having sex with each other. Nevertheless, don't give in to the temptation to rush. Let the relationship take the lead; take the path of no resistance.

If the relationship is going to be successful, you won't ruin it by taking your time. In fact, you can often increase a partner's interest by going slowly. The biggest problem early in relationships is the panic that results when one person is feeling pressured or smothered by the other. Perhaps you can identify with the following story.

Jane, twenty-seven, is a competent professional woman, stylish in dress. She sat in my office, frustrated and disgusted.

> I met Ruby at a meeting, and we talked a little over coffee. She was nice enough, and I liked her looks. When she asked me for my number, I said yes. The next day she called. That was nice; I was flattered. She asked me out to dinner. That seemed a little sudden, but I couldn't make it, so it was okay.
>
> At the next meeting, she sat next to me. By then I was beginning to feel a little crowded. Then she began calling me every day, saying she'd go to dinner anytime I wanted to. That was way too much. And when I got home from work today, there was a present at my front door from her.
>
> I don't want this—it's going way too fast. I don't want to hurt her feelings, but I just want you to tell me how to brush her off. She's too needy—I can't take it.

I happen to know Ruby. She's not really a pushy or obnoxious person; she just doesn't know how to let other people go at their own pace. She gets too anxious, and then she goes too fast. By now, she's been rejected many times. As her anxiety rises, she pushes even more—and is rejected yet again. Don't make Ruby's mistakes. Take your time.

After several dates (and a few weeks or a month), begin doing some more everyday things together—pulling the weeds in the garden, jogging or working out, spending long, lazy afternoons of talk and silence. Once you've established a basis for relating, you can begin to do some reality testing to see how far you and your partner can go together.

HOW LONG WILL IT LAST?

Early in the dating stage, your impression of your partner is made up of a small percentage of fact and a larger percentage of speculation and fantasy. How well you have paid attention to what your partner says, how he or she behaves, and how the two of you interact determines how much fantasy is in the mix. My own experience, and that of many of my gay clients, has convinced me that people can be highly aware of what kind of a person a partner is even in the very early stages of romance.

As noted earlier, people constantly give out clues about their habits, their attitudes, and their feelings. By paying attention, we can identify a person who is:

- chronically angry or abusive (argues frequently with the boss, yells at other drivers in traffic, always blames "the other guy")
- unable to give or receive emotionally (has to be coaxed to show any affection, "freezes" when hugged, won't hold hands even in a safe setting)
- financially irresponsible (keeps getting money from Mom, doesn't pay parking tickets, bounces checks)
- addictive (gets drunk or high, feels out of control, says "I can't help it" when confronted)
- immature or passive/aggressive (makes a joke out of serious things, not responsible, seems helpless a lot)

When my gay and lesbian clients come to me brokenhearted or outraged about being used, manipulated, or lied to by a lover, I ask a lot of questions about the lover's behavior in the early stages of the relationship. Usually, these clients realize that in fact they knew about the potential problems very early but had ignored the warning signs or convinced themselves that they could change the other person.

Recently, I conducted a workshop on interviewing other people and paying attention. One young woman raised her hand and said, "But I don't think like that when I meet someone new. I'm worrying whether that person likes me." Then she paused, considered what she had just said, and said: "Oh—that's how I keep getting involved with alcoholics, isn't it! I know they've had too much to drink, but I don't *notice* it. Now I understand."

There is really no reason for nasty surprises and drastic, dramatic breakups. If fantasizing about who you'd *like* your partner to be, or worrying too much about whether he or she likes you—and not whether *you* like what you see—is getting you into relationships that become disasters, learn to open your eyes. Hope and anticipation are wonderful, exciting feelings and appropriate for you and your new lover to share. But hanging on to a fantasy that denies the truth is dangerous.

In her book *A Fine Romance,* author Judith Sills writes:

> Time together, which offers both variety and repetition, practically invites a more realistic picture to develop. It's only an invitation, though. Lots of us, with plenty of opportunity, do not R.S.V.P. We cling to our fantasies because they are sweeter or safer. Spend time and force yourself to notice. You may not love everything you see, but you will see more realistically. The strongest bonds are forged when you are able to love what is so, not just what you hope is so.

It's better to find out as early as possible if your partner has a problem such as addiction, homophobia, or instability. If you find that you cannot negotiate with each other or that the reality is too flawed, it is important to change the nature of the relationship or end it before you become more emotionally invested.

If you feel that a new relationship has become too strained or unproductive, perhaps it's time to let go. Danger signs may include the following:

- Your lover is not able to give you the affection you want.
- You constantly disagree about basic things, and/or you argue frequently.
- The initial excitement has disappeared but has not been replaced by deeper feelings.
- You sense that your partner wants out.

If you're not sure whether to disengage or to try to save the relationship, you need to explore the possibilities with your partner. While it's a tough subject, not discussing it will be tougher in the long run. Following are some guidelines:

- Use the problem-solving and communication techniques in chapter 4.
- Discuss what each of you wants and is willing to give.
- Be as gentle as you can, but don't be afraid to be honest. If you can't be honest about your feelings at this point, your relationship doesn't have much of a chance, anyway.
- If your partner wants more of something than you can give (sex or affection, openness about your homosexuality and coming out, space and freedom, approval, or communication), admit it. Try to understand that your partner has a right to want what you cannot give.
- If you want things your partner does not seem able to give you, admit this, too. Tell him or her exactly what you want. Make it as specific as you can (not "I want more time together" but "I want to spend at least four nights a week with you").

Sometimes a frank, open discussion will help you to realize that you've just been misinterpreting each other and that you really *can* fix what's wrong. If not, the discussion will at least help you to clarify why the relationship is not likely to work. If you can reach an agreement together on what to do next, it's an accomplishment you can be proud of.

Saying Good-Bye

For many of us, the ending of a relationship—no matter how brief it has been, or how much of a problem—is often experienced as a personal failure. "Success" is defined as a long-term relationship, and any ending short of death implies that someone has done something wrong. This viewpoint ignores the fact that many relationships are circumstantial, existing because two people have met on vacation or have been working together for the summer. It also ignores the fact that it takes time for two people to get to know each other well enough to determine whether their relationship has long-term potential. Perhaps the two of you would make better friends than lovers, and it has just taken a while to find this out.

Sometimes it's difficult to allow your relationship to be what it truly is. Often, we either try to manipulate a relationship in an attempt to make it match our fantasy, or we stay in a relationship that really doesn't satisfy us because we're afraid to let go and look for someone else. The relationship then becomes "stuck": while it may really be best suited to being a casual friendship, we insist that it be more. We begin to pressure each other to meet our expectations; we complain about being dissatisfied and unappreciated. Eventually, the situation becomes so stressful that we spend most of our time being angry and frustrated with each other. What could have been a lovely friendship has become a disaster, with neither of us wanting any more contact with the other.

If you come to a mutual agreement not to go any farther as lovers, honor that agreement with a formal good-bye. Saying good-bye is a ceremony that creates closure. It puts a specific end to one phase of your relationship (romance), allowing you to begin a new phase (friendship). Here's how to say good-bye:

- Set a time when you can be alone together.
- You may want to exchange some possessions. Don't separate all your worldly goods at this session; it's better to get that out of the way beforehand. Just exchange some symbolic tokens. Give back jewelry, or exchange good-bye gifts.
- Talk about your past time together, reminding each other of the good times. Let each other know that you do care. This may bring up emotions; that's good. Let yourselves cry or feel frustrated that things didn't go where you had hoped they would. You're saying good-bye to that dream.
- Talk about how you feel: relieved, sad, disappointed, hurt, scared.
- Formally say good-bye: you may want to hug, shake hands, light and extinguish a candle, or ceremoniously burn some symbol of your previous relationship, such as a picture of the two of you together.
- Then leave, planning to spend some time apart before you attempt to get together again on your new terms. Make an agreement to contact each other in a month or so, to see how you both feel.

Earl and Sam, both lawyers in their forties, dated for about a year. When they tried living together, it just didn't work. All the joy went out of their time together. I helped them figure out that they really needed to just be friends, and I suggested that they say good-bye in the way outlined above. Later, Earl said to me:

> I just had the good-bye ceremony you suggested with Sam. It was sad. We talked over all the good times, we cried, we realized how much we care about each other, and we recognized that we need to move on. We gave each other our rings back. I thought I would feel terribly sad, but to my surprise, I feel good. I feel that Sam and I will always be friends. We're going to need some time apart to adjust, but we have a new bond—we know we can do something really difficult together. I think the friendship will always be there. It was hard, but I'm so glad we did it.

Moving Forward in Your Relationship

For many of you, saying good-bye won't be necessary. If all goes well, your relationship will deepen and begin to move through other stages. You'll find that you and your partner are spending more and more time together, and dating will begin to feel too awkward and too formal. You'll want to begin sharing the everyday, not-necessarily-romantic times together. You'll begin to make small commitments: leaving clothes and possessions at each other's places, reserving weekends for each other, exchanging tokens of affection, buying items together, attending groups and activities as a couple.

Allow these small commitments to happen gradually. Restrain yourself, if you can, from bypassing this stage and forcing an early commitment. This slow growth establishes a solid foundation for your later commitment. Just as it's necessary for a baby to learn to creep and then crawl before it can walk, it's necessary for a relationship to pass through gradual stages on the way to greater intimacy. In the next chapter, I'll describe these stages and discuss how to know when it's time to commit.

CHAPTER 3

From Dating to Commitment

You've been dating for a while, and things are going well. The two of you are good together. Now what? How far will it go? Is it love?

Perhaps you can relate to the feelings of my client John, a friendly, outgoing gay man in his mid-twenties, who told me:

> I really like Ed. I feel good around him. We have fun and we like the same things, but I don't know if it's love. The last time I was with someone, I was sure I was in love, and it was a disaster.
>
> Gary—my last lover—and I moved in together right away, and then I found out that we really didn't have enough in common. Everything he said sounded great, but he never followed through. I'm excited about Ed in the same way that I was excited about Gary and about other relationships that didn't work out. I don't want to make another mistake. When do I know it's right to make a commitment? How can I tell if it will last?

Or perhaps you feel like Linda, who is dating Cindy. Both women are in their mid-thirties and are well educated. Linda came to see me with a dilemma:

> I met Cindy just a few months ago. Compared to my last relationship, this one is going pretty well. We're taking our time, developing a friendship, and getting to know each other. Sex is pretty good and seems to be getting better, and we get along. I just don't know if this is real—if it's true love. What if I decide it is, and I'm wrong? I've been wrong before. I don't want to go through telling my folks about my being

gay and all that, only to have my relationship with Cindy fall apart. Cindy wants to meet my family, but that's a lot like coming out, and I don't want to do that until I'm really sure.

These two stories illustrate a hazardous course that every gay relationship must take: the transition from dating to a committed relationship. Many gay people in dating relationships that last for any period of time find themselves under constant subtle pressure—from friends, from the environment, and from their own internal feelings—to "up the ante." If you're dating once a week, the expectation is that you'll begin to spend weekends together. If you're spending weekends, the push is to "go steady" and be exclusive with each other. Going steady is supposed to lead to moving in together. Traditional rules say that anything less than marriage is not good enough. We are urged, by both inner and outer forces, to declare ourselves, to make a commitment. For many of us, the decision of whether or not to commit is very difficult and raises a number of issues that must be dealt with honestly.

Commitment itself has different meanings to different couples. For some, it simply means seeing even more of each other, usually on a regular basis. For others, it can mean being sexually exclusive. For still others, it can mean living together and planning a lifelong relationship, even getting married. In any case, the issue of commitment involves stronger relationship bonds and greater expectations than dating.

This transitional phase is particularly difficult for many people because it brings up feelings of fear, anxiety, and tremendous uncertainty. As I've mentioned before, commitment is particularly difficult for gay men, because their cultural role training—and perhaps their instincts—influences them toward random sexuality and away from settling down with one person. On the other hand, many lesbian women have a tendency to overreact about commitment, often rushing into relationships without taking the time to develop a solid foundation based on love, mutuality, and an in-depth knowledge of themselves and their partners.

In addition, for both gay men and lesbian women, facing the responsibilities and life changes of commitment can sometimes aggravate latent homophobia and raise the issues and fears of coming out to family, friends, and coworkers.

As a result of all of these issues, many gay people suffer needlessly from a kind of approach/avoidance dance about commitment. My work with gay and lesbian couples has convinced me that they can, indeed, have long-term, meaningful, enjoyable relationships that result in living together, lifelong companionship, and marriage. Gay couples do not have to follow the accepted heterosexual patterns—traditional gender roles, monogamous marriage, divorce—nor do they have to buy into the homosexual stereotypes of short-term, unsatisfying love relationships or promiscuous, purely sexual encounters. For homosexuals, creating healthy, successful commitment means both revising the old rules and devising some new ones unique to gay relationships.

This chapter is about the transition from dating to commitment. I will not be analyzing the pros and cons of commitment here. Rather, I will be helping you to decide whether or not to commit in your current relationship, and to know when and how to develop commitment.

THE ISSUES OF COMMITMENT

As discussed in the last chapter, dating and "going together" are exploratory steps through which two people get to know each other. During the early stages of a relationship, the focus is generally on having fun; both partners are usually careful not to stress the bonds too much. As the level of trust builds, the couple begins to relax, allowing their less attractive aspects to be seen, and they start to do more ordinary activities together. In this way, they begin to "test" the relationship to see how well it can survive small difficulties.

If all goes well, the couple's confidence increases. They begin to trust that the relationship will be successful. At the same time, however, the increased emotional investment raises feelings of vulnerability—there is more to lose. Eventually, the investment becomes important enough that the couple begins to feel the need for some security, some reassurance that the relationship will last.

If the small problems remain unresolved and the couple gains no confidence in their ability to survive them, they begin to feel uneasy about the possibilities of commitment. One or both of them will question whether the relationship is worth continuing.

In either case, there is a necessary transition going on. The precommitment phase of a relationship is a natural part of the courtship process.

If you've been dating for a while, you have two options: to end the relationship and move on, or to continue it and hope that it will lead to further growth. You and your lover are probably asking yourselves (and maybe each other) questions like the following:

- Can our relationship last?
- Is the relationship healthy?
- Should I be cautious and start (or continue) to see other people?
- Am I ready to take the plunge and be exclusive with my partner?
- Do I know who this person really is, or might he/she change after we've committed?
- Am I rushing into this?
- Am I dragging my feet?
- How will being committed to this person change my life, and am I ready for it?

Asking questions such as these is a useful part of the development of a healthy gay or lesbian relationship.

There are four main criteria to be considered when assessing a relationship at this stage. These criteria, and the order in which I believe they are most effectively considered, are:

Love
↓
Judgment
↓
Mutuality
↓
Responsibility

By moving from one level to the next and asking the questions appropriate to each level, you can gain a perspective on your relationship that will support your decision to commit or not.

Is It Love?

There are so many outside factors putting pressure on a gay or lesbian couple that it's very easy for them to focus on whether or not they should commit rather than on whether they're actually in love. On the other hand, many gay people get so caught up in the feeling of being in love that they may forget to consider whether they have a solid basis for commitment.

Love is the underlying motivator that provides a commitment with strength and durability. It is the source of the energy that will keep you honoring your commitment through all the rough spots you'll encounter in your relationship. The question is, how do you know whether you are enough in love to sustain a commitment?

This is a difficult question, one that cannot be answered with some simple, quantifiable measurement. Although I've spent a large part of my life learning about love, its total nature is probably beyond the scope of our understanding. The minute I *think* I understand it, it moves beyond what I already know, leading me to further experience and study.

The concept of love is often reduced to meaningless, misleading platitudes—"love at first sight," "love conquers all," "love is blind," "love makes the world go 'round." Confusion also arises because we use that one word, *love,* to describe several different conditions and circumstances: in addition to the complex dynamic that exists between two people who share romantic and sexual bonds, we use the word *love* when referring to the bonds of friendship, the feelings between parent and child, devotion to a spiritual source, and affection for pets and possessions.

Following are two quotes that I feel describe the kind of love that must be present in gay and lesbian relationships in order for them to survive. These writers point out that love is the giving of oneself to another without conditions—that is to say, we love because the other person deserves our love, not because we ourselves need love.

In *We: Understanding the Psychology of Romantic Love,* Robert Johnson says:

> Love is the power within us that affirms and values another human being as he or she is. Human love affirms that person who is actually there, rather than the ideal we would like him or her to be or the projection that flows from our minds. . . .
>
> Thus, love is by its very nature the exact opposite of egocentricity. We use the word *love* loosely. We use it to dignify any number of demands for attention, power, security or entertainment from other people. . . . Love is utterly distinct from our ego's desires and power plays. It leads in a different direction: toward the goodness, the value, the needs of the people around us.

Hugh Prather, in *The Quiet Answer,* writes that

> Love is a state of mind or a vision that handles all things equally. . . . Love can only accompany what is given away, and since all of love must be given in order for all of it to remain, there can be no range to our giving. There is only one kind of love, the uncalculated kind.

The mystery of love is what keeps it ever exciting and never boring. Understanding, exploring, and discovering love and how it connects us is a lifetime task, so don't expect yourself to be absolutely clear about your love. For now, it's enough if you believe you're in love. The rest of the information and exercises in this chapter will help you to discover whether the love you feel for your partner can be a solid basis for a long-term relationship.

Chemistry and the Myths about Love

In *A Fine Romance,* Judith Sills writes:

> Chemistry is the magic that makes one person exciting to you and another irrelevant. . . . You must feel it to connect, but you can't control where you might feel it—or for how long.
>
> Chemistry can mean the click that occurs when two personalities intrigue each other . . . the magic of sensing the potential in someone else. . . . It's also a feeling of excitement that someone has come into your life who could change it forever.

In all my years of counseling, I have never encountered a gay or lesbian client who didn't recognize chemistry—the feeling of being in love. Chemistry is the rush, the high, that we experience when we get together with someone who mysteriously "turns us on." Everyone I've talked to seems to know the difference between loving someone in a familial, friendly, platonic, or parental way and being in love, which implies romantic, sexual love.

Chemistry is usually the first thing that must be present in order for a relationship to exist. No one would have the energy for the sometimes difficult journey of love without the excitement of that bodily "knowing." Chemistry is the motivation, the energizer, the reason for our interest. It is enthusiasm and excitement. It can be a positive, creative force, one that grabs your interest and that can perhaps hold onto it long enough for deeper, more significant feelings to emerge.

While excitement about and strong sexual urges toward a lover can be simply a positive indication of physical and emotional attraction, they can also be signs of unresolved inner conflicts for which we are seeking resolution. We all fantasize about love, but for some of us the myth obscures the reality. In such cases, chemistry projects us toward fantasy objects fraught with problems.

Jodie is a good example of someone who repeatedly lets chemistry lead her into trouble. An attractive lesbian of thirty-eight with an eleven-year-old son, Jodie has been "married" eight times, twice to men and six times to women. She came to me because her sister, on whom she relies for advice, insisted that she get help.

> I don't know what happened. This time, I thought I'd found the right person. Molly and I clicked from the start—it was love at first sight! My son, Josh, loved her, too. We had lots of fun together. She and I moved in together after the first two weeks. But she left me, like all the others. I thought she loved me, just like I did with all the others. But just like them, she didn't really love me either. Why won't anyone ever love me?

Unfortunately, Jodie believes the myth that every time chemistry calls, it automatically brings along lifetime love. There are several such myths to watch out for on your way to a solid gay or lesbian relationship:

Myth #1: Love happens instantly. The ideas that you must be absolutely sure from the beginning, that you'll recognize love immediately when you find it, and that "chemistry" is all you need are heavily promoted in movies, on television, and in novels. Such a romantic idea of what it means to fall in love can be great entertainment, but it usually doesn't work well in real life.

Myth #2: Physical lust is always the same as love. While love can include physical excitement, there can also exist purely physical and/or circumstantial attractions that fade quickly. With such an attraction, the more you get to know each other, the less exciting it is; with love, the excitement grows.

Myth #3: You can't fall in love with someone you are not immediately excited about. Sometimes love grows slowly, as we get to know someone. Falling in love with the inner person is often different from falling in love with the outer person (that is, that person's physical appearance and style). Sometimes we see an old friend in a new light, and chemistry suddenly happens. Excitement and physical response develop where there was once only friendship.

Myth #4: Relief is the same as love. When we're very lonely, or hurt, or grieving, we appreciate positive, caring attention—but our feelings of appreciation should not be confused with love. Neediness alone will not sustain a relationship over the long haul.

Judgment

Judgment is the balancing factor that can help you to rationally assess the quality of your love. We often fail to use our ability to judge because we love in childlike ways that reflect the uncritical sense of love and relationships we developed as children. Long before we learned to think rationally and logically, we learned patterns for loving and being a "family." For example, if you had a cold, unexpressive father, as an adult you might unconsciously seek out cold, unexpressive partners.

Without judgment, unexamined natural attraction can lead to problems. Chemistry alone cannot help you to evaluate whether the attraction is sensible; it is simply a response to certain signals. For these reasons, it's necessary that you think clearly about your immediate sexual responses so that you can choose partners with whom success is possible and commitment worthwhile.

Because intimacy reminds us of childhood feelings, it may not occur to us that we have choices. Like Jodie, many of the gay clients who show up in my office devastated by love have attempted romantic adventure by leading with their childlike, feeling aspect; their rational, critical thinking seems to have been lost. Love has a much better chance of being realized if you make your choices mentally as well as with subconscious and physical responses. You need to step back from your excitement and evaluate your partner using your rational judgment: think, observe, evaluate, ask, remember, experiment, speculate, and empathize.

Dr. Sonya Friedman wrote her book *Men Are Just Desserts* for heterosexual women, but the following piece of wisdom applies equally well to men choosing men or women choosing women:

> If you choose a [lover] on the basis of romance, idealism, salvation or "chemistry," the result will almost always be

> eventual bitterness and hurt. In the early stages of courtship, romance is dazzling. When you think you're falling in love, your vision blurs and you develop selective hearing. To your slightly malfunctioning senses, reality is distorted. You see what you want to see and hear what you need to hear. What happens? You miss the clues that are laid out before you. A man reveals himself very early in the relationship, and you need all your faculties to be attuned to him. . . . When the veil of romance drops from your eyes, the man you are looking at will be in sharp focus. By seeing him clearly, you can evaluate him not by what he *says* ("I can't live without you") but by how he *behaves* (he sees other women while insisting all the while that you're his only true love).

When doubts about your love arise, don't push them away. Instead, use them to help you mentally evaluate your chances of success. If you feel nervous and unsure, chances are that you're going too fast. Your inner wisdom is asking you for a safety check; listen to it, and take the time to make an informed decision.

Similarly, don't reject a relationship too quickly just because the chemistry isn't powerful and immediate (see Myth #3). If your judgment suggests that the relationship has possibilities, hang in there a little while longer to see whether a bond develops.

Before making a deeper commitment to a lover, take a look at any obvious problems (for example, signs of drinking too much, outbursts of rage, profligate spending, frequent criticism of you, and rude or humiliating behavior toward you or others). If problems such as these are present, your odds of having a successful relationship with this person at this time are very poor. Consider ending the relationship, or at least minimizing your involvement until you have had a chance to see whether your lover can make some changes. Be aware that whatever problems exist now won't go away if you get more involved; instead, they're likely to become more severe. Taking a good, hard, objective look at your relationship now can save you needless pain later on.

Chemistry and Judgment Exercise

Part I:

Divide a piece of paper in half vertically by folding it or drawing a line down the middle. On the left half of the paper write the heading "Chemistry"; on the right, write the heading "Judgment."

Now write down some of your reactions to your lover, putting your feelings in the "chemistry" column and your thoughts and evaluations in the "judgment" column. For example:

Chemistry	*Judgment*
Has black, curly hair; my favorite!	Intelligent, but does not like verbal sparring; I do.
Too dramatic; scares me sometimes.	Has had several good jobs, but says she was unhappy in all of them—is she stable?
I melt when I look into her eyes.	
Lovemaking is wonderful, but it can get too intense	We communicate well; she understands me.
Reminds me of my first lover—that worries me.	Seems to be very closeted, which I am not.

Fill the page, and then fill as many more pages as you wish. This will give you practice in separating your subconscious motivations from your conscious thoughts. Once you've finished both columns, put the list away for a day or two.

Part II:
Take your list out and look at it again. Which column has more entries? Which one is most positive?

Now fold the paper so that you can see only one column at a time. Look at the chemistry side first. Do you feel there's enough there? How long do you think these things will last? Which of the items on this list is the most fun? Which is the best dream-come-true item? Does the "child" part of you like this list?

Next, look at the judgment side. Your security and stability are reflected here. What would a wise, loving parent say about this match? Imagine the future of the relationship. What is your opinion of that future? If anything is missing in your picture of it, talk about this with your lover.

Don't be afraid to listen to your own judgment; it may yield a more positive picture than you expect. If not, and you can see that significant problems exist, you'll save yourself a lot of pain by keeping the relationship casual or ending it. On the other hand, if your judgment says "go for it," you'll have the security of knowing that the decision you've made to go deeper has been carefully considered and logical as well as emotional.

Mutuality

The next criterion for assessing your relationship is mutuality—that is, whether you both feel love for each other and are approximately equal in your motivation. Lack of mutuality is one of the pitfalls into which gay and lesbian clients of mine regularly fall. If you want commitment very much, it can be easy to lose sight of how your lover feels. However, true commitment can arise only from the free and conscious choices made by *both* partners.

Remember John and Ed, from the beginning of this chapter? In talking about his ex-lover, Gary, who couldn't follow through on his promises, John painted a picture of a lover who probably didn't care as much as John did. John is worried that the same thing will happen with Ed.

Jodie, in her eight different "marriages," had never even considered whether her lovers cared as much as she did. She moved right in, disrupted her and her son's lives, and in each case soon found that her lover didn't meet her needs.

In each of these cases, the mutuality of feelings and chemistry—and, therefore, the motivation to stay together—was unequal. Both John and Jodie were left hurt and confused, although for different reasons. Many other gay and lesbian clients have come to me feeling excited and in love, saying that they've found the perfect potential mate. They are worried, however, that the relationship isn't moving fast enough, or that their lover isn't initiating enough sex, or that he or she is resisting some step toward commitment (such as introducing them to family and friends, making the relationship monogamous, or moving in together).

There are four major areas of mutuality that must be present if a relationship is to succeed and grow: love, trust, benefit, and support.

Mutual love. Love is the constantly renewing energy that keeps a commitment alive. When both partners feel loved, and both feel appreciated for being loving, commitment can thrive.

Mutual trust. During the dating and courtship process, both partners get to demonstrate their trustworthiness. As promises are kept and feelings respected, the trust grows. In order for equal commitment to exist, the two partners must experience roughly the same degree of trust.

Mutual benefit. The benefit we gain is based on what each person knows he or she will get out of the relationship, and how each person is enhanced by being in the relationship. While each partner may perceive different benefits to differing degrees, the total benefits must feel approximately equal to the two partners; if not, it is likely that resentment will develop.

Mutual support. Although commitment can involve a certain amount of stress, when we feel committed, we feel willing to face the difficulties and the challenges of working things out. Implicit in a commitment is the understanding that the two partners will support each other—emotionally, financially, mentally, spiritually—to the best of their abilities, through both good times and bad. Also implicit is the expectation that each partner will be responsible for himself or herself and will thus not lean too heavily on the other.

When the above four conditions exist, the condition of mutuality necessary for true commitment exists. Recognizing this is especially important for gay men and lesbian women who persist in relationships in which their needs are not being met. Jodie, after considerable therapy, came to understand the need for mutuality; in her subsequent relationships, she has made choices based on love, judgment, and mutuality rather than on chemistry alone.

Understanding the importance of mutuality is also important for those people who don't know whether they're ready for commitment. If this is the case for you, you may be so afraid of not having your needs met that you are reluctant to commit to anyone. Or perhaps you are not looking closely enough at your partner to see what he or she has to offer that *does* meet your needs—in other words, maybe you don't recognize a good thing when you see it!

If you're really paying attention to whether you and your partner *both* feel love, trust, benefit, and support, your intuition will probably be a pretty good indicator of whether mutuality truly exists. Most of my gay and lesbian clients report that they are aware when their relationships are unfair and unequal. Following are guidelines to help you create or build on the mutuality in your relationship.

- *To build mutual love:* Let each other know when you feel loved, and show your appreciation for it. If you're not getting the kind of love you want, use the problem-solving techniques in chapter 4. If you're worried that your partner is not feeling loved or appreciated, don't let it pass. Ask about it.
- *To build mutual trust:* Only make agreements that you can actually keep. If something unavoidable is going to prevent you from keeping a promise, renegotiate in advance. Be willing to say no when you *mean* no, and help your partner to feel free to do the same.
- *To build mutual benefit:* Ask yourselves what's in the relationship for each of you. Consider whether the decisions you are making will benefit both of you. For example, if one of you decides to work to put the other through school, what will the payoff be for the wage earner?
- *To build mutual support:* Discuss what support means to each of you (for example, support can be emotional, mental, or financial in nature). Experiment with new ways of giving support to each other.

If you're feeling that one or more of the criteria for mutuality—love, trust, benefit, or support—is not shared or equal, say so. It's always best to tell your partner, no matter how uncomfortable you may feel about doing so. If you do not, resentment and anger can build and, sooner or later, explode; what is perhaps only a small and easily solvable problem now can thus become a major issue later on, blown out of all proportion.

Remember, you're establishing behavior patterns here for the rest of your relationship.

Your relationship should change in a mutual fashion, and in small stages. If one partner makes a move toward greater commitment, the next move should be made by the other person. For example, if you're the one who has made the first sexual move, hold back a little on the next likely occasion so that your partner has a chance to initiate sex. By maintaining equal involvement in the movement toward commitment, you can establish mutuality in your relationship.

Note that there is no universally "right" timing for commitment. Some people are ready for commitment after a few months;

others need a few years. The key is mutuality: do you both want it, and are you both ready?

The next exercise can help you and your partner to determine the level of mutuality in your relationship.

Mutuality Quiz

You and your partner should do this exercise separately, then compare your answers to see how closely you are in agreement. Fill in the blanks with "none," "some," "most," or "all."

My lover and I are now spending ________ of our free time together.

We solve ________ of our problems without having them escalate into fights.

We both know how to request enough time apart ________ of the time.

We both know ________ of the reasons why we want to make a bigger commitment.

If it doesn't work out, I know ________ of my lifestyle will still be intact.

I still spend time with ________ of my old friends.

My lover still spends time with ________ of his/her old friends.

Our relationship fills ________ of my needs for support.

Our relationship fills ________ of my needs for intellectual stimulation.

Our relationship fills ________ of my needs for romance.

Our relationship fills ________ of my needs for companionship.

Our communication is open and clear ________ of the time.

We have clear agreements about ________ of our financial issues.

We have discussed ________ of the domestic issues, such as cleaning, car repairs, and yard work.

If you find that your perceptions and feelings are very different on one or more of these issues, take the time to discuss these differences and how you both feel they should be resolved. If you find sharp, unresolved disagreement on several answers, it's likely that your relationship is not yet ready for the commitment stage.

RESPONSIBILITY = RESPONSE-ABILITY

Love and commitment require responsibility on the part of both partners. Often, people react to the word *responsibility* in the same way they would respond to the words *fault* or *blame,* as though saying "you're responsible for your life" means that you should feel guilty and at fault for mistakes. This sense of responsibility is childlike, and it can cause you to act as though an angry parent were standing over you, angrily asking, "Who's responsible for this mess?"

Adult responsibility is something else altogether. I like to think of it as *response-ability*—that is, the ability to respond to life. Seen in this way, it's clearly not a matter of blame. Rather, this view simply acknowledges the fact that each person, in every circumstance, has the ability to respond. Accepting responsibility is recognizing that we have choices. Out of many possible responses, you can choose the one you'll make; choosing not to respond is also a choice. Like it or not, the results of your responses shape your life.

As an illustration of the concept of "response-ability," imagine what would happen if you took a three-year old child into a big, shiny supermarket and then abandoned him. Although the child might have a wonderful time for a short while, before long he would be in lots of trouble and would be very upset. Every small child needs an adult in charge to meet his needs and keep him safe.

When you enter the seductive "supermarket" called love, you must be response-able for yourself. If you pay attention to your needs and make carefully thought-out choices, you won't become lost or panicky. And as a responsible adult, you'll find yourself making nourishing selections—not piling your cart full of emotional junk food!

Your prime response-ability can only be to yourself—that is, you can't make your partner's choices or make your partner more stable, honest, caring, or loving. It does little good to worry about what your partner's responsibility toward you should be, because you really haven't any say in how your partner views responsibility. It is your responsibility to take care of yourself; no one else can do this for you, not even the lover of your dreams. When you respond in an adult manner to the events that occur in your relationship, you will protect yourself and preserve your own integrity.

THE "WAFFLE"

You now have a number of tools to use to evaluate your readiness for commitment. We have examined love and chemistry, judgment, mutuality, and responsibility. The process of becoming committed is progressive; at each transition—going from dating occasionally to dating frequently to "steady" dating, to intimacy, to spending all your time together, to living together—you must reevaluate whether further commitment is appropriate.

It is very possible that at any point on this continuum, either you or your lover may feel undecided. Even people who have a strong urge to commit can waffle now and then. This can be very frustrating for the other partner, who may feel tempted to try to make up the partner's mind *for* him or her. Since this is, of course, not possible, the paragraphs that follow offer advice on how to deal with a partner's waffling, or with your own.

If Your Partner Is Waffling

Don't push. Here, as in squirrel hunting, patience is the best policy. If you are the one who is ready for commitment first, and you're tempted to try to coerce or persuade your partner, reconsider. If you want an equal investment and sincerely felt love, you need a partner whose commitment is free and clear. If you try to sway his or her feelings with guilt ("After all I've done for you . . .") or with fear ("If you don't commit to me right now, it's over!"), you'll never know whether your lover has his or her own reasons to be with you. You'll also be setting a precedent for a pattern that will be hard to break: putting more than your share of the energy into the partnership.

Be willing to see the truth. If your partner is waffling, don't automatically assume that he or she is "afraid of commitment" or just "needs a push." Back off a little and look for the truth. Could it be that your partner doesn't care as much as you do? Are you just straining to make a fantasy come true? Seek to understand your lover's hesitation, without pushing or being accusing. It's much better to learn at this point about any ambivalence your partner has than to wait until you're more heavily entangled.

Give your partner some time. In the case of John and Ed, earlier in this chapter, John was waffling. He had been hurt in his previous relationship and so was unsure now. In therapy sessions with John, I helped him to see that his fear was based on a combination of his past history and his not knowing how to evaluate whether it was likely that he'd be hurt again. In his last relationship, he hadn't known what to do when his partner was waffling, and he ended up pushing too hard. As a result, his lover left, and John was hurt. This time, it was John who was feeling undecided. Ed, however, had more patience. He saw that John was in therapy and working to sort out his confusion, so he just bided his time. Today, the two are living together happily.

If your partner is hesitant, he or she may feel frightened by commitment. There may be abuse or difficulty in your lover's history, or the problem may concern homophobia. Such issues take time and patience. *Decide how important more commitment is to you, and how impatient you are.* How much time are you willing to put into this relationship if your lover is never able to commit more deeply? Make that decision for yourself, by yourself. Then, once you've set your limit, relax and let your lover have time to make a decision. It's up to you to decide whether to tell your partner about the limit. That limit is really intended to help prevent you from waiting forever. It will help you relax. However, if the waffling continues and your limit is fast approaching, or if you're already too impatient and frustrated, tell your lover what decision you've made.

Recognize coming-out issues. Remember, gay men and lesbian women have a lot at stake in making a commitment, since doing so usually involves coming out. Waffling can thus be caused by uncertainty about what commitment will mean in terms of actual behavior. Your lover may require some extra time, and extra patience on your part, to come to terms with these issues.

The case of Linda, whom I introduced in the first part of this chapter, is a good example of waffling that arises from uniquely gay issues. When Linda's lover, Cindy, pushed to be introduced to

Linda's parents, Linda recognized that there was a lot at stake. While her parents were aware that she was gay, they had never actually seen her with a lover. Before confronting them with the issue, Linda understandably wanted to feel more secure in her relationship with Cindy. After some couples counseling, Cindy understood Linda's reluctance better and agreed to give her more time. The two were eventually able to work things out, and last year Cindy spent Christmas with Linda and her parents.

Back off quietly. If you feel you're being pushed away, go quietly—no drama, no scenes, no accusations. Make it easy for your partner to have space, since it's especially important for someone frightened by commitment to have the necessary space.

Backing off like this takes a great deal of patience (and you'll probably need to have someone outside the relationship whom you can lean on for support), but it can be incredibly effective. When you give your lover some room, he or she is more likely to come to the realization that commitment does not mean being trapped, and that the pressure comes from internal sources—not from you. Back off as far as you're asked to, as easily and calmly as you can. Then stay at that distance until you're invited back in.

If You Are the One Who is Waffling

Listen to your hesitation. If you are being pushed by your partner, or if you are pushing yourself ("We've been dating for a year—I should want more by now"), you need to respect your own inner wisdom. Ask yourself how you truly feel about your relationship and about the idea of making a commitment to your partner. For example, are you committed enough to this person to declare it openly? How much involvement do you want? Are there conditions attached to your commitment? If so, what are they?

Keep reevaluating your position. Just because you have initial hesitation, don't despair and decide it's all over. Give yourself a few days or weeks, and then reconsider how you feel.

Talk to someone who is objective. It can help a great deal to bounce your concerns, hesitations, and fears off a trusted friend. Unlike your lover, your friend won't be frightened or upset by your indecision. You might ask your friend to play devil's advocate, coming up with reasons why you *shouldn't* make a commitment. Such a debate, in a safe environment, can help you to see things more clearly.

Keep your partner informed. No matter how confused you are, telling your partner how you feel and what you're thinking is reassuring. Both you and your lover will feel calmer; as a result, you'll feel less pressure.

The following exercises can help you to sort things out.

Waffling Exercise #1

To find out whether you really want to commit or just think you should, it is essential that you separate your own thoughts from those of everyone else. In a notebook, make a list of all the things you know, or imagine, that others feel you should do regarding your current relationship. For example:

> My lover (mother, father, best friend) thinks I should ________ . (Fill in as many responses as needed.)

Next, make a list as long as you like in which all the items begin "What *I* want to do is . . . ," finishing each sentence with your *own* wishes. It's important that you be completely honest with yourself.

Now compare the two lists. How alike or different are they? Making these two lists will help you to clarify your thoughts and will enable you to determine whether your confusion is partly the result of outside pressures, either real or imagined.

Waffling Exercise #2

Divide a piece of paper vertically by folding it or drawing a line down the middle. On the left side, write the heading *Pros,* and on the right, *Cons.* List your feelings about commitment on the appropriate sides. This exercise may seem simplistic, but it works.

Put the list away for a day, and then take it out and review it. Notice which side seems to make the most sense to you. Which of your arguments do you feel really need serious consideration? When you've sorted out the issues you feel are important, talk them over with your lover.

Whether the hesitation is yours or your lover's, approach the barriers gently and thoughtfully. Don't just bulldoze over them or ignore them, as any reservations that are not dealt with now will likely return to haunt you later.

DECIDING NOT TO COMMIT

Not every gay or lesbian relationship benefits from change. More time and more involvement may bring not more pleasure, but more pressure. Many formerly committed and now separated gay couples have found, to their surprise, that they began to get along much better after separating. In these cases, the couples broke up because the changes brought about by commitment were too difficult for one or both partners to handle.

You may have to face the possibility that you'll decide not to go for further commitment; you may even decide to break up. However, if you feel that you do not want to change the nature of your relationship right now but you think that the commitment issue might come up again, set a time limit—for example, "We'll leave things as they are for three months (until my job transfer comes through or until I finish school), and then we'll discuss it again." A clear agreement about when to raise the issue again can prevent anxiety.

If you've decided not to commit, you have essentially three options: you and your partner can revert to open dating, you can decide to be just friends, or you can take a break from each other and then decide later what kind of relationship—if any—you'd like to have.

Open Dating

This is usually the most difficult option, because most of us have trouble allowing a relationship to go "backwards" from exclusive to nonexclusive dating. It is possible to make such a transition, however, if the emotional level of the relationship is relaxed and casual. For example, you may have been dating each other steadily due to circumstances or simply to a lack of effort to find others.

It's important that both partners be in agreement on whether to have an open-dating arrangement, and on how this will be handled. Part of your agreement may involve what you will tell friends who know that you've been dating steadily.

Being Just Friends

As I've mentioned elsewhere, gay couples sometimes mutually discover that they do much better as friends than as lovers. While the new situation can feel awkward at first, this kind of friendship can feel very close and safe; such a friend knows all about you, and loves you for you. Again, discussion and agreement are key.

Taking a Break

Most often, the transition from being lovers to having any other kind of relationship (dating or being close or casual friends) takes time. Getting completely away from each other for a while can give both of you a chance to experience your emotions about the situation and come to terms with the changes.

If you decide to take a break, an ending ceremony can be helpful. If you're on good terms, you may even want to have a last dinner or walk on the beach together. Set a date to meet again later (in two or three months) and discuss how you feel. At that time, you can consider what new direction you want to take, if any, with each other.

DIFFERENCES BETWEEN LESBIAN AND GAY COMMITMENT

As I've mentioned, lesbian women sometimes have a tendency to commit too fast, while gay men frequently have trouble committing at all. These are not absolute truths, of course, for all men and women in same-sex relationships; they are merely patterns I've observed. On the basis of these observations, I will offer a few hints for overcoming such partners. Feel free to follow the advice given for the other sex if it applies to you and your situation.

Advice for Lesbian Women

I know that dating is tough, and you've been trained to want to settle down. But remember the old cliché that anything worth doing is worth doing well! Before you jump into a relationship, talk to lesbian women who have long-term, solid relationships. Most of the gay women I've spoken to who have been badly burned by love did not take the time to define their relationship agreements before committing to a lover and moving in together.

It's important that you overcome any reluctance you may have to talk frankly about love and commitment with your partner. As we've seen, dating is the relationship stage during which two people can find out whether they're compatible. Respect and value this period of courtship, and allow it to run its full course. Insist that trust be earned, and work to earn your lover's trust.

Your personal life should be secure enough that you can feel happy and healthy *without* a relationship. Then, before committing, make sure you're clear about how you expect your new relationship to improve your life. Be sure to keep your own lifestyle intact: keep your friends, your source of income, your favorite activities and organizations. Suggest that your potential lover do the same.

Advice for Gay Men

For many of you, the idea of committing to a long-term arrangement may seem to go against your instincts. In my practice, I see many gay male couples who are reluctant to commit or who are unsure about when commitment is appropriate.

Men in our society have been conditioned to respond sexually to visual cues and to flit "from flower to flower to flower," to quote from *The King and I.* Such behavior is also believed to have a biological component (researchers are currently debating the question of just how much influence is exerted by nature and how much by nurture). Further, our culture generally has not given men permission to develop deep emotional ties with others, especially with other men.

With this biological/cultural push toward promiscuity, commitment can feel like a trap. As a gay man, you may see the potential hazards of commitment more quickly than you see its potential rewards. Intimacy is your challenge. Learning to open up, to share feelings, and to be mutually supportive with a partner are the necessary skills for intimacy. Since you will be doing this in a masculine way, your emotional communication will look different from that of most women.

Finally, gay men, more than lesbian women, are often concerned that further commitment will ruin a good friendship. When Dave and Alan came into my office they were both worried, although they were having no serious relationship problems. They'd been dating exclusively for several months and now felt that it might be time for them to try a deeper commitment. Alan explained his concerns this way: "What worries me is this: What if it doesn't work? What if we don't like each other as much when we live together? Will we lose what we have now?"

I explained to them that if they took their time and allowed the relationship to go through several gradual levels of commitment, they would be able to see how being more involved affected the relationship. I suggested that they first try spending a few weeks at each other's houses. This worked well, and they decided they were ready to move in together. I suggested that they view living together as a trial phase preparatory to making a permanent commitment. The one-step-at-a-time process was very reassuring for both of them, and they now live together and own their house. They are considering having a commitment ceremony to make a public declaration of their status as a couple.

THE PAYOFF OF COMMITMENT

By now, you probably know whether commitment is the step you want to take. If it is, as the years go by and your love grows and matures, you and your partner will likely see this early period of your love in a different light. If it has been a relatively smooth progression, you'll probably join the ranks of those who claim to have felt "love at first sight," and any little doubts you're having now will be forgotten. If the early stages have been rocky, you'll be able to laugh later about the difficulties from the secure stronghold of your experience and mutual understanding; whatever problems you have had in the beginning will be seen as just one phase of your growth as a couple.

Making a carefully considered, deeply felt commitment is a great joy. It's worth the time and effort, the confusion and the struggle to be honest with yourself and with each other. Commitment accomplished in this way becomes the secure foundation for everything else that you will build together.

CHAPTER

4

Dynamics of Gay Relationships

James and Mark, both in their mid-thirties, met a year ago at a friend's party and have been living together for five months. James is an administrator at a local hospital and deals with many personnel problems; Mark works with AIDS patients in a hospice. Since both have demanding jobs in the health-care field, they share many of the same concerns and frustrations. Their relationship has generally been good, but they came to me because they were beginning to have a lot of arguments.

Mark was especially upset, and he expressed his fear that the relationship might be falling apart. "James never wants to talk to me," he told me. "When he comes home from work, he disappears into his study." Mark nervously twisted his hands together as he talked. "I know he's tired, but I've been waiting two hours for him to come home, and I want to talk to him."

When I asked James to tell me his side, he said, "When I get home from work, I just want to relax, to unwind a little. Mark won't let me. He keeps badgering me, beginning the minute I walk in the door. He has to know *everything* about my day. I can't stand it anymore. I just want him to leave me alone."

Sally and Mary, who have lived together for two years, both work for the military although they themselves are civilians. They are in their late twenties, fit and athletic. Both dress in a unisex but attractive and stylish way: slacks, jackets or sweaters, and boots. They came to see me because they had been having physical fights. "I can't help it," Sally says. "I get angry, and then I lose control. I don't know what comes over me." Mary says, "I try not to make her angry, but sometimes I just have to tell her off. Then she gets mad, and we're at each other before I know what happened."

cheat can have similar results. Following are a few other hidden expectations that often occur in homosexual relationships:

Every other gay person will understand you.

All gay people are sexually open.

You and your lover will have no power conflicts because you are the same gender.

Your gay male lover will automatically understand if you cheat.

Your lesbian lover will automatically be faithful.

Your relationship will likely fail simply because you're gay.

Your lover will automatically reject his or her family if they don't accept your relationship.

You and your lover will automatically want to adopt roles, such as "butch" and "femme."

To avoid the problems of conflicting expectations, it is necessary to recognize when hidden expectations are present and learn how to bring them into the open. Recognition is not as difficult as it sounds. Hidden expectations are probably at work if one or more of the following situations exist:

- A simple mistake or misunderstanding leads to a big blowup.
- You or your partner is more upset about something than a situation seems to warrant.
- Such words as *should, ought, always, never, right,* and *wrong* are frequently used by you or your partner during disagreements.
- One or both of you are generally suspicious, guilt-ridden, or hopeless about your relationship.

Bringing a hidden expectation into the open is often more difficult. You and your partner need to think about what your expectations might be, share them, and then find out how each other sees the same issues. Let go of any inclination to feel that your expectations are right and your partner's are wrong; try to accept the fact that you are simply different. If the beliefs seem to be homophobic in origin, use the information in Appendix C to help you deal with homophobia.

George and Al, both in their fifties, have been lovers for five years, but they have not had sex in a year. Both men were formerly married and have families who are grown. They're quite distinguished-looking, with a little gray around the temples. George, who owns a store, says, "We used to have great sex, but I feel too tired now. There's a lot of stress at my business. I'm just not interested, and Al is too demanding."

Al, an electrician, looks hurt. "I can't take it anymore. I work just as hard as he does, but I still want sex. I've tried being patient, but I'm not going to just go without sex. Either we get this solved, or I'm going out to look for someone else."

All three of these gay couples are experiencing conflicts that reflect their *relationship dynamics*—a term used to refer to the way in which two people interact with each other. The dynamics of a relationship result from the styles of both partners in making requests, communicating ideas and opinions, and expressing emotions. For example, some people are silent when they're angry, some yell, and some show a tight, forced smile. Some people show love through tender words and gestures; others express it by giving their lover constant attention; and still others show love by giving their lover emotional space. In short, the language we use, the gestures we make, and the ways in which we approach conversation and problem solving all reflect our individual styles of expression. The degree of difference in styles between partners in a relationship determines the quality of communication and ultimately plays a role in whether the relationship will succeed or fail.

Several major dynamics of relating—such as expectations and speaking and listening skills—are universal, regardless of the sexual preferences or relationships of the people involved (heterosexual or homosexual lovers, friends, colleagues, boss and employee, or parent and child). However, because of homophobia and because of a lack of rules and role models, certain dynamics are experienced only in gay and lesbian relationships.

For example, some gay couples have adopted the media's focus on sex as the major aspect of the gay lifestyle, and as a result they can more easily express sexuality than love and tenderness. Gay males, in particular, may not have much knowledge of relationship dynamics beyond knowing how to communicate their sexual needs. In addition, the lack of support and acceptance gay people feel from society—on the job, in public, and at home with family and relatives—can increase their level of anger. This anger often ends up being expressed as hostility and violence within the relationship dynamics. When you're under stress, your tolerance for disagreement is reduced, and you may find it especially difficult to overcome conflict with your lover through peaceful means such as negotiation and problem solving.

Finally, the taking on of roles among gay couples reflects a special dynamic. In lesbian or gay relationships in which one partner plays a "butch" or macho role, communication problems often exist due to an unequal division of power in the relationship. The expectation in such a partnership is that the decisions are to be made by the dominant lover. On the other hand, when both partners in a gay or lesbian relationship play more traditional feminine or "nelly" roles, the couple may end up avoiding conflict altogether if both partners shy away from expressing anger or are unwilling or unable to articulate their needs.

Troublesome relationship dynamics can make a couple feel stuck—locked in combat, and helpless or hopeless about the future. Usually, however, such problems in dynamics are not as unsolvable as they may seem. Some problems can be avoided through the development of better communication skills; others can be resolved through the use of negotiation techniques. Mastering techniques for improving relationship dynamics will improve not only your relationship with your lover but all of your other relationships as well.

In a gay relationship with healthy dynamics, partners can:

- discuss problems and disagreements without fighting.
- allow each other to have different opinions and styles.
- recognize and acknowledge homophobic issues without laying blame or making accusations.
- speak for themselves and make their wants known.
- hear and understand each other, even during disagreements.
- relax their roles when necessary to make negotiation possible.
- find enough time to communicate on a regular basis.

EXPECTATIONS: OVERT AND HIDDEN

Many problems of relationship dynamics can be traced back to expectations—assumptions we make about how things *should* be.

Often, we are unaware of our own expectations. According to Paul Williams, author of *Waking Up Together,*

> A "belief" is an assumption that is so automatic that we don't know it's there. Many of our daily actions are controlled or affected by our beliefs. Acting out of a belief (whether it is "right" or "wrong") is the opposite of being in the moment.
>
> The important thing to do with a belief is: *know that it's there.* Identifying and being aware of beliefs is the only way to avoid being controlled by them.

We all have expectations, because knowing what to expect is comforting. When we were children, the approval of adults was important to us, so we learned to anticipate other people's actions in order to know which behavior of ours would be appropriate. We thus have become so accustomed to looking for patterns that as adults we automatically make assumptions about others. In themselves, expectations and assumptions are not wrong. The problems arise when our expectations are not met and our assumptions come into conflict with our partner's.

Some of our expectations are overt—that is, out in the open. "I want you to call me when you're going to be late" is an overt expectation. This type of expectation usually does not lead to trouble, because it can be clearly discussed and negotiated; it is not necessary to "read minds" or guess what is expected.

Hidden, or covert, expectations are a different matter. We all bring hidden expectations to our relationships. Such expectations are a part of life, and their existence cannot be avoided. They can, however, cause problems. For example, suppose it's very important to you that your partner come home for dinner every night, but you have never actually said this because up until now your partner *has* been home every night. But if he or she calls up one day and says casually, "I'm working late tonight, so I'm going to eat out," you might react with disappointment and anger—to your partner's surprise. Hidden expectations often result in feelings and reactions that seem out of proportion or inappropriate to wha has happened.

In gay relationships, some hidden expectations can be th result of unresolved homophobic feelings. A lesbian woman wh believes that homosexual relationships can't work may doubt h lover's sincerity and act so guarded that she makes it difficult f her partner to love her. A gay man's belief that gay men alw

The rest of this chapter is devoted to teaching you how to uncover hidden expectations and solve the problems they can cause by improving your communication style, developing negotiation skills, and learning more about how you and your partner express love.

COMMUNICATION: A TWO-WAY STREET

In my counseling practice, one of the most frequent complaints I hear from gay clients is "My lover doesn't communicate!" Nonsense. Everyone communicates, constantly—*but each of us is unique and communicates differently.* We all express our ideas and emotions in different ways; we listen (or ignore) in different ways. We may be verbal, visual, or physical in our style of expression and in our way of thinking.

Individual differences in communication are compounded by the fact that we often tend to choose people who are our opposites in style. People whose personalities are different from ours may seem refreshing and thus attractive. For example, a quiet, relaxed person may be strongly attracted to someone with high energy; a very verbal person might be attracted to a good listener or a silent type. While the opposite styles may at first complement each other, they can later become a source of communication difficulty.

Communication problems are usually the culprit if you experience any of the following in your relationship:

- When a problem needs to be solved, you have a fight instead.
- One of you is silent and won't talk.
- Your partner becomes upset because of something you've said, but you don't know why.
- You get angry, and your partner can't understand why.
- One of you feels misunderstood, taken for granted, or ignored.
- Ordinary conversations frequently turn into arguments.
- Your previously good sexual relationship has begun to show problems.

Good communication is an essential skill for making your relationship survive on a long-term basis. Differences in style can make it necessary for you to learn how to communicate from scratch. Doing so can seem almost like learning a new code or language; the greater the differences between your mode of expression and your partner's, the more essential it is that you learn each other's codes. With patience, practice, and a willingness to learn, you and your partner can improve your ability to communicate with each other.

There are four main responsibilities that each partner must assume in order to develop good communication:

1. Expressing ideas and feelings clearly.
2. Paying attention.
3. Listening actively.
4. Allowing time for communication.

The more equally the two of you share these responsibilities, the more you will ensure mutual understanding, effective problem solving, and fair negotiation in resolving conflicts.

Expressing Yourself Clearly

Communication is the art of sharing your thoughts and feelings with someone else. To do this most effectively, learn to use "I" messages—that is, to state whatever you want to say in terms of how *you* feel and what *you* want. In the book *Straight Talk,* by Sherod Miller et al., the authors write:

> The first and most important step in connecting with others is to begin by speaking for yourself. Whatever personal pronoun you use—*I, me, my,* or *mine*—your intention is to claim ownership of your perception and your actions. There should be no question that you're [not] describing any experience other than your own. . . .
>
> Most of us were raised to consider such I-statements improper because they seem egocentric, vain, even imperious. [However,] we don't believe that speaking-for-self is at all selfish as long as your intention is accuracy and clarity . . . . Self statements tell others that you are responsible for your thoughts, feelings, and deeds, that you speak from personal awareness and allow others to do the same.

George and Al, both in their fifties, have been lovers for five years, but they have not had sex in a year. Both men were formerly married and have families who are grown. They're quite distinguished-looking, with a little gray around the temples. George, who owns a store, says, "We used to have great sex, but I feel too tired now. There's a lot of stress at my business. I'm just not interested, and Al is too demanding."

Al, an electrician, looks hurt. "I can't take it anymore. I work just as hard as he does, but I still want sex. I've tried being patient, but I'm not going to just go without sex. Either we get this solved, or I'm going out to look for someone else."

All three of these gay couples are experiencing conflicts that reflect their *relationship dynamics*—a term used to refer to the way in which two people interact with each other. The dynamics of a relationship result from the styles of both partners in making requests, communicating ideas and opinions, and expressing emotions. For example, some people are silent when they're angry, some yell, and some show a tight, forced smile. Some people show love through tender words and gestures; others express it by giving their lover constant attention; and still others show love by giving their lover emotional space. In short, the language we use, the gestures we make, and the ways in which we approach conversation and problem solving all reflect our individual styles of expression. The degree of difference in styles between partners in a relationship determines the quality of communication and ultimately plays a role in whether the relationship will succeed or fail.

Several major dynamics of relating—such as expectations and speaking and listening skills—are universal, regardless of the sexual preferences or relationships of the people involved (heterosexual or homosexual lovers, friends, colleagues, boss and employee, or parent and child). However, because of homophobia and because of a lack of rules and role models, certain dynamics are experienced only in gay and lesbian relationships.

For example, some gay couples have adopted the media's focus on sex as the major aspect of the gay lifestyle, and as a result they can more easily express sexuality than love and tenderness. Gay males, in particular, may not have much knowledge of relationship dynamics beyond knowing how to communicate their sexual needs. In addition, the lack of support and acceptance gay people feel from society—on the job, in public, and at home with family and relatives—can increase their level of anger. This anger often ends up being expressed as hostility and violence within the relationship dynamics. When you're under stress, your tolerance for disagreement is reduced, and you may find it especially difficult to overcome conflict with your lover through peaceful means such as negotiation and problem solving.

Finally, the taking on of roles among gay couples reflects a special dynamic. In lesbian or gay relationships in which one partner plays a "butch" or macho role, communication problems often exist due to an unequal division of power in the relationship. The expectation in such a partnership is that the decisions are to be made by the dominant lover. On the other hand, when both partners in a gay or lesbian relationship play more traditional feminine or "nelly" roles, the couple may end up avoiding conflict altogether if both partners shy away from expressing anger or are unwilling or unable to articulate their needs.

Troublesome relationship dynamics can make a couple feel stuck—locked in combat, and helpless or hopeless about the future. Usually, however, such problems in dynamics are not as unsolvable as they may seem. Some problems can be avoided through the development of better communication skills; others can be resolved through the use of negotiation techniques. Mastering techniques for improving relationship dynamics will improve not only your relationship with your lover but all of your other relationships as well.

In a gay relationship with healthy dynamics, partners can:

- discuss problems and disagreements without fighting.
- allow each other to have different opinions and styles.
- recognize and acknowledge homophobic issues without laying blame or making accusations.
- speak for themselves and make their wants known.
- hear and understand each other, even during disagreements.
- relax their roles when necessary to make negotiation possible.
- find enough time to communicate on a regular basis.

EXPECTATIONS: OVERT AND HIDDEN

Many problems of relationship dynamics can be traced back to expectations—assumptions we make about how things *should* be.

Often, we are unaware of our own expectations. According to Paul Williams, author of *Waking Up Together,*

> A "belief" is an assumption that is so automatic that we don't know it's there. Many of our daily actions are controlled or affected by our beliefs. Acting out of a belief (whether it is "right" or "wrong") is the opposite of being in the moment.
>
> The important thing to do with a belief is: *know that it's there.* Identifying and being aware of beliefs is the only way to avoid being controlled by them.

We all have expectations, because knowing what to expect is comforting. When we were children, the approval of adults was important to us, so we learned to anticipate other people's actions in order to know which behavior of ours would be appropriate. We thus have become so accustomed to looking for patterns that as adults we automatically make assumptions about others. In themselves, expectations and assumptions are not wrong. The problems arise when our expectations are not met and our assumptions come into conflict with our partner's.

Some of our expectations are overt—that is, out in the open. "I want you to call me when you're going to be late" is an overt expectation. This type of expectation usually does not lead to trouble, because it can be clearly discussed and negotiated; it is not necessary to "read minds" or guess what is expected.

Hidden, or covert, expectations are a different matter. We all bring hidden expectations to our relationships. Such expectations are a part of life, and their existence cannot be avoided. They can, however, cause problems. For example, suppose it's very important to you that your partner come home for dinner every night, but you have never actually said this because up until now your partner *has* been home every night. But if he or she calls up one day and says casually, "I'm working late tonight, so I'm going to eat out," you might react with disappointment and anger—to your partner's surprise. Hidden expectations often result in feelings and reactions that seem out of proportion or inappropriate to what has happened.

In gay relationships, some hidden expectations can be the result of unresolved homophobic feelings. A lesbian woman who believes that homosexual relationships can't work may doubt her lover's sincerity and act so guarded that she makes it difficult for her partner to love her. A gay man's belief that gay men always cheat can have similar results. Following are a few other hidden expectations that often occur in homosexual relationships:

Every other gay person will understand you.

All gay people are sexually open.

You and your lover will have no power conflicts because you are the same gender.

Your gay male lover will automatically understand if you cheat.

Your lesbian lover will automatically be faithful.

Your relationship will likely fail simply because you're gay.

Your lover will automatically reject his or her family if they don't accept your relationship.

You and your lover will automatically want to adopt roles, such as "butch" and "femme."

To avoid the problems of conflicting expectations, it is necessary to recognize when hidden expectations are present and learn how to bring them into the open. Recognition is not as difficult as it sounds. Hidden expectations are probably at work if one or more of the following situations exist:

- A simple mistake or misunderstanding leads to a big blowup.
- You or your partner is more upset about something than a situation seems to warrant.
- Such words as *should, ought, always, never, right,* and *wrong* are frequently used by you or your partner during disagreements.
- One or both of you are generally suspicious, guilt-ridden, or hopeless about your relationship.

Bringing a hidden expectation into the open is often more difficult. You and your partner need to think about what your expectations might be, share them, and then find out how each other sees the same issues. Let go of any inclination to feel that your expectations are right and your partner's are wrong; try to accept the fact that you are simply different. If the beliefs seem to be homophobic in origin, use the information in Appendix C to help you deal with homophobia.

The rest of this chapter is devoted to teaching you how to uncover hidden expectations and solve the problems they can cause by improving your communication style, developing negotiation skills, and learning more about how you and your partner express love.

COMMUNICATION: A TWO-WAY STREET

In my counseling practice, one of the most frequent complaints I hear from gay clients is "My lover doesn't communicate!" Nonsense. Everyone communicates, constantly—*but each of us is unique and communicates differently.* We all express our ideas and emotions in different ways; we listen (or ignore) in different ways. We may be verbal, visual, or physical in our style of expression and in our way of thinking.

Individual differences in communication are compounded by the fact that we often tend to choose people who are our opposites in style. People whose personalities are different from ours may seem refreshing and thus attractive. For example, a quiet, relaxed person may be strongly attracted to someone with high energy; a very verbal person might be attracted to a good listener or a silent type. While the opposite styles may at first complement each other, they can later become a source of communication difficulty.

Communication problems are usually the culprit if you experience any of the following in your relationship:

- When a problem needs to be solved, you have a fight instead.
- One of you is silent and won't talk.
- Your partner becomes upset because of something you've said, but you don't know why.
- You get angry, and your partner can't understand why.
- One of you feels misunderstood, taken for granted, or ignored.
- Ordinary conversations frequently turn into arguments.
- Your previously good sexual relationship has begun to show problems.

Good communication is an essential skill for making your relationship survive on a long-term basis. Differences in style can make it necessary for you to learn how to communicate from scratch. Doing so can seem almost like learning a new code or language; the greater the differences between your mode of expression and your partner's, the more essential it is that you learn each other's codes. With patience, practice, and a willingness to learn, you and your partner can improve your ability to communicate with each other.

There are four main responsibilities that each partner must assume in order to develop good communication:

1. Expressing ideas and feelings clearly.
2. Paying attention.
3. Listening actively.
4. Allowing time for communication.

The more equally the two of you share these responsibilities, the more you will ensure mutual understanding, effective problem solving, and fair negotiation in resolving conflicts.

Expressing Yourself Clearly

Communication is the art of sharing your thoughts and feelings with someone else. To do this most effectively, learn to use "I" messages—that is, to state whatever you want to say in terms of how *you* feel and what *you* want. In the book *Straight Talk,* by Sherod Miller et al., the authors write:

> The first and most important step in connecting with others is to begin by speaking for yourself. Whatever personal pronoun you use—*I, me, my,* or *mine*—your intention is to claim ownership of your perception and your actions. There should be no question that you're [not] describing any experience other than your own. . . .
>
> Most of us were raised to consider such I-statements improper because they seem egocentric, vain, even imperious. [However,] we don't believe that speaking-for-self is at all selfish as long as your intention is accuracy and clarity . . . . Self statements tell others that you are responsible for your thoughts, feelings, and deeds, that you speak from personal awareness and allow others to do the same.

By using "I" messages, you express what *you* think, feel, see, and hear without projecting your feelings onto the other person—for example, by saying "I'm unhappy because we don't go out often enough" instead of "You never want to go out with me anymore." Similarly, it's preferable to say "I want some time to myself right now" instead of sighing and saying (passively) "Gee, it's so hard to get enough time alone" or (indirectly) "Don't you have to make dinner now?"

While putting your thoughts into "I" messages can sometimes be hard, doing so

- will help you to clarify what you want to say.
- will make it easier for your lover to hear you without becoming defensive.
- will help you to bring hidden expectations into the open and thus avoid disagreements.

Another important technique of good communication is that of asking direct questions about what your partner wants or thinks, rather than trying to read his or her mind. For instance, "Is this a good time to talk?" will elicit a better response than "I know you don't really want to talk now, but . . ."

James and Mark, whom we met in the beginning of this chapter, are a good example of a gay couple who learned to benefit from speaking clearly. In Mark's original statement, "James never wants to talk to me," Mark was not speaking for himself but was instead projecting his assumption onto James. I suggested that Mark learn to use "I" messages and direct questions—for example, "James, I like to find out what your day was like when you come home" or "How do you want to be greeted when you come home?" James, for his part, learned to let Mark know what he wanted.

After some negotiation, they decided that Mark would leave the house and go to the gym for an hour just before James got home. This would eliminate Mark's waiting around, bored, and would give James some time alone to unwind. This solution worked well, and the couple is once again able to share and enjoy discussions about their work.

Expressing yourself clearly doesn't mean that you won't sometimes be a bit unsure about what you want to say. Just let your partner know this: "I don't know why I get so angry about messes in the kitchen. Will you listen to me talk about it for a few minutes, so we can both understand it better?" If you admit your confusion, your lover will be much more motivated to be patient and listen.

The same directness works if you're afraid that what you want to say will come out wrong, or that your partner will be hurt by it. Don't be embarrassed to announce that you may be clumsy or that you're afraid your partner will misunderstand. It might be useful to first check out *why* you're worried. Do you perhaps have some unexpressed resentment, or do you fear your lover's anger? If so, use the techniques in this chapter for recognizing covert expectations before you attempt a conversation with your partner.

Although speaking directly is crucial, being too worried about doing it right will get in your way. It's more important that you make a genuine attempt to get your point across than that you follow some prescribed rules for communicating. The connection you establish with the person with whom you're communicating is far more important than how you say what you say. Begin with the attitude that you want to understand your partner as well as to be understood, and you'll be halfway there.

When You Want to Be Heard, Pay Attention

Most of us, when we're talking, concentrate only on what we're saying. In order to get your point across, however, you must also pay attention to how the other person is *receiving* what you're saying.

Watch your partner's face and body as he or she listens to you. Focus your attention on what's actually going on with your partner, without speculating about what he or she might be thinking or feeling. Your partner's facial expressions, body movements, and posture all provide clues that can help you to know whether you're being understood. If you get a response that seems unusual or inappropriate, ask a question—for example, "I thought I just gave you a compliment, but you look annoyed. Did I say it wrong?" Or, "Gee, I thought you'd be happy to hear this, but you look upset. Please tell me what you're thinking." Or, "I'm angry about what you said, but you're smiling. Did I misunderstand you?"

If your listener becomes fidgety or looks off into space as you talk, either you're in uncomfortable territory or you've been talking too long. Toss the ball to the other side: "What do you think?"

or "Do you see it the same way?" or perhaps "Am I talking too much (or too fast)?"

If you're paying attention, incomprehension is also easy to spot. If your partner begins to have a blank or glassy-eyed look, you may be putting out too many ideas all at once, or you may not be explaining your thoughts clearly enough. Blaming your listener—for example, by insisting that he or she just isn't paying enough attention—will only exacerbate the problem. Instead, ask a question, such as "I don't think I'm explaining this clearly—have I lost you?" or "Am I bringing up too many things at once?" Phrasing questions to show that you're looking for ways to improve your style and clarity invites cooperation and encourages teamwork.

It's not necessary to be an expert on body language to decipher silent messages; we were all born with built-in "antennae." When you know what to look for, you can read your partner's signals easily.

Most gay men and lesbian women are aware that we can "read" one another and so can tell when a stranger is gay. In doing so, we're deciphering nonverbal communication by paying attention to such nonverbal cues as attitudes, gestures, clothing style, posture, and so on. The same skills you use to spot a gay sister or brother can be used to improve communication with your lover.

Active Listening

You can encourage communication, even from a usually quiet partner, by using good listening skills. Active listening establishes a supportive environment that makes it inviting to talk about anything. When you are both willing to listen to each other, you create a safe haven for meaningful communication, whatever the topic to be discussed.

For instance, the problem of my clients George and Al, introduced at the beginning of this chapter, had to do with listening, not sex. Although Al claimed that he tried to be patient about George's job stress and lack of interest in lovemaking, he always discounted what George said by claiming that he was under pressure at work, too. The implication was that if he could handle the pressure, George should be able to handle it, too. In this way, Al made it nearly impossible for George to openly discuss his job problems. In reality, Al wasn't listening.

When I put this couple through an active listening drill and they began to really hear each other, some important information emerged. It turned out that when Al had been out of work, George had supported him financially—and George now wanted some emotional support in return. George was able to say directly that he wanted some comforting when he was under stress from work, and Al was relieved to know that this emotional support would even the score between them. George was then able to reassure Al that he hadn't lost his sexual desire; he was just feeling hurt. The two were soon able to renew their sexual relationship.

Active listening means doing for your partner what you'd like to have done for you. First, learn to recognize when your partner has something significant to discuss. While some people have no problem saying "I have something important to tell you," most of us usually aren't so clear. Everyone, however, has methods that let others know they need to talk. By observing your partner, you can become aware of his or her style. If you notice a sudden change in your partner's pattern of behavior (for example, your normally talkative lover suddenly becomes very quiet), he or she is probably troubled about something. You can make the situation easier by asking, "Is there something you want to talk about?"

Second, do your best to pay attention to what your lover is trying to say. Ask questions if you don't understand. You might say, "Could you stop a minute? I want to be sure I understand your last point before you go on to the next." Don't let yourself be overwhelmed; ask for explanations when you need them. Try to determine whether there is a hidden expectation, like Fred's need for comfort and support, at the root of your conversation.

Third, remember that listening to your lover does not necessarily mean agreeing. Even if you don't like what you're hearing, develop the habit of saying "Tell me more about that." Find out as much as you can about what your partner is thinking before you disagree or counter with your own viewpoint. You may find that you simply misunderstood what your partner first said, or that you're not as opposed to your partner's point as you had thought. Even if you find that you still disagree, you'll have a better chance of solving the problem if you have a clear understanding of the opposing ideas.

If it seems to you that I'm asking you to take responsibility for *both* sides of the conversation, you're right. Communication works best when both speaker and listener take responsibility for being heard and for hearing. While this may sound like a lot of work, it's a lot easier than having arguments and battles. I'm not suggesting that all of your conversations with your partner must be at this level of awareness and intensity. There will obviously be times when you can joke around, interrupt, talk at the same time, or doze off in the middle of a discussion, and it will be funny or endearing. But try to recognize situations in which joking is really masking a message or when a seemingly light conversation has the potential to become an argument. Such dynamics are an indication of hidden expectations, and it's time to pay attention. Be particularly aware of "faggot" or "dyke" jokes or remarks, which can indicate homophobic insecurity or fear.

If communication is an ongoing problem, or if you and your partner are simply having a problem understanding each other on some issue, try the following exercise.

Active-Listening Drill

Draw straws or flip a coin to see who will go first (Partner A). Then do the following steps:

1. Partner A says just one sentence, without interruption.
2. Partner B then repeats back what was said, in his or her own words.
3. Partner A then either acknowledges that B heard correctly *or* goes back to Step 1 and tries again.
4. Once Step 3 is successful, Partner B replies to A's original statement (again, keeping it to one sentence).
5. Partner A paraphrases B's reply statement.
6. Partner B acknowledges that the reply was heard correctly or goes back to Step 4.

Once both partners feel that they have been heard on this one sequence, the partners switch places, and the exercise is repeated.

If you become stuck at Step 3, take your time and work through it one word at a time. If you find that one of you is actually angry and simply won't admit to being understood, take a break and allow a cooling-off period.

Does this exercise seem too simple? It's a demonstration of how simple communication truly is when we stop mind-reading and begin listening. When my gay and lesbian clients are not communicating, keeping it simple is usually the cure.

Providing Opportunities for Communication

One of the biggest barriers to communication encountered by the gay couples who come to my office is lack of time. With careers, outside activities, a busy social life, and, in some cases, children, many gay couples find that opportunities for discussion do not appear automatically. I suggest that you set aside specific times to talk with your lover about wants, needs, important issues, and problems.

Such communication opportunities can help you and your partner to develop cooperation, enthusiasm, honesty, security, and trust in your relationship. By planning communication times you establish a distinction between casual time and time for serious talk, so that during a romantic dinner or just before a party you won't be squabbling about a difficult issue that requires in-depth discussion. Also, scheduled meetings for frank discussion can keep problems from accumulating or being ignored until they've become critical. Of course, not every such conversation will need to be scheduled in advance; spontaneous conversations will also happen. However, these can't be counted on for regularity. Find your own frequency for scheduled talks—be it once a day or once a week—and choose a time when you will both be available to talk without interruption.

You can use these communication opportunities to work out simple domestic problems (such as the division of chores or schedule conflicts) or to discuss important relationship issues that need to be negotiated (such as lifestyle differences or issues of homophobia). Scheduled times for talking can be used not only for problem solving but also for sharing your joys and successes.

Begin the communication session by getting comfortable. Start by saying what's good about your relationship and each other. Then, if you've been busy and haven't had a chance to talk for a while, catch up on recent events.

Next, discuss anything that's not working for you. Are there any little hurts or irritations that need clearing up? Each of you gets a few minutes to talk, *uninterrupted.* Use the communication techniques discussed earlier to resolve these feelings.

Once the complaints are understood, work together to solve them using the problem-solving techniques discussed below. If the root of some of your difficulties seems to be deep-rooted insecurity because your relationship is gay, use the techniques in Appendix C for dealing with homophobia.

With regular communication sessions, you can keep most problems minor, and resolving them won't be hard. Once you've reached a resolution and the air is clear, celebrate! This is a lovely time to develop a celebration ritual. You've just done a great job of relationship maintenance—a reward is in order.

PROBLEM SOLVING THROUGH NEGOTIATION

Contrary to the "happily ever after" myth, problems do exist in healthy relationships. In fact, a lack of disagreements often means that you and your partner are avoiding issues. To deal with problems effectively, you both need to learn problem-solving skills. The main element of such skills is negotiation, through which you can minimize conflicts and prevent them from escalating.

Negotiation is not a contest in which one or both of you must give up what you want. Rather, it is a means of working together to solve a problem in such a way that both of you are satisfied with the results. Negotiation is the essence of teamwork, and as such it reflects the equal power and status of each partner in a long-term relationship. In short, negotiation is the means for maintaining the mutuality you established earlier in your relationship.

I have often heard people say that negotiation means compromise. However, I see these two terms as having clear distinctions. My dictionary defines *compromise* as "a settlement of differences reached by mutual concessions"—that is, each person has to give something up. I believe that negotiation means that you can *both* get what you want—in other words, problem solving becomes a win-win challenge. My professional experience has shown me that compromise doesn't work, but negotiation does.

When one person feels compelled to give up part of what he or she wants, to make concessions, there is a tendency for that person to feel resentful. I call resentment the great destroyer. Love can survive anger, fear, hurt, and long separations, but it can seldom survive resentment. When you resent someone, you feel that you've been unfairly treated, that the other person has done you wrong. He or she begins to feel like an enemy, not a lover.

You can avoid competition, compromise, and resentment by solving problems cooperatively. Successful problem solving is a key skill for developing and maintaining a long-term relationship. The negotiation techniques involved are equally effective for conflict resolution at work and with family and friends. The following cooperative problem-solving steps are adapted from those I developed with Riley K. Smith for our book *How to Be a Couple and Still Be Free.*

Step 1: Identify the problem. Obviously, it's easier for you to communicate your feelings about a problem to your partner once you've taken some time to understand it yourself. Before you begin negotiating, identify and write down the main points that are bothering you. Might there be a hidden expectation (either yours or your partner's)? Make sure that you're thinking and evaluating as well as feeling emotional reactions. While your emotions let you know that a problem exists, they can't help you to solve it. When you are thinking clearly and are ready to focus on finding a solution, it's time to talk to your partner.

Step 2: Make an appointment. Making the appointment reassures both of you that the problem will be faced, not ignored. Choose your problem-solving time and place carefully. Negotiation is an important part of the process of building trust and confidence between you and your partner. It deserves quality time, with no distractions. Make an actual date with your partner to talk about the problem. *Don't* choose the last five minutes before bedtime or before you have to leave for work in the morning. Instead, choose a time when you'll both be relaxed and able to concentrate. If you've already set a regular time for communication opportunities, this can also be a good problem-solving appointment time.

Step 3: Present the problem. Begin by telling your partner what the problem is, using "I" messages. Don't project your assumptions of the cause of the problem by saying such things as "You hurt me" or "You tried to mislead me." Instead, tell your partner your own observations and feelings—for example, "I feel hurt" or "I thought we had an agreement." Then wait to see if your partner also thinks that a problem exists. Over and over again, in my counseling sessions with gay and lesbian couples, I have seen one partner launch into a one-sided explanation of a problem without pausing to find out whether his or her lover also feels that there is a problem. When I turn to the partner and ask, "Do you agree that this is a problem?" I often get a stunned look.

Step 4: Agree to negotiate. Make sure that you have an agreement to negotiate before you begin. Remember, this is a mutual process. Establish goodwill by reminding each other that while the relationship is important, you are also important as individuals, and you want each other to be satisfied with the solution.

Step 5: Negotiate—don't wage war. Arguing over who's right or wrong has nothing to do with problem solving; neither do accusing your lover, defending yourself, crying, or angrily pounding your fist on the table. While most of the above can be beneficial within a controlled therapy setting, they are detrimental to the process of negotiation and will discourage cooperation between you and your partner.

After presenting the problem and giving your opinion of it, give your lover a chance to evaluate the issue and to express his or her opinion. Some points to remember while negotiating:

- You can allow your partner to express his or her opinion without necessarily agreeing with it.
- Listening is *not* the same as giving in.
- The best way to be heard is to also be willing to hear.
- Discussing problems in a relaxed atmosphere, with the problem-solving process presented as mutually beneficial, can be tremendously effective.

Step 6: Explore options. Once each of you has had the opportunity to describe your view of the problem, you both need to state what would solve the problem for you. Allow yourselves to be creative and even outrageous about the solutions. Explore impossible dreams, and talk about other people's solutions to similar problems. Stir up an atmosphere of adventure.

It is in this step that your cooperation truly gives you team power. It probably won't be easy at first to reach solutions that seem to work equally well for both of you. As a gay man or lesbian woman, you may have learned to be competitive with your partner. In addition, thoughts such as "I don't really deserve to have what I want, so I'm going to have to fight for it" indicate low self-esteem or perhaps homophobia. (See Appendix C for help with issues of homophobia.) You may be tempted to give up or give in; you may become anxious and try to coerce or overpower each other.

In exploring solutions, avoid threats and attempts at coercion. Aside from the fact that they cannot work in a healthy relationship, such efforts reflect your own belief that it's not possible to reach a cooperative solution, and they therefore destroy any mutual trust in your ability to solve the problem as a team. The minute you say something like "I'd leave you if I found out you were having an affair," you have shut down any possibility of solving the problem, and you are asking to be lied to. Instead, you could say something like this: "I'm not sure if monogamy is as important to you as it is to me. Let's talk about it—I want to know how you feel."

If you can't come up with a permanent solution right away, try to reach a temporary one, and make an appointment to come back to the problem a few hours or days later. Sometimes, a temporary solution can give you a new perspective on the problem.

Don't worry if it takes a few days or even weeks to solve a problem. If a problem is particularly difficult to solve, have several sessions about it. The more time you devote to the solution, the more your creativity will open up.

There may be times when a solution seems to be out of reach despite your best efforts. You and your partner may be too close to the situation or too locked into old ways of thinking. Perhaps one or both of you have some hidden expectations that haven't yet been uncovered. In such cases, it can be very helpful to take your problem to a counselor or therapist. Just one session could save you months of struggle.

Step 7: Confirm your agreement and celebrate. Once a solution—permanent or temporary—has been found, confirm the agreement by taking turns by stating it out loud, as each of you has understood it. By doing this, you will increase the likelihood of understanding and reduce the chances of miscommunication.

When the agreement has been confirmed, do something simple to celebrate it. Shake hands, hug, make a toast with your coffee cups, or go out for a celebration lunch.

Negotiation has the greatest chance of succeeding when:

- You don't approach problems as though they are disasters.
- You use your sense of humor.
- You don't try to control or overpower your partner.

- You are willing to find and drop hidden expectations.
- You want both of you to be satisfied with the solution.
- You are willing to tell the truth and to say what you want.
- You use your imagination and creativity to find possible solutions.
- You are open to new ideas.
- You make celebration an important part of the process.

My clients Mike and Tom provide a good example of the power of successful negotiation. When they came in to see me some time ago, they had been living together for several years and were doing quite well. Previously, with my help, they had worked out an agreement to live together indefinitely, to be each other's primary partner, and to have a sexually open relationship within careful guidelines.

Then Tom got an excellent job offer in a foreign country, with an initial contract of two years. The couple came right in to see me. Tom began by expressing his confusion:

> I have such mixed feelings about this. The job is fantastic—it would make my career. I want it a lot. And living in Europe would be great, too.
>
> But I don't know what to do about Mike. I love him, and I want to take him with me—but he wouldn't know the language, he'd have to give up his career for a couple of years, and we don't know what the laws about homosexuality are over there.

Mike, too, had ambivalent feelings:

> I'm scared. I wouldn't mind giving up my work here, and the foreign experience and travel would be an asset. But I may not be able to get a job—I work in the entertainment industry here, and I don't know if those skills are transferable—and I wouldn't want to be financially dependent on Tom. Also, I hate to leave my friends. I'm afraid I'd feel trapped in the relationship if we were isolated in Europe.

We discussed all the problems and possibilities over a few sessions. I encouraged them to find out as much as they could about the laws in the other country, as well as about language classes and job opportunities for Mike. After a couple of weeks of research, the picture became much clearer to them. Mike and Tom did some very honest and tough negotiating. They drew up a financial contract, and they agreed to renegotiate their sexual contract if it seemed necessary to do so in their new situation. Mike gave up his job, and Tom agreed to support him for a maximum of six months while he learned the language and found a job. Mike agreed to be in charge of all domestic chores during that time. Tom also decided to set aside money in a special savings account to pay for Mike's flight home and resettling expenses if things didn't work out in Europe.

Tom accepted the job offer, and the two moved to Europe. Mike was able to find a good job after only about three months, and at last report they are both very happy with their new situation.

COPING WITH ANGER

Anger is the energy that arises naturally within you when something seems intolerable and needs to be corrected. Properly applied, anger is a natural force for change in your life; it does not have to lead to violence. By acting thoughtfully upon your anger, you can reduce your sense of helplessness and frustration. Only when anger is bottled up does it lead to self-destructive anxiety and violence. If you learn to handle your anger in healthy ways, you will find that it can become a great ally and a source of personal strength.

If you have difficulty in dealing with anger, the following exercise can be of help to you.

Anger Exercise

Whenever you feel angry, try taking these steps:

1. ACKNOWLEDGE that you're angry. Instead of launching into a tirade, simply state, "I'm angry" or "I'm really upset at you right now" or "That makes me so mad."
2. EXPRESS how you feel. Stay away from cataloguing who did what, defending yourself, or going over the story.

Stick with "I feel" messages: "I feel rejected," "I feel like my feelings don't count," "I feel scared that ______." If it is difficult for you to put your feelings of anger into words, or if your anger feels overwhelming, physical movement can help you. For example, you could stomp around your room, go for a brisk walk, or pound on a pillow. Whatever physical movement you use, make sure that you are not endangering yourself or others or being destructive of property.

If your feelings have been unexpressed for a long time, practicing this step when you are alone or in a controlled situation (such as a counseling session) even when you are *not* angry can help you learn to deal with your angry feelings. Repeat this step until you have achieved an emotional or psychological release of pressure and are feeling calmer. You may even feel exhausted, since the mental and physical release that follows the expression of pent-up emotions is often experienced as exhaustion.

3. THINK about solutions. Now that the storm is past and you're feeling more clearheaded, think about what would alleviate this anger for you.

   If your anger has arisen because you are dealing with death, serious illness, childhood abuse, or any other issue that's not easily handled, be good to yourself and get help. There are some problems we were not meant to handle alone.

4. COMMUNICATE with others who are involved. Please notice that *communicate* does not mean the same thing as *express*—that's why it is the last step here, after the emotional storm has passed and you have had a chance to think about the issue. Now you are ready to problem solve and negotiate.

Some gay couples have a problem with anger that gets out of control and leads to violence. The roots of violence often lie in childhood, when children who witness violent arguments or who are abused learn that violence is part of life. If you find yourself being violent or verbally abusive with your partner, or you have a history of choosing partners who are abusive toward you, chances are good that your childhood involved violence or abuse.

My counseling experience with gay and lesbian couples has included several cases of violence. Although many experts believe that men are more violent than women, my clinical experience is that women become physical in their fighting as often as men do. Some lesbian women who are abusive may have taken a macho or "butch" role to an unhealthy extreme, while the nondominant partners may feel that their lovers have a "right" to abuse them, that they somehow "deserve it." Some gay men with a problem of being abusive have been taught, perhaps through sports or the military, to react to problems violently.

Alcohol and drug abuse play a large part in domestic violence. Without exception, all of my clients who have become violent had been drinking or using cocaine just beforehand. The use of alcohol and drugs clouds rational thinking and removes inhibitions, making it possible for anger to explode and become unmanageable.

Sally and Mary, who were introduced at the beginning of this chapter, had repeated episodes of violence in their relationship. In answer to my questions, they revealed the following similar patterns: First, both had alcoholic fathers who had been violent and verbally abusive toward the family when they were small, and both had witnessed many fights between their parents. Second, either Sally or Mary had been drinking prior to each episode of violence.

I requested that they separate until they could learn to control the violent behavior. They objected, saying that they could handle the situation—but when they came in the next week, Sally's arm was in a cast. It had been broken during an argument between the two, but because both had been drinking, neither woman was clear on just how it had happened. This episode was enough to convince them that the violence was out of control, and they agreed to separate. At my further suggestion, both began to attend meetings of Alcoholics Anonymous and Adult Children of Alcoholics. With this support and further counseling, Sally and Mary decided that a permanent split was necessary. Today, they are friends. Both are nondrinkers, and both are learning how to solve problems by negotiating rather than by exploding into violence.

If violence or other abuse has been a part of your relationships, a competent counselor or therapist with experience in abuse issues can help you to learn why this is so and can show you how to change violent relationship patterns.

If you become violent or abusive toward your partner, the first thing to do is to seek professional help. In addition, whenever you feel in danger of a violent emotional outburst try the following: Say "I need a time-out," and get away from your partner. Go to another room, or, if possible, go outside and walk around the block (*do not drive*—you are probably not clearheaded enough). After the violent feelings subside, go back and talk about the issue, using the seven problem-solving steps presented earlier. If the rage rises again, take another time-out. If violent anger is a persistent problem for you, practice taking time-outs when you're not angry so that it will be easier for you to do so when you're upset.

If you are being abused in your relationship, *seek help immediately.* If the abuse is physical, it is important that you leave—*do not remain in any situation in which you have been battered, even once, without getting help!* Call a hot line, get a referral, and begin to change the pattern now, before it gets worse. Do *not* wait for your partner to change. Keep in mind that abuse

- can be physical, verbal, or mental;
- damages the victim, the abuser, and the witnesses (such as children);
- follows a cyclic pattern and inevitably repeats itself until the pattern is changed; and
- will *not* "go away" by itself, but requires professional help.

DEALING WITH SUBSTANCE ABUSE

Substance abuse—especially alcohol abuse—is a frequent problem in many gay and lesbian relationships. Substance abuse is obviously a special issue, and your relationship can go no further until the addiction is under control. The most effective therapy is replacement of the addiction; trying to go "cold turkey" is not only less effective but can also be dangerous. Get help from drug clinics or from such programs as Alcoholics Anonymous, Narcotics Anonymous, Cocaine Anonymous, and Adult Children of Alcoholics. If it is your lover who has the substance-abuse problem, I urge you to attend Al-Anon meetings or seek therapy to help you learn how not to be part of the problem, as well as how to take care of yourself.

When addiction is part of the relationship dynamics, the lovers become addicted to each other as well as to whatever substance is involved. Such relationships are called "codependent" relationships. In her book *Codependent No More,* Melody Beattie defines a codependent person as someone "who has let another person's behavior affect him or her, and who is obsessed with controlling that person's behavior." A codependent relationship is dysfunctional—that is, it does not function properly; it does not do what a relationship is supposed to do, which is to support and nurture those involved in it.

Among people who grew up in addictive atmospheres, the family-relationship patterns can continue to exist even in the absence of an actual substance problem, since the codependent patterns have been unconsciously learned. Codependent relationships can be fixed if the partners recognize that they are being mutually dependent and seek help. If you are in a codependent relationship, you can begin the process of recovery by using the information in this book aimed at helping you and your partner to be mutually independent and personally responsible for your actions by

- developing cooperative rather than competitive interactions;
- using good problem-solving and communication techniques;
- being honest; and
- realizing when old family patterns are interfering with the healthy functioning of your relationship.

If your family history is heavily dysfunctional or codependent, you may need extra help. In the back of this book you'll find references for books and organizations that can help you to overcome these destructive patterns. Becoming aware and educated is crucial to the process of resolving substance-abuse issues.

EXPRESSING LOVE AND TENDERNESS

As I indicated earlier, many gay and lesbian couples find it easier to express sexuality, hostility, or violence than love and tenderness. Many gay males, especially, have had more experience with sex than with expressing love.

Love is an art, and so requires all the learning and dedication of any other art. No one learned to play concert piano in a day! Love, too, requires practice, technique, and style.

Further, most of us unconsciously know only one way to express love, and that is the way we were taught within our families. Some people, for example, grew up in very angry or unsupportive families, where the expression of love was negative or nonexistent. Such people must learn how to express love. As adults, some might give overly frequent (and perhaps awkward) demonstrations of affection, support, and caring, and they expect the same from their partners. Others from such families might not express love at all and may be uncomfortable when a lover shows them affection. Or, they may want only to *give* love or sexual pleasure, but never to receive it.

On the other hand, some people grew up in extremely expressive families in which there were frequent displays of affection—kisses, pats, and embraces—as well as a keen interest in the sharing of one another's daily experiences and problems. Some gay people from this type of environment want to keep such closeness in their adult relationships but find that their partners are resistant. Others from such families want only to escape what they perceive to be a smothering atmosphere, and they may view a lover's desire for such closeness as a threat to their independence.

Being gay or lesbian in an unaccepting environment also affects your style of expressing love. First, as discussed earlier, you probably had few—if any—role models to illustrate what homosexual love can be. Your own homophobia can also be a major obstacle to feeling and expressing your love. If you feel that you don't deserve love, or that you can't succeed at love because you're gay, your expression of love is likely to be extremely limited. Lastly, when you encounter hostility on the job, among friends and relatives, and in social situations, the resulting frustration and anger you may feel can have a negative impact on your communication of love.

In my practice, I often see gay couples who are at odds in the ways in which they express love. Karen and Ellen are both professional women in their mid-thirties. When I met with them, Karen said, "I don't know what more Ellen could want. I love her as much as I can. I'm always there, I show affection, and I ask her to tell me what she thinks. But I don't get any attention back from her!"

When I asked Ellen how she felt, she said, "Karen never leaves me alone! I don't get any privacy. She wants to own every minute of my time. I love her, so I give her plenty of space—but she won't give *me* any!"

Clearly, Karen and Ellen express love in different ways. Karen is very affectionate and expressive, with a need for a high degree of closeness. Ellen, on the other hand, requires a lot of private time, and one way she expresses her love for Karen is by giving *her* a great deal of space and privacy, too. I helped these women to understand their differences and to learn to adjust their behavior to each other's responses. Ellen learned to initiate more interaction with Karen; for her part, Karen learned to enjoy having time alone. The two have have now established clear ways to communicate their love for each other, and their relationship is running smoothly.

The key to a successful gay relationship is the effective communication of love. Begin by accepting that you and your partner must get to know each other in order to love each other successfully. One partner's idea of tenderness might be the other's idea of aggravation. As with communication, it takes time to learn each other's styles; to achieve true intimacy, it is important that you accept your differences and avoid getting stuck in a struggle about "right and wrong" ways of expressing love.

Fear of rejection, low self-esteem, the belief that we're unlovable, memories of past relationship problems and mistakes, and confusion about how to show our love—all of these can get in the way. Don't let your fears be in charge. If you're afraid, admit it to yourself and to your lover. Talk about your doubts. For example, you might say, "I'm afraid I'm not loving you right, and that you can't feel my love for you" or "I don't know what to do to show you that I love you." Give up any need to be an expert. When you are both open, you and your partner can learn to love each other as fully as possible.

You can help your gay or lesbian relationship to flourish by following these suggestions:

- Take the time to learn to express your love in ways that your lover understands and is familiar with. The best way to learn your lover's style of expressing love is to observe him or her around family and close friends.
- Talk about what love means to each of you. Tell your lover what makes you feel loved and what you think of as being loving toward him or her. Ask questions, and volunteer information.

- Experiment with new kinds of affection and caring to find out what works best for the two of you. Take some risks, and have a sense of humor about it.

The next exercise can help you and your partner to enhance your mutual understanding of love.

Expressing Love Exercise

Make an extra copy of the list below and give it to your partner. Now, working separately, check off those things that make you feel loved. If an item on the list sometimes feels like love to you but at other times does not, write down what the difference is between one instance and another. You may also add items of your own to the list.

I feel loved when my partner:

______ fusses over me when I'm sick
______ brings me flowers
______ calls me at work
______ cleans the house
______ lets me make a mess sometimes
______ greets me and talks to me about his/her day when I come home from work
______ gives me space when I come home from work
______ buys me presents or takes me out on birthdays and anniversaries
______ kisses, hugs, and touches me often
______ lets me know I turn him/her on
______ lets it be okay if I don't want to make love
______ phones me if he/she is going to be late
______ takes me out on "dates"
______ shares my favorite sport or activity with me
______ gives me time alone
______ notices what I'm wearing
______ doesn't seem to notice if I've gained a few pounds
______ encourages me when I have problems at work

______ helps me to forget work and relax
______ celebrates my successes and achievements with me
______ is nice to my friends
______ does some of my chores if I'm especially tired
______ listens to me when I'm angry
______ tells me when something is bothering him/her
______ holds me when I cry
______ makes me laugh
______ doesn't take it personally if I'm feeling crabby
______ cares about my wants and needs

Now go back over the list and place an asterisk (*) after those things that you think feel like love to your partner. Swap lists with your lover, and discuss the choices you have both made. This sharing can be fun, warm, and intimate, as well as very informative.

Save each other's lists, and take note of other expressions of love your partner seems to particularly appreciate. Being able to express your love to each other effectively will help carry the two of you through difficult times.

You and your partner can learn to communicate effectively, to solve problems together, to handle powerful feelings, and to express your love for each other. As you grow together and practice what you learn, experimenting with new techniques, your communication skills will improve. As your skills increase, your pleasure and pride in your relationship will also grow. A sign I drew up for my office wall sums up the lessons of this chapter:

IN THE BEGINNING, LOVE TAKES COURAGE.
THEN, IT TAKES OVER.

CHAPTER 5

Gay Relationships and Sexuality

Many of my gay and lesbian clients ask me for assistance in making the decision of whether to be monogamous or sexually open in their relationships. If properly approached, either choice is possible for homosexual couples today.

There are two primary factors to consider in making your choice. First, in a committed relationship it is crucial to avoid conflict over sexual intimacy and trust. Second, whatever decision you make, your most important guideline must be sexual safety; the chances of contracting AIDS are far too great to risk endangering your life or your lover's.

In addition to the question of monogamy or openness, many of my clients are uncertain about just what healthy sex is in a relationship. Because of the lack of social rules and role models, gay people often pattern their behavior on sexual stereotypes.

This chapter is intended to answer many of your questions about sex in gay relationships. In it I will examine in detail the concept of sexual contracts and the choice between monogamy and open sexuality. I will then cover the issue of sex between friends. Finally, I will present some guidelines for healthy sex and discuss the difference between sexual games and destructive compulsions.

NEGOTIATING SEX: FIDELITY CONTRACTS

Before examining the pros and cons of monogamy and open sexuality, let's examine how a clear sexual contract can serve both partners. Many people take the word *fidelity* to imply monogamy. Actually, *fidelity* means honoring one's agreements, whatever they are. I therefore call a sexual agreement a "fidelity contract," because the issue is that of adhering to your promise.

Regardless of its specifics, a fidelity contract clarifies each partner's expectations and provides a basis for honesty. Developing the agreement is a careful, mutual process that must suit your individual personalities. Following are the steps you need to take to jointly establish one's sexual contract.

- *Approach the discussion as a problem-solving session.* If you've been successfully practicing negotiation in other areas using the techniques in chapter 4, it will be easier for you to deal with this sensitive issue. Begin with reassurance and goodwill, reminding each other of your love and of your desire that the relationship be fulfilling for both of you.

  If your relationship is new, this discussion can be another step toward more intimacy. If you haven't established a way to begin discussions about sex, try reading portions of this book aloud (for instance, excerpts from this chapter—from the section on "Open Sexuality" to the end of the chapter—and Appendix B, "Safe Sex Information"), or discussing a news item on AIDS.

  If you've been together for a while but discussions about sex are still not easy for the two of you, this is a prime opportunity to improve your communication in this area.
- *Share your wants, needs, and ideas.* It's important that you be honest in discussing your sexual needs. Your lover may or may not feel as you do, but you'll never know unless you're willing to express your feelings and to hear what your partner's feelings are. Keep in mind that being honest means not only telling the truth but also being willing to hear the truth from another.

  Making truth-telling okay is the key to clear sexual contracts. The only attitude that works is this one: "I may not like what you tell me, and I may have trouble hearing it, but I will still love you and be willing to work together to come to an agreement that satisfies both of us."
- *Avoid using threats or pressure to get what you want.* Comments such as "If you ever had sex with anyone else, I'd leave you" or "Don't ever look at Jan like that again at a party—I won't stand for it" close down discussion. Further, they don't change feelings—they just send them underground.
- *Allow room for mistakes, confusion, and renegotiation.* It is important that your contract allow for flexibility so that it reflects

the growth in your relationship as time passes. I recommend that as part of the contract you and your partner set up regular communication meetings to talk about your contract and to review how it is working.

GAY RELATIONSHIPS AND MONOGAMY

Our culture places a positive value on monogamy. The relationship rules and role models held up to us when we were children all involved idealized heterosexual couples living together in monogamous arrangements.

In actuality, Western culture has been somewhat hypocritical about monogamy. In many Western societies, it has long been generally—though quietly—accepted that men can have sex outside of their marriages. The extent of the social permissiveness has varied according to the strengths of the religious and cultural convictions of each society. Research shows us that our sexual behavior has, in fact, changed little over the centuries. What *has* changed is how overt or covert we are about infidelity.

Our contemporary culture has not escaped this hypocrisy. While we incorporate vows of monogamy into marital agreements and, in general, treat nonmonogamous sexual arrangements as taboo, many of our television programs, films, and popular novels depict a glorified view of nonmonogamous behavior. Recent surveys have indicated that more than half of the heterosexual men and women in monogamous marriages have had sex outside their relationships—and these findings do not take into account the vast numbers of people in homosexual relationships. The differences between our idealized beliefs and our behavior indicate that the desirability for monogamy is a social myth, one that causes a great deal of confusion.

It is essential now, more than ever, for gay couples to be honest and responsible in deciding whether they will or will not choose monogamy and in establishing a mutual understanding about whichever choice is made. Because of AIDS, more gay people will be seeking long-term commitment and lifelong partnership. Some will choose to practice monogamy willingly and voluntarily. For those who choose a nonmonogamous lifestyle, honesty is a better policy than hypocrisy.

All of us must begin to rationally analyze our sexual beliefs and, with our partners, to confront our fears and our needs. Men and women in gay relationships today can break ground in developing new attitudes and lifestyles that reflect our sexual behavior. On one hand, we don't need to think about monogamy in the same way as straight couples do, since the pros and cons are not exactly the same. For example, we do not share the fear of some heterosexuals that monogamy is a trap leading to narrow husband-and-wife roles, since these roles are virtually meaningless in same-sex couples. Instead, we can view a monogamous relationship as a door opening to a greater pride in our individuality and homosexual lifestyle.

On the other hand, because we are already distanced from the pressure of social acceptance, we can also choose open sexuality *without precluding marriage.* For many of us, a lifelong partnership can incorporate a nonmonogamous agreement as a means of meeting our needs for variety and excitement.

There is no easy answer to the question of whether to choose monogamy or open sexuality in a relationship. Every gay couple must find the solution that works best for them. We'll now look more closely at the pros and cons of each choice.

MONOGAMY OR OPEN SEXUALITY: MAKING THE DECISION

There are many positive and negative aspects to both monogamy and open sexuality for homosexual couples today. Assessing the pros and cons before making a decision will ensure that your decision is based on your own relationship needs, not simply on an assumption that one solution or the other is the only one that will work for you.

Monogamy: Pros and Cons

Pros

If handled conscientiously, monogamy can:

- help a couple delve more deeply into their relationship
- guarantee safety from disease
- provide a feeling of security

- increase bonding
- be emotionally comforting

Cons
If allowed to deteriorate, monogamy can:

- be boring
- lead to a feeling of being trapped
- lead to a feeling of being taken for granted
- lead to cheating
- diminish your sexual desire for your partner
- encourage apathy and negligence about behavior and appearance

The example of one lesbian couple I counseled illustrates well the power and pitfalls of monogamy. When they came to see me, Sue and Judy, both in their fifties, had been living together for fifteen years. Their monogamous relationship had become lifeless and boring. Sue, looking hurt and sad, began her story. "Judy never wants to talk to me anymore. She doesn't look at me or touch me. We don't make love. I feel as though we're sisters, not lovers."

These two women shared a powerful love that had kept them together for an extended period of time. For them, monogamy was an expression of their mutual devotion and loyalty. Their intimacy, however, was showing signs of deterioration; like many monogamous couples, they had begun to take each other for granted.

I suggested that they begin a three-point plan of action. First, both Sue and Judy needed to begin exercise programs to improve their physical condition and appearance. Second, each needed to develop some interests to renew her excitement and pleasure in life, as well as to have something to share with her partner. Third, and most difficult for them, they needed to consciously set aside time for romance and affection. I suggested, for example, that they get into the habit of talking about their feelings while massaging each other. After a few such sessions, they began to be physically affectionate with each other once more. We gradually worked through some additional exercises to help them open up even more to each other.

Within six weeks, they began to make love again. We discussed the benefits of using different sexual toys (for example, vibrators and flavored lotions), changing old routines (switching "leader" and "follower" positions), and taking the pressure off during lovemaking (by making fantasies okay, and by not focusing on achieving orgasms every time). The strength of this couple's bond gave them the motivation they needed and made it possible for them to renew their sexual energy.

Afterward, Judy said, "I never realized that a relationship really had to be maintained. I know now that I got lazy and took Sue for granted because I knew she loved me. Now I understand what it takes to keep us going well. It takes work, but it's worth it."

Open Sexuality: Pros and Cons

Pros
If handled conscientiously, open sexuality can:

- provide a sense of personal freedom and choice
- enhance autonomy and individual responsibility
- create excitement and new energy
- provide a means of healing old abandonment issues
- prevent lovers from becoming complacent
- create a deep feeling of trust
- provide a sense of sharing and unconditional love
- provide needed personal space

Cons
If allowed to deteriorate, open sexuality can:

- bring up feelings of jealousy and fears of abandonment
- take too much time and energy from the relationship
- increase the risk of disease
- damage self-worth
- be used as a way to avoid intimacy
- be a vehicle for sexual addiction

The experience of Floyd and Rich, both twenty-six, demonstrates well the problems and rewards of having a sexually open relationship. This couple wanted to make a commitment but didn't want to be monogamous. They came to me because they had heard I could help them to create a healthy open relationship.

Floyd said,

> I tried being with only one person before, and it didn't work. I kept thinking about what I couldn't have, and then I'd get angry. After a while, I didn't even love my lover anymore—I just saw him as a jailer, someone who was keeping me trapped. Still, I do want to have a real relationship with Rich. I love him, and we have great sex. I think we could build a good relationship together.

Then Rich spoke:

> I always thought I wanted an open arrangement, but I tried it with my last lover, and we had a lot of problems. I'm not sure it can work, but I've heard about other people who've been helped to do this, so I thought we'd try it.

After an extended discussion, I found that what Rich and Floyd wanted was to maintain within a permanent, committed relationship the excitement and variety of having occasional sexual contact with other men. I explained that there were several factors to consider. First, they had to have a clear, honest contract that both were willing to keep. Second, they had to be very concerned and responsible about the issue of safe sex. Third, they had to consider each other's feelings and allow for times when they might feel insecure.

For the first two sessions, I assisted Floyd and Rich in talking very frankly about AIDS and safe sex, fear of abandonment and of being taken advantage of, and what commitment meant to both of them. Then we began to formulate an agreement. Regarding sexual safety, Rich and Floyd agreed to limit sexual activity with other men to masturbation only. They decided that there would be no sexual activity with mutual friends. They agreed to tell all outside partners about their committed relationship so that there would be no misunderstandings, and they also agreed to tell each other in advance if either one wanted to change any aspect of the agreement. Included in their contract was the provision that they would have a weekly meeting with me during the first few months to talk about how things were going.

Floyd was the first one to act on the contract, and Rich did get a little uneasy. In their next meeting with me, he said,

> It felt funny, knowing everything, and I know Floyd felt funny talking about it. I sort of felt that I had to go out and do the same thing. But after I'd thought about it, I decided I'd rather go work out at the gym and then go out to eat with a friend. Once I'd made that decision, I felt great! I talked some more with Floyd, and we actually had a great time talking about his "date." We got turned on and made love, so I feel I got something out of it, too!

A year later, Floyd and Rich have settled in together and report feeling very solid about their relationship. One or the other of them has sex outside the relationship about once a month, after which they usually discuss it and then use the discussion to stimulate their own lovemaking. While they agree that an open relationship requires extra work, they like the excitement it provides.

Now that we've looked at many of the pros and cons of monogamy and open relationships, following are some essential points to consider when making your decision.

Choosing Monogamy

If the idea of monogamy seems to you to automatically imply boredom and a sense of being "trapped," take a look at why you feel this way. Perhaps you think that sex can't be exciting or different with the same person. Or perhaps homophobia is an issue here: do you think your sexuality is wrong, that your love can't last, or that you're restricted to certain activities because you're gay? For example, some men won't kiss another man, and some men believe that one partner always has to be on "top"; also, some women will not use sex toys. Or are you reacting to pressure you feel from your friends and social environment to avoid permanent relationships? In fact, monogamy can be very rewarding. If you take care of your monogamous relationship, your mutual pleasure and excitement can last a lifetime.

If you think you want monogamy, you must be honest with yourself about the following issues:

- *Be absolutely certain that you can honor the agreement.* Honesty begins at home. Maintaining monogamy does not mean simply rejecting sex outside your relationship; it also means keeping sexuality and intimacy alive and well within the relationship. Nothing contributes to infidelity more than sexual frustration and dissatisfaction. Don't let yourselves relax into the security of monogamy to the point where you no longer have fun. Monogamy is a choice, not a necessity. If you take it seriously and keep it healthy, it can be a choice with which you'll be satisfied.
- *Make sure your decision is mutual and voluntary.* The choice to be monogamous must not be made with hidden expectations, such as using monogamy as a means of getting your lover to make a commitment. You can't force intimacy. If your partner is not ready for monogamy, this does not necessarily mean that he or she doesn't care about you; instead, it may simply be that the relationship hasn't developed enough yet for a commitment to be made.
- *Don't use monogamy to avoid discussing open sexuality, especially if your partner is interested in that option.* Find out what your lover thinks, and share your own opinions. Examine your feelings about open arrangements. If your lover would like to be open, what is it that he or she is looking for? Can you provide it instead? For example, you may be able and willing to provide sexual fantasy play, but not the variety your lover seeks. If this is the case, you will need to delve honestly into your conflicting views of monogamy.

If you and your partner decide to choose monogamy, be careful not to fall into static sexual roles, such as "husband" and "wife," "top" and "bottom." Make sure your sexual play has some variety in it. If you get lazy about this, you will find your sexual excitement for each other fading rapidly.

Choosing Open Sexuality

If the idea of a sexually open arrangement is disturbing to you, examine your feelings. Do your religious beliefs conflict with the idea of open sexuality? Do you fear disease? Or are you afraid you'll lose your lover to someone else? In my experience, gay couples who make clear open-sexuality agreements are not likely to be "broken up" by third parties. What *can* destroy such relationships are poorly made agreements, which are prone to misunderstandings and resentment. With a properly made and maintained open agreement, the partners do not risk losing each other, because their primary relationship is healthy and fulfilling.

In choosing open sexuality, keep these guidelines in mind:

- *Approach your agreement responsibly and honestly.* I don't recommend contracts based on the philosophy of "You can do whatever you want—just don't tell me about it." Such an arrangement is not only likely to lead to shock and pain, but it also deprives you and your partner of the chance to make a clear, honest, and mutual contract about sexual behavior. You need to decide when and how you will discuss your actions. How often is outside sex acceptable, and with whom? How will you handle jealousy and insecurity if these arise?
- *Don't consider your primary commitment unimportant because you are open, and don't use your agreement to escape from the problems of your relationship.* For example, don't go out on a night when you and your lover are not getting along. Never go out to get even or to make your lover jealous, angry, or more attentive to you.
- *Be sure to practice safe sex.* I recommend limiting your outside sexual contact to sensual touch and massage, "petting," and mutual masturbation. Appendix B provides information on safe-sex practices, and information is readily available in most gay communities.

Considerations for Either Decision

Whatever your decision, I encourage you to do the necessary work to ensure that your agreement is mutual. Think through and talk about your reasons for wanting monogamy or open sexuality. Don't make a decision because you're feeling pressured to do so, either by yourself or by your partner.

If at any point one of you becomes uncomfortable with the contract you have made, talk about your feelings in your communication meetings. Has sex become less inviting, less exciting? Is one (or both) of you feeling bored or jealous? Use the problem-solving techniques in chapter 4 and the sexual-discussion techniques in this chapter.

If one of you breaks the agreement, seek to find out what caused the conflicting behavior, without making accusations. Was the agreement made freely and clearly, or were there some hidden expectations? Was the partner who broke the contract angry or hurt and trying to get even or inspire jealousy? In any case, it is important to recognize that the conditions that led to the breach already existed. Perhaps the relationship was deteriorating, or the partner who broke the contract was not ready to make the agreement in the first place.

Finally, the success of your contract depends to a large extent on your ability to maintain a joyous sexuality in your relationship over the "long haul." Just as you need to develop communication and problem-solving skills, you need to know how to handle long-term sex. Probably the two most important things you can do are to make sure that you allow enough time for intimacy and to keep your sexual relationship fresh. Every lasting relationship needs sexual variety; this can be achieved in either a monogamous or an open relationship. Chapter 9 will deal in more detail with the issue of intimacy and sex in long-term gay relationships.

SEXUAL TRUST AND FREEDOM

Trust is the real issue in all sexual matters of relationships. Do you trust yourself, and do you trust each other? Trust, like all emotions, is difficult to define. On a surface level, a trusting relationship is one in which both partners feel secure that agreements will be honored. Behind this, however, is a much deeper issue: self-esteem.

In order to have a trusting, reliable relationship with another person, it is essential that you be reliable and trustworthy yourself. If you make a promise to yourself, do you keep it? If you're unable to keep an agreement with yourself, others cannot trust you and will always be suspicious and dissatisfied. After all, why should they treat you any better than you treat yourself? In addition, your own untrustworthy behavior will lead you to believe that others are also unreliable. Your trust of your partner thus begins with your own self-esteem and self-control. The trust between you needs to develop in a reciprocal fashion, with each partner demonstrating to the other that the trust expected is the trust given.

For some gay couples trust can be difficult to develop if either partner has a history of short-term or exploitive relationships.

Gwen and Martha, a lesbian couple I counseled, were both in their mid-forties and had gotten together after each had been in a relationship with an alcoholic partner. Both were emotionally scarred and were only beginning to heal.

At first, their relationship had been wonderful and had seemed finally to be fulfilling their needs for mutual love. But when Gwen made plans to go to another state to visit her children from a prior marriage, the trust they had in their relationship was put on the block. In my office, Gwen explained, "I just need to visit my family, but Martha seems to have gone crazy. She won't listen to me; she seems to think I'm trying to leave her. I'm beginning to think I should end the relationship." Martha sat still, looking terrified. Gently, I asked her what she was feeling. She began to cry and said, "I don't know what's wrong with me. I know I should trust Gwen, but she won't tell me what's going on, and when she talks about going away, I just panic."

In therapy sessions I later had with Martha, I discovered that like many other gay people I have worked with, her memory of her previous partner's extreme unreliability kept her constantly wary of her new lover. It took some time, but Martha eventually saw that she had not taken care of herself in her last relationship. While she had actually known when her old partner was lying to her, having affairs, and even taking her money, she had let herself be used out of her desire to be loved. Martha needed to learn to develop her trust slowly, rather than either handing it over too quickly or withholding it completely.

Gwen did go away to visit her children. When she returned, the couple broke up and reunited several times over the next year. With work, they were able to eventually resolve their issues of trust and make a permanent commitment to each other.

Trust is crucial to the success of your relationship. If you're not sure how much you can trust your partner, slow down and begin to build that trust before going any further. Find out if there is a homophobic or personal issue at the root of your uncertainty. If you don't feel you can trust yourself yet, keep your relationship low-key until you have taken care of your own problem. If you and your partner had built a trust together that has somehow been damaged, you will need to work to rebuild that trust.

How do you build trust? Make agreements that are sensible, and keep them. Be on time, pay your debts, and treat both yourself and your partner with respect. The process is much the same whether you're building trust with yourself or with another person.

GUIDELINES FOR BUILDING TRUST

- *Make sure that you both feel comfortable with your agreements.* Don't frighten your partner or yourself by testing too hard, demanding the impossible, or risking too much. Keep in mind that fear breaks down trust. If you begin to feel frightened, talk about it, and encourage your partner to do the same.
- *Keep each other informed.* Lying to your partner about whether you have broken an agreement does more damage than breaking the agreement. If you slip up, tell the truth. If it's your partner who has slipped, be open to listening to him or her without flying off the handle so that the two of you can negotiate a solution to the problem. If you or your partner continuously breaks the trust between you, you need to reevaluate your relationship.
- *Give yourselves time.* Whether you choose monogamy or an open arrangement, learning how to carry out your agreement successfully takes practice and experience. Patience and communication are your best allies. As you make mistakes and learn, trust gradually builds. As trust grows stronger, you can begin to relax the rules and allow yourselves more spontaneity.

Because most of us are very vulnerable and at our most insecure with regard to sexual issues, sexual trust is among the most difficult types of trust to build. The following exercise can help.

Sexual-Trust Exercise

Begin by asking your partner to risk telling you one small truth. The truth can be about anything: something he or she likes or doesn't like about sex; a fear about your friendship with someone; concerns about body image. Then take whatever time is necessary to be able to respond calmly. Take a few deep breaths if you get anxious or if your feelings are hurt. Respond by repeating in your own words what was said, or ask for more explanation if you need it. Once you and your lover agree that you understand, then share your feelings about the truth your partner has expressed. Put as much gentleness and understanding into this process as you can.

Then share a truth yourself, and give your partner time to hear it and react to it. Ask for a guarantee of gentleness; don't share your truth until your partner can guarantee this. After you have shared your truth, listen calmly and openly to your partner's feelings about what you have said.

Repeating this process a few times in one session will give you a sense of what sexual honesty feels like. If you and your partner practice doing this exercise over several months, you'll find that your confidence will grow. Once the two of you have developed a loving atmosphere free of fear, being honest and trusting about sexual matters will come more naturally.

An important side benefit of this exercise is that your sexual encounters will improve. Trust between partners provides a sense of security and an environment conducive to relaxed, open, and free sexual expression. When you both know you can say whatever comes to mind without fear of getting a negative response, you open mental doors that can lead to very close connections.

INCESTUOUS FRIENDSHIPS

The issue of sexual relations with friends can be a problem in gay relationships. This situation comes up so often among my gay and lesbian clients that I feel it deserves special attention.

When the breaking of a sexual contract involves a couple's friends, the damage done can be similar to that seen in families in which incest has occurred. I draw this parallel because a close group of friends can often develop dynamics similar to those of a family, complete with a "mother" and/or "father" figure, "sibling" rivalries, and feelings of power and powerlessness. If members of the group have come from families that were sexually unclear, incestuous, or abusive, these patterns can recur in the form of partner-switching, clandestine affairs, or heavy flirtation. In such cases, the normal boundaries of friendship are violated, and the result is distrust, pain, and trauma.

One of the most interesting series of clients I have had was a group of lesbian women who worked for the same company. The first person I saw was Carol, a twenty-two-year-old who was extremely upset and hurt because her lover was having an affair with Carol's best friend. In due time, Carol referred several of her other coworker friends, who were in similar situations. After a few sessions with several of these women, it became clear to me that much of the turmoil they were experiencing was caused by frequent partner-switching. One couple would break up, and the two ex-partners would immediately begin to have "secret" affairs with members of other couples in the group. In fact, the group was so close-knit that no secrets were possible. Eventually, the women involved began to feel tremendous emotional pain. Several of them became severely depressed, despairing, and even suicidal.

The correspondence of their feelings to those of incest survivors and perpetrators was remarkable. There was a similar mélange of guilt, rage, love, and attachment. Several of the women—again, acting like members of an incestuous family—were unwilling to discuss the subject for fear of losing the support of the "family" group.

When I told these clients of the similarities I had noticed, I learned that several of them had been the victims of incest or sexual abuse as children. Through individual and group therapy sessions in which I helped them to heal the old incest scars, most of the women were able to work through their incest issues and to separate from the few women who were not willing or able to take responsibility for their behavior.

Honesty within all intimate relationships is important. Friendships must be nurtured and kept functional, especially if friends fill the role of family, as they do for many gay couples. If friends and lovers are the same gender and sexual preference, it becomes essential to make clear distinctions between partners and friends.

Friendship "Contracts"

Learn to make solid agreements with your friends as well as with your lover about what is on and off limits. If sexual feelings arise in a friendship (and it is natural for this to happen), be willing to discuss them with both your friend and your lover. Above all, take responsibility for your sexual decisions. For example:

- If a friend constantly tempts, coerces, or pressures you to become sexually involved, reconsider the value of the friendship.
- If you have considerable trouble with this problem, consider that your primary relationship may be lacking something or that you have an issue you need to deal with.

- If you decide to have open sexual relationships with friends, it is obviously essential that this be part of an agreement you have made with your primary partner.
- If it is important to you that you be free to have sex with friends, but your partner is not in agreement, the two of you should renegotiate the status of your commitment. Perhaps it would be better for you to revert to dating, if possible, or perhaps you need to consider breaking up.

HEALTHY SEX: SOME GUIDELINES

Most gay people learn about gay sex "on the street" and by trial and error. Information gained in these ways can be not only confusing but incorrect. When they first come into my office, many of my clients are shy about discussing sex. Once trust is established, they usually have questions about what is considered "normal" sex for homosexuals. So, we spend some time "talking dirty with the therapist," as one of my clients put it!

Among the questions I commonly hear from my gay and lesbian clients are these:

Am I sexually normal?

What is healthy sex?

(From men) Sometimes I dress up like a woman. Is that sick?

(From women) How important is having an orgasm?

Is it okay if my lover has an orgasm, and I don't?

Is it okay to play fantasy games, such as nurse/patient or teacher/student?

Are sex toys and special outfits okay?

Are bondage and "water sports" normal?

The answers to these and to other questions about gay sexual activity can be found only by learning the facts and opening up discussion. The opportunity to learn the facts about sex is greater now than it was just a few years ago. More and more respected professionals are researching human sexuality, and new information is available each year. Sex-information hot lines abound in major cities (volunteers for such hot lines often report that the training they receive provides them with a first-rate course in both sex and communication). Many couples are finding it useful and fun to enroll in human-sexuality courses, which not only are educational but often can be a turn-on as well.

To open up the discussion about sexual activity, begin by talking to your partner. Between the two of you, you may have a fair amount of past experience from which you can both learn. You may then want to extend your discussion by comparing sexual experiences and information with some close friends.

In the rest of this section, I'll answer the questions I hear most often from my clients and cover the issues that I find cause the most confusion among them.

What Is Healthy Sex—Or, How Weird Am I?

Healthy sex is any sexual activity between two consenting adults that is not harmful to them or to others. "Consenting" means that both parties must agree freely. An "adult," under most state laws, is defined as someone eighteen years of age or older. And, because of the current epidemic of sexually transmitted diseases (STDs), including AIDS, "harmful" must now be considered in a medical as well as a physical and a psychological sense. (Note that harmless, mutual sexual play between children is considered normal, or at least not pathological, if the children are within two years of each other's ages and their actions are voluntary, involving no coercion and no adult influence.)

Whatever the sexual issue or activity, it's important not to take things too seriously. Following is an excerpt from a column I wrote for gay newspapers on healthy sex:

> I believe that it's possible, and possibly even necessary, to have sex in a healthy and responsible manner and still be lighthearted about it. Sex without pressure ("We have to do it this often and this way"), without goals ("It wasn't good if we didn't both have the orgasm of a lifetime"), without record keeping ("I initiated last time—now it's your turn"), without competition ("Am I as good as your last lover?") might just turn out to be sex with more joy and more love, and it's bound to be a lot more fun!
>
> In these terms, it's not the *sex* that counts, it's the love. Sex is a fine and glorious way to communicate love and to share all aspects of ourselves. . . .
>
> When I hear clients complaining that their partners

"withhold" sex from them, I wonder: What happened to make it not fun? When did it get to be work? . . . When I hear people bragging about "size" or "beautiful bodies" or the duration and "score" of the experience, I wonder: Where is their pleasure, their joy? What happened to the love? Why is it not okay to mention the tenderness, the pleasure of being held and touched? When clients come in afraid of sex and surrender, I wonder: What has been done to create this fear?

God has done a great thing: We come fully equipped, no batteries needed, to share our joy and our human be-ing—physically, mentally, emotionally, and physically. The only restriction we have been given is inherent in the equipment: keep it healthy, don't abuse it, "play nice," and respect each other's toys.

I have been practicing surrender, including surrender to my sexual self. And do you know what? I find that this means I must surrender to joy, to love and laughter, to letting it happen "the way it wants to." This also means surrendering to the times when I'm not enjoying it—to respect myself and my partner enough to admit it, and to change what's needed—and surrendering to my fears enough to double-check to make sure I'm safe.

I wish you peace and joy in sex, and in all ways that you live.

Sexual Games: B&D, Cross-Dressing, and Other Amusements

Bondage, role-playing, cross-dressing, and fetishism have traditionally been regarded as "weird" or "kinky." Since the arrival of AIDS, however, they have achieved status as safer-sex practices (which demonstrates the arbitrary nature of many of our taboos!).

Any such activity is okay as long as it meets the definition of healthy sex. However, if an activity becomes compulsive or threatens to disrupt your lifestyle, this is an indication of a problem. Sometimes the sexual activities we choose represent deflected expressions of overwhelming or unsatisfied feelings. In discussing each activity below, I'll give you guidelines to help you know when you're stepping over the line from play to problem.

Bondage and domination (B&D). Many people experience a thrill in being dominated or in dominating someone else. B&D is a harmless cousin to sadomasochism (S&M). Whereas S&M has an unhealthy emphasis on inflicting or receiving pain (physical, mental, or emotional), B&D is just for fun.

B&D games involve lots of costumes and props (usually rubber, leather, and studs). These games are played by women and men of any sexual persuasion. Players can be couples, trios, or groups. Some aficionados have complete "dungeons"—elaborately decorated rooms with whips, chains, and restraints used for decor. B&D does not always involve sexual intercourse. Sometimes it's a prelude to sex, sometimes it includes sex, and sometimes it's a completely separate event.

To avoid problems with B&D, you must know how to keep it from slipping into S&M. Following are the rules for safe and healthy B&D that I developed for a discussion group at a gay therapy center:

- Get to know your partners *before* playing.
- Agree in advance on a word or phrase that can be used to end the game instantly. If anyone says this word or phrase at *any* time, all bonds or restraints should be released immediately (much as the phrase "King's X" is used by children to end a game).
- Be sure you enjoy the game. If you're unsure about it or have never done it before, let your partner(s) know this, and go slowly.
- Be very careful not to obstruct breathing or otherwise endanger your partners or yourself. Know the difference between pretend role-playing and real reluctance. Never coerce an unwilling partner, and never force yourself to do something you don't want to do. This game centers on trust—so be sure to keep your promises, and play only with people who keep theirs.
- If any injury (mental, emotional, or physical), however minor, occurs, or even if there is a close call, STOP PLAYING. Before playing this game again, determine the reasons for the occurrence, preferably with the help of someone knowledgeable, such as a therapist or counselor.

B&D does not mix well with self-destructive tendencies or with a reluctance to take care of oneself. If you're not following the above rules, it is *vital* that you seek professional assistance to find out why, before you hurt yourself or someone else.

Cross-dressing. Many of my gay male clients have asked me about cross-dressing, a term used to refer to the wearing of clothing that is generally associated with the other gender. In the larger society, there's an interesting double standard about cross-dressing. While women who engage in it are seen as "cute" or eccentric, men who cross-dress are usually seen as "sick" or, at the very least, strange. As a result, male cross-dressers have more difficulty in understanding what is healthy.

Many male performers, both gay and straight, make their living cross-dressing. Because it's done to entertain, cross-dressing in this way is generally considered acceptable and amusing (particularly in the cases of big-name stars). The movie *Tootsie,* for example, was a box-office smash, and two recent Broadway plays—*La Cage aux Folles* and *Torch Song Trilogy* (both also made into films)—featured gay cross-dressing.

Cross-dressing can be fun, and it's harmless. I know of many groups of gay men who get together for a day and dress up as women, just for a lark. Cross-dressing is considered a Halloween ritual by many gay people. The strong social taboo about men wearing dresses, heels, and makeup invites this sort of rebellious play.

When cross-dressing is a psychological compulsion, it's called transvestitism. Transvestites cross-dress not to have fun but to relieve some internal psychological pressure.

If you cross-dress, only you know which category you fit into. If you're just having fun, don't worry. But if your cross-dressing places you in any danger or is upsetting to you or your mate, or if you feel a need to cross-dress at inappropriate times and places, you may need professional guidance. In addition to therapy, you can get help through one of the many transvestite support groups across the country. In such supportive settings, you can learn to understand yourself better and to manage your compulsion.

Paraphilias. Until recently, finding one's sexual turn-on in objects, animals, children, and body secretions instead of in other adult human beings was termed *perversion, deviation,* and/or *fetishism.* However, because these forms of sexual arousal occur with some frequency in our society, sex researchers have reconsidered the terminology, now using the term *paraphilia* to refer to any alternate kind of sexual turn-on.

Paraphilias are a compulsion, not a choice. Like all compulsions, they can range from the harmless to the obsessive and self-destructive. There are some paraphilias that are considered pathological or illegal. For example, to fantasize about having sex with children or animals is a paraphilia, but to actually engage in sex with children or animals is considered pathological. This is a gray area, since homosexual acts are still often declared illegal but no longer pathological.

The rule of thumb for deciding whether your favorite sexual habit is a problem is the same as that for any other substance or activity that might be abused: Are *you* in charge, or does the activity or substance dictate your actions to you? Also, are you or anyone else being harmed by your practices?

The following activities all fall within the range of "usually normal":

- Using toys (dildos, vibrators, ticklers, and so on)
- Urinating on each other in the shower
- Wearing leather and/or rubber costumes, high heels, and handcuffs
- Role-playing (teacher/student, nurse/patient, and so on)

Many of my gay male clients ask me about "water sports"—that is, sexual activity that involves urine. It is important to be cautious here, as bacterial and viral diseases can be contracted when one partner's bodily secretions come into contact with another partner's sores, wounds, or other orifices.

If you are in doubt about *any* of your sexual practices, consider discussing them with a trained sex therapist, who will be open and nonjudgmental as well as knowledgeable about sexuality and health. Sex-information hot lines can also answer many of your questions.

What Are Healthy Sex Roles?

Healthy sex roles, in general, are sexual behaviors that are renegotiable, not harmful to either partner, and mutually agreed upon. In talking to my gay clients who have sex-role problems, I find resistance to change and feeling "stuck" in a role are the biggest problems.

As I mentioned earlier, many gay and lesbian couples tend to follow predefined patterns in lovemaking, based on stereotyped roles of "butch" and "femme" or "nelly." Most people like some variety in sex, just as in other activities. One of the skills necessary for making your long-term gay relationship successful is the art of creating new and exciting experiences with the same partner.

If you are interested in changing your sexual routine, the first step is to discuss your feelings with your partner. Choose a time when the mood is relaxed. To begin the discussion, you might say something like, "You know, we've never really talked about sex—what we like and don't like. I feel sort of nervous about bringing it up, but I'd really like to talk about it. What do you think?"

You may need to talk about sex in general a couple of times before getting to specifics (Appendix B, "Safe-Sex Information," can be of help to you in your discussion). Before talking about something you don't like, say what you do like. This will make the negatives easier to take and will reassure your partner that you don't dislike *everything* about his or her style. Then let your partner know what you want, and invite a response.

Keep in mind that sex is just one form of interaction among many in your relationship. When you open up discussions about it, you are not damaging your spontaneity but rather giving it a chance to flourish. It's another way to "come out of the closet" and allow your true self to be known. Healthy and pleasurable sexuality is a key ingredient in successful gay and lesbian relationships.

CHAPTER 6

Living Together

You are a couple, and your friends speak of you in one breath—"Tim and Joe," "Fran and Beth." You're always invited to parties together, and you're introduced as a pair. A friend who runs into you alone will likely ask, "Where's Gail?" or "Is Nick with you?" You and your partner spend most of your time together. One of you stays at the other's apartment on most weeknights and every weekend, and you're finding that it's getting tough to live in two places. You begin to think about moving in together. After all, you say to yourselves, you're practically living together already.

For most gay couples, living together is the primary goal and the ultimate relationship step, because marriage has generally been perceived as being either impossible or unnecessary. I view marriage as a practical and desirable goal for gay and lesbian relationships, and I will further discuss options for formalizing your relationship in chapter 7. But because so many couples see living together as the ultimate step, and because most gay and lesbian couples who do marry live together first, it's important to know how to make the decision to move in together. Based on my experience with my clients, I believe that many homosexual people do not adequately manage the decision to live together. Rather than reaping the rewards of greater intimacy and commitment, they end up in unhappy, short-term situations with their lovers.

Many of the issues involved in deciding to live together echo the commitment issues discussed in chapter 3. For example, some homosexual couples—particularly lesbians—jump right into cohabitation without much forethought and are thus often unprepared to handle the new challenges and more intense dynamics of living together. Others—particularly gay males—may resist taking the step of living together because they fear they will lose their individuality and sexual freedom. They may struggle with the decision for months or even years, getting stuck somewhere between separation and increased commitment.

Other homosexual couples who do move in together may short-change themselves of the benefits because they still have gay issues to resolve. Issues of homophobia ("I'm gay, so it's not right") and of coming out ("If we move in together, then everyone will know we're gay") can create so much fear that living together is joyless and stressful.

The following two stories typify the problems that can occur when gay and lesbian lovers do not squarely face the decision to live together.

Pete, twenty-two, and Craig, thirty-five, met at church, where they both sang in the choir and worked on committees. They often got together at Pete's apartment to prepare the church newsletter, and they would linger over coffee. Pete admired Craig's knowledge and experience, and Craig enjoyed the attention. Soon, the meetings began to be more than just get-togethers for church business. One night, they made love.

When Pete's roommate left to move to another city and Pete found that he couldn't afford the apartment alone, Craig suggested that Pete move in with him temporarily. "Temporarily" stretched on for weeks, then months. Pete began to feel overpowered and "nagged at" by Craig; Craig thought Pete was irresponsible. By the time they came to see me, they were both angry and confused.

Craig did all of the talking at first: "I never wanted this. He was just supposed to live with me temporarily, but he won't get out and find an apartment. He could have a better job, but he doesn't care. Now everyone in the church knows we live together. It will be awful if we break up."

Finally, Pete got a few words in: "I don't know what he's so upset about. We're doing okay. We have a good time, when he's not nagging at me. If he'd just relax, things would be fine."

Suzanne, twenty-three, and Valerie, twenty-five, were both proud that they had been exclusive lovers since their first date. Within six weeks, they had moved in together. Six months later, they came to see me. "I think we made a mistake," said Suzanne. "I thought Valerie was the one, but now I think I was wrong." When I asked why, she said,

> The magic is gone. We're not excited about each other any more. She doesn't like the way I clean the bathroom. I don't like how she spends all her money. We're always arguing. We

think we should split up, but neither of us wants to be single again, so we thought we should talk to a counselor.

Whatever your situation with your partner, it is important to jointly analyze the decision to live together. Moving in *is* a new step in your commitment, and it creates relationship dynamics that are very different from those of dating. You will need to confront such issues as personal space, privacy, domestic chores, and relationship roles, all of which will become more intense and difficult to negotiate.

As with any other step in the process of courtship, there is no universally right time to take the step of living together. Some gay and lesbian couples may need only a few months of dating before they are ready for this stage, but many will benefit from considerably more time.

Let's look now at some guidelines for making your decision and at the major issues to consider *before* you move in together.

LIVING TOGETHER: THE PROS AND CONS

Like the reality of marriage, the reality of living together is often obscured in a mist of romantic fantasy. The truth is that living with a lover does not in itself improve the quality of life. If you are unhappy alone, you are likely to be equally miserable when you are living with your partner. Living together successfully requires the same effort and skill needed to make your individual lives satisfying.

Living together obviously has many advantages, but for some gay couples it can have an equal set of disadvantages. Consider the following list of possible pros and cons.

Pros

- better lifestyle due to shared income and expenses
- no hassles in getting to see each other
- possible ease of communication and sharing
- trial run before gay or lesbian marriage
- more efficient use of time
- possible learning opportunity about intimacy skills

- chores and responsibilities are shared
- contact and possibly intimacy are facilitated
- possible end to loneliness
- readily available companionship, support, and affection
- possible encouragement toward better habits

Cons

- risk of being "taken for granted," apathy, and loss of excitement
- more pressure and stress on the relationship
- harder to break up if necessary
- more discussion and negotiating necessary
- struggles over space and privacy
- possible conflicting styles in housework, money management, work, and leisure
- loss of freedom and independence
- more difficult to get personal time and space
- need to always consider someone else's feelings before acting
- loss of financial freedom
- less time for hobbies and projects
- single friends may drift away

In addition to these pros and cons, there are a few other special issues that you may need to consider in making your decision. If you are concerned about coming out, living together can complicate your ability to remain closeted. Since it's more difficult to hide your relationship, having family nearby or living in an area where people are openly hostile to homosexuals will likely generate further stress and anxiety.

Further, if you have a lot of emotional baggage (a demanding career, children from a previous marriage, or difficult family dynamics), living together can involve your partner too closely in your personal problems and can be too overwhelming to him or her.

Finally, if your relationship is already troubled, living together could create more problems than it solves.

Understanding all of the above factors can help you to avoid unrealistic or hidden expectations about living together. In the end, each couple must decide for themselves based on their particular situation and their personal needs. The rest of this chapter contains specific guidelines to help you handle the most difficult dynamics of living together, should you decide to take that step.

PRIVACY, DOMESTIC CHORES, AND MONEY

Even if you have had roommates before, it's important to recognize that sharing your space with a lover is very different. No matter how much you love each other, each of you has different—and perhaps hidden—attitudes, beliefs, and habits that can influence the success of your living together. The greater the difference in your definitions of living together, the more critical it is that you discover and share your wants and needs before shifting your relationship into higher gear.

Living together effectively changes the emphasis in your relationship from "When can we get together?" to "When can we be apart?" In essence, it turns your dating relationship upside down. For example, one partner's strong requirement for time alone can be a major source of conflict, for two reasons: First, our cultural value system makes us believe that lovers should want to spend all their time together, so wanting to be alone is often interpreted as selfish or insulting. Second, there may no longer be a convenient place for either partner to go to be alone.

One general strategy I recommend for preparing to live together is to review with your partner the previous living arrangements you both had with family, roommates, or old lovers. You can use what went right and wrong in those situations to guide you in your new adventure.

Privacy

Much of the turmoil gay and lesbian couples experience in living together centers around privacy. I have seen many clients who believe that moving in together provides them with a license to know everything about their partners' lives.

We all need privacy, and we all have different styles and attitudes about personal space and possessions. It is absolutely essential for every couple to learn how to deal with privacy issues and to negotiate their individual needs.

One lesbian couple I counseled, Marlene and Suki, had totally different perceptions about several privacy issues in their relationship. Their family backgrounds had given them very different values on such issues as sharing, respect, and politeness.

Their dilemma started when Suki came home one day and was horrified to find that Marlene had borrowed a blouse without asking. They told me that the ensuing conversation had gone something like this:

Suki: I can't believe you just reached into my closet and took the blouse when I was at work!

Marlene: Well, I couldn't find anything to wear with these pants. I didn't mean any harm.

Suki: But you just went into my things! How can you do that?

Marlene: I don't understand what the big deal is! I gave the blouse back, and I even washed and ironed it. I didn't hurt it.

Suki: And you always walk in on me when I'm in the bedroom. You don't even knock!

Marlene: Knock? You want me to knock on my own bedroom door? That's crazy!

Suki: And you have friends over without telling me! You don't care about my feelings at all! I can't live like this!

When I helped Marlene and Suki examine the roots of this disagreement, I learned that in Marlene's family, she and her two sisters had borrowed clothes from each other, crammed into the bathroom at the same time, and invited friends over constantly. Meanwhile, in Suki's Japanese-American family, politeness and consideration had meant *never* infringing on another person's privacy. When someone was on the phone, Suki stayed out of the room until the conversation was over. Before entering a room with a closed door, she always knocked and sought permission.

Once I had helped Suki and Marlene to understand their individual differences, they ultimately decided that they would be better off separating. Although it was difficult for them to move out, their relationship actually improved after they did so. Clearly, if they had talked about privacy before moving in together, they could have avoided a great deal of pain and struggle.

While your values about privacy may clash less than Suki and Marlene's did, you probably both have some minimum limits that you need to establish. You may have already considered privacy issues, but if you haven't, the following exercise can help you to discover your individual needs and learn to handle any differences between you.

Space and Privacy Exercise

First, take some time to review your perceptions of privacy, beginning with childhood. For example, if you were an only child and your lover had siblings, it would be useful to ask whether your partner shared many things with his or her brothers and sisters. Also, review your previous experiences with former roommates and lovers.

Then ask each other the following specific questions:

Is it okay for me to borrow your clothes?

Is it permissible for me to read your magazines or newspapers first?

Can I listen to the messages on your answering machine?

Can I read your mail from friends and family?

Can I open your dresser drawers to put laundry away?

Do you want to be in the bathroom alone, or can I come in even when the door is closed?

Should I knock before coming into your study or into the bedroom?

Can I invite friends over without checking with you first?

As you discuss your answers to the above questions, consider these guidelines:

- Tell the truth about your needs. Even if you feel guilty or embarrassed about how much privacy or togetherness you want, this is the time to tell your lover about it. Otherwise, it will likely come out in anger later.
- Respect your partner's needs, no matter how trivial or uptight they may seem to you. This is the person you're going to live with, so mutual respect is essential.

- Consider the space you'll be living in. If you both need a great deal of privacy, it may not be workable for you to live in a studio or one-bedroom apartment. Perhaps you should consider renting in a lower-priced neighborhood to get more space.
- If one of you is planning to move into the other's established space, be *extra* thorough in your discussion of privacy needs. Make sure you can set up special areas for each of you and that shared space contains items belonging to both of you.
- Don't panic if you find that your needs for privacy are very different from your partner's. Chances are that with honesty, respect, and thoughtful negotiation, the two of you will find a workable solution.

Remember that your respect for each other's privacy reflects your level of trust. People who intentionally "pry" or "snoop" into their lover's private life or belongings are usually insecure about some aspect of the relationship. There may be a hidden issue such as homophobia, addiction, financial trouble, or unresolved anger. For example, it's important to know beforehand if your lover has any large debts or obligations (alimony, etc.). You don't need to see detailed financial statements, but you do need to know where you and your lover stand economically. The methods discussed earlier for developing and negotiating sexual trust can also be applied to the area of privacy. Discussing things frankly now can help you to avoid problems later on.

Domestic Chores

No matter how organized or disorganized you thought you were when you were living alone, you did have a routine. When you live with someone else, however, your personal routine may no longer work. Each chore will need to be discussed, and a new routine must be designed that suits both of you.

The best time to review your housekeeping arrangements is *before* you move in together. It should be part of your precommitment discussion, as it will help both of you to get in touch with the reality of living together. You can avoid many arguments by talking honestly about your cleanliness requirements, how you feel about the sharing of chores, and what sort of atmosphere you want your home to have.

If you're already living together and are having problems with domestic issues, it's still possible to renegotiate. Recognize that you've already established patterns together, so you will need to restructure the ones that don't work. Think of it as starting over, and seek to revise your agreement from today on rather than arguing about issues of the past.

Establish an awareness of your own attitudes about domestic chores. Perhaps your habit in the past has been to leave everything to someone else (Mom, a maid, or a roommate who liked housework). Perhaps you've preferred to do everything yourself, or to let cleaning go and live "casually." Or perhaps you've preferred to share chores more or less equally when living with others. If you have particular likes and dislikes, these need to be part of the discussion. Such things as allergies (are you allergic to cats? dust? smoking?) and little personal quirks (for example, you may like to drape clothes on a chair when you're tired and put them away in the morning) can be a future source of major battles if they're not discussed now.

In analyzing attitudes about domestic chores, you and your partner should be sure to consider only your own and each other's needs and habits, not those of family and friends. While your mother might have waxed the floors every Saturday, that solution may not be the best one in your own household.

The possible solutions to handling the issue of domestic chores are numerous. For example, you could do one of the following:

- divide the tasks equally, or according to preferences
- alternate doing all the work each week or month
- assign each chore a point basis, and keep a tally
- agree to a reduction in rent for one partner, in exchange for that partner's doing a larger share of chores
- hire out some of the work (this is more affordable than you might think, particularly if you both work and time is precious)
- barter your own business or service in exchange for outside help

Toothpaste Tubes and Other Trespasses

Idiosyncrasies you hardly noticed in your partner when you were dating can suddenly become unbearably irritating when you're living together. Don't be unduly alarmed. All couples go through this, and the problem usually passes. Working it out requires problem-solving skills, as well as a willingness to accommodate each other and to tolerate each other's quirks. Use these helpful hints for dealing with pet peeves and trespasses:

- *Talk to each other.* If you're feeling frustrated, don't keep it to yourself. The only way for the two of you to learn about each other's needs is to share your thoughts and feelings.
- *Take responsibility.* Don't blame your partner for your own irritation. Make it your responsibility to let your lover know what doesn't work for you, and why.
- *Seek balance.* Although a habit of your partner's may loom large in your eyes, avoid becoming an unreasonable nag. Pay attention to your tolerance level: if it seems low, you may be using little things to disguise your fears of relationship failure. You might tell your lover, "I know I've been on your case a lot about housework, but it's not the real problem. I think I'm scared about something else. Can we talk about it?"
- *Acknowledge successes.* As you solve minor problems together and become more comfortable with doing so, acknowledge these small triumphs. Remember, too, that nothing will motivate your partner to be more thoughtful than your show of appreciation whenever he or she does something nice.

Finances

Money is a very personal thing. We use it as a symbol of success, as a reward, and as an indicator of self-esteem. Everyone handles money differently. Because of these differences in attitudes and styles, money is an emotionally charged issue. In fact, struggles about money are a problem for most of the gay and lesbian couples I see in counseling.

There are two main aspects of finances for couples: practical and legal. The practical aspect is best handled through negotiation, while the legal aspect is dealt with through the use of such contracts and arrangements as joint tenancy, wills, designated insurance beneficiaries, and so on. The legal questions will be addressed in chapter 7, which deals with how to give your relationship legal status. For the purposes of the discussion here, we'll explore the practical, day-to-day issues of a couple's financial arrangements.

There are several ways to negotiate your financial arrangement. You can split the household expenses equally, or, if one of you earns substantially more than the other, you can split expenses on a percentage basis. For example, if you earn 60 percent of the household income and your partner earns 40 percent, you might choose to split the expenses at the same percentages. This allows the two of you to live at a higher level than the lowest-earning partner can afford, without straining his or her finances. You may also have to take into account one partner's much higher expenses (for example, child support, car-insurance premiums, or loans). When negotiating your financial arrangement, don't offer to pay more than you want to or to pay a larger amount if your partner is careless with money. Doing so will only lead to resentment later on.

I often recommend that couples separate their personal money, especially if both of them work. My experience with gay couples is that their financial arrangements work best when each partner keeps an individual checking account, with perhaps a joint account for household expenses. Such an arrangement allows for a degree of financial autonomy and freedom for each partner.

Finally, keep in mind that with finances, as with other areas, you can use the problem-solving steps in chapter 4 to work out differences as they come up.

THE NEED FOR HONESTY

Because living together makes it difficult, if not impossible, to ignore each other's attitudes and behavior, it becomes even more essential that you communicate honestly. When you attempt to hide your feelings, they become like time bombs waiting to go off. Whether you're hiding resentments, broken agreements, or personal secrets, if the truth comes to light accidentally, your relationship will be undermined and the trust between you will be damaged.

Prying or attempting to coerce your partner into revealing the truth will do equal harm. My experience with many gay couples indicates that pressuring a lover to be honest can often backfire, creating even greater distance and secrecy.

In the end, it's much easier and more productive to be honest and to invite honesty. While it is not possible to force another person to be trustworthy, it is very possible to make being honest an attractive option. To invite honesty from your partner, be supportive and nonjudgmental whenever he or she opens up to you, *even if you don't like what you hear.* Take the role of a friend, not a parent, and do your best to put yourself in your partner's shoes. Rewarding honesty by reacting positively to it will send the message that truth-telling is productive.

Don't expect a lover to be more honest with you than you are with yourself. As I've said before, honesty really begins with yourself. This means that your responsibility is to tell the truth, whether or not your partner does so. Are you willing to face difficult truths about your relationship or your partner, or do you find yourself making excuses for your or your lover's actions? For example, some people have a difficult time facing up to their own or a lover's addiction problems. Others want so much to be loved that they refuse to acknowledge that they are being abused.

If you suspect that your partner is not telling you the truth, don't beg or nag. Instead, protect yourself: don't surrender your money, health, secrets, or heart to anyone you cannot trust, and take the following precautions until the situation changes:

- Don't excuse, rescue, loan money to, or otherwise "make it better for" a partner who is repeatedly irresponsible or untrustworthy.
- If you suspect that your lover is not being sexually responsible, either decline sex or insist on following safe-sex guidelines until you can be *sure.*
- If your partner is reckless with your car or careless with your other belongings, don't allow her or him access to these.
- If your mate spends wildly, separate your bank accounts, credit cards, and so on, and deny him or her access to your funds.
- If your lover has an addiction and you want to stay together, you'll need support. Attend meetings of Al-Anon or other

Twelve-Step programs to learn how to avoid being co-dependent.

- If your mate does not keep agreements, make sure there are consequences for breaking them.

The above recommendations are called "tough love," because these steps are tough to take but can be effective in difficult situations. If you've been using the criteria of love, judgment, mutuality, and responsibility, and your relationship has progressed to the point at which you're living together, you'll probably never need to use such difficult methods. I mention them here only in the event that inviting openness is not enough or that a relationship crisis arises.

ROLES PEOPLE PLAY: "BUTCH" AND "NELLY" REVISITED

In chapter 5, we reviewed many aspects of sexuality in gay relationships. A related issue is that of the roles we take on according to our beliefs about how men and women are supposed to act.

As I've said earlier, there is a fair amount of confusion among many gay couples over sexual roles, due largely to early training. As children, many of us learned that men work and women do housework, men are in charge of money and women are in charge of the house, and men make decisions and women carry them out. This paradigm of sexual roles is clearly changing today, but it is surprising how much influence it still has, even in gay and lesbian relationships. Despite the problems of applying these roles to same-sex couples, few homosexuals have escaped thinking in terms of "husband and wife," and their images of these roles are intimately bound up in their sense of what it means to be a gay couple. In living together, many gay and lesbian partners—particularly those over forty—dramatize and exaggerate these traditional roles, with one partner taking the aggressive masculine ("butch") role and the other playing the passive feminine ("femme" or "nelly") role.

Playing such stereotypical roles can become a way to avoid the responsibility of a relationship. When you model yourselves after Mom and Dad or after the ideal heterosexual couple on television, you limit your possibilities both as individuals and as a couple. While having roles can eliminate the need to make decisions about who does what in a relationship, they deprive the partners of choice and growth.

Instead of limiting ourselves to predefined and perhaps ill-suited roles, we can choose our roles according to our personalities. A lesbian woman who is mechanically adept, assertive, and career oriented may play the traditional "husband" role, but this doesn't mean that she can't cook or clean. Her partner may enjoy doing domestic chores, being the emotional caregiver, and generally taking on the role of a traditional "wife," but there's no reason she can't also take responsibility for the finances and for equal decision making in the relationship.

One lesbian couple I counseled learned to negotiate their responsibilities according to their interests. In the beginning of their relationship, Patty and Barbara had taken on husband-and-wife roles. Patty, a real-estate broker, made ample money for them both to live on, and Barbara really enjoyed taking care of the house and being home to look after her and Patty's children from previous marriages. This arrangement worked fine for a while, but as the children got older and needed her less often, Barbara began to feel restless. The couple found themselves squabbling frequently, and the relationship eventually became so tense that they came to me for help.

After listening to their stories, I pointed out that their original roles were no longer appropriate, and that they needed to experiment with a new division of responsibilities. Following several months of discussion, Barbara decided to take a job outside the home, and Patty decided to work less and to spend more time with the children. As a result, both women were happier, and their arguments ended.

Like Patty and Barbara, all gay and lesbian couples can learn to reexamine the roles they may have unconsciously adopted and to make more practical agreements for dividing their relationship responsibilities. Following are some guidelines to help you and your partner in defining your relationship roles.

- Negotiate your division of responsibilities, and don't make your roles mutually exclusive or irreversible. If a particular role is very important to you, make sure that your lover understands why. Take the time to discuss what you expect from each other, and use the problem-solving techniques in chapter 4 to work out an arrangement that is satisfactory to both of you.

- We all get tired of our roles from time to time. Be flexible and open to change, and trade roles whenever you or your partner needs a break.
- Everyone occasionally needs the comfort of a parent figure. We all need to cry in someone's arms, be soothed when we're troubled or sick, and have someone to lean on in times of difficulty. While it can be very satisfying for both partners to take turns supporting each other, it's important that you do not begin to consistently feel like parent and child. If one of you feels too dependent or too responsible, talk about it and negotiate a more mutual agreement.
- Don't get into role-playing by default—that is, don't fall into doing the same things all the time simply because you haven't bothered to think about it or to negotiate your responsibilities. If you find yourself wondering why you *always* do the cooking or why your lover *never* initiates sex, the two of you have probably fallen into unquestioned roles. It's time to renegotiate.

Whatever roles you play now, be prepared to outgrow them. Although you may have recently arrived at a comfortable balance in your relationship, new challenges will certainly appear. Don't be surprised or alarmed when you or your lover begins to look for new directions in your relationship. This is a natural aspect of any healthy, growing relationship.

We who have chosen a gay lifestyle have already veered from the traditional path and must make our own way. In defining how we are to live, we need support, both from each other and from organized groups. We need education and information. We need to be willing to learn and to challenge our own assumptions. I believe that today's gay men and lesbian women will be seen in the years to come as those who radically altered homosexual love and relationships. It's a big job, but one that's most certainly worth doing.

PANIC! AND PROBLEM SOLVING

Many gay couples experience some form of panic in the early stages of living together, when the inevitable problems intrude into their rosy "happily-ever-after" views of their relationship. When we fail to see problems as a normal part of a healthy relationship, we may come to believe that the entire relationship is a disaster, and we panic.

Whether that panic is about the added responsibility of shared living or about doubts that the move wasn't a good idea after all, there are ways to deal with it. Panic itself can make problems worse, because we can't think clearly when we're upset.

If you are feeling panicky, the following suggestions can help you to deal with your panic so you can get on to solving the problem:

- *Deal with yourself first.* You can't get anywhere with your partner until you understand what your own feelings are. Take a little time alone to think about the problem as you perceive it.
- *Recognize that all problems are solvable.* Focus on the solution, not just on the problem. Use your problem-solving skills to come up with possible answers.
- *Take responsibility.* Explain to your partner that you know your panic is *your* problem, and that you want help with it. Blaming, accusing, complaining, and nagging lead nowhere. Every relationship conflict involves two people; when you take the responsibility for your share of the difficulty, your partner is invited to do the same. Standoffs can thereby be avoided, and the way is paved for working toward a solution.
- *Use good communication skills.* Ask questions and listen actively to the answers. Seek to understand your partner's position. Many arguments consist of two people trying to make the other person understand, with neither one really listening. If you are a good listener to your lover's side of things, you'll find that he or she will be a better listener for you and will be more willing to help.
- *Ask for what you want.* Whether what you want is space, reassurance, or understanding, give your partner a chance to be generous and helpful by letting him or her know what you want.
- *Don't go too fast.* Panic has a way of making us rush blindly

forward. If you can't get the problem solved right away, simply take a break! Calm down, and then tackle the problem again.

- *Remind each other of what's going right between you.* Don't let your panic make you feel that absolutely *everything* is terrible in your relationship. Remind each other of your love—which is, after all, the most important part of your relationship.

- *Don't make drastic decisions, announcements, or threats when you're upset.* Most likely, you won't break up over this problem. But if you do, that decision must be made calmly and carefully. Think about it for a few days before taking any action. (You may want to review the section on breaking up in chapter 3 to determine whether you're thinking clearly about it.) Don't allow your panic to turn a relatively small problem into a disaster.

MOVING IN

Although gay marriage is a real possibility, as you'll see in chapter 7, many homosexual couples don't consider it an option because it has not been legalized for gay relationships. Moving in together has therefore taken on a special significance. Whereas heterosexual couples are usually clear that living together is not marriage, gay and lesbian lovers often see these two situations as synonymous.

As a result, it's critically important for you and your partner to decide what living together means to you before you take this step. If one of you approaches it as just a lark or an experiment but the other interprets it as evidence of a deep commitment, you're obviously setting up a problem. Before you move in, talk about your views of the purpose and meaning of living together, and discuss what it means to each of you in terms of commitment and marriage.

If you and your partner mutually decide that your moving in together symbolizes a stronger commitment, you may want to mark the date with an appropriate celebration or ritual (such as lighting candles, exchanging rings, or having a party). Especially if ceremonies and special occasions are important to you, don't deny yourselves this one. Your relationship is significant, and the move is a major change in your lives. You deserve to acknowledge the joy and spirit of the occasion. The exercises in the next chapter can help you to design a moving-in celebration that's meaningful to both of you.

CHAPTER 7

Commitment Ceremonies, Marriage, and Legal Issues

If moving in together doesn't satisfy your need to express the importance of your commitment, or if you feel "cheated" out of traditional commitment rituals because you're gay, you and your lover may want to have a commitment celebration or wedding. With a little imagination and your mutual efforts, you can create a ceremony that will enhance your relationship, clarify your goals, and celebrate your love.

Gay and lesbian weddings *are* possible and actually happen quite often, especially within the membership of the Metropolitan Community Church (MCC), a Protestant denomination begun by the Reverend Troy Perry in Los Angeles on October 6, 1968.

Because the terminology regarding homosexual commitment and marriage is new and so is not yet standardized, I will be using several terms here. *Holy Union* refers to a homosexual wedding in the Metropolitan Community Church; *wedding* means any religious gay marriage ceremony; and *commitment ceremony* applies to any celebration of a committed gay relationship, religious or not, that is designed by the couple.

The fact that homosexual marriage is not legally recognized should not discourage you from having a formal celebration.* There are ways for a gay or lesbian couple to make a lasting

*While it's true that homosexual marriage is not legally recognized by any state in the United States, it *has* been made legal in a few cities—notably, San Francisco, Berkeley, and West Hollywood, California. In these cities, any two people can register as a "domestic partnership," and they are then entitled to hospital visitation and any city-controlled privileges normally afforded only to married heterosexual people. Such registration is still mostly symbolic, however, because a city controls very few of these privileges; most rights are regulated by the state or federal government.

commitment that gives them most of the benefits and privileges afforded heterosexual couples. In fact, since such a commitment is not legal and is preestablished, you can design your own commitment package and so gain some advantages over the "automatic" legal rights and responsibilities that heterosexual marriage brings.

Commitment ceremonies, Holy Unions, and weddings are not to be taken lightly. Taking such a step indicates that you are serious about spending your lives together and publicly announces the committed nature of your relationship. The following information will help you to understand the significance of gay and lesbian commitment ceremonies, and will give you guidelines for designing a celebration, getting your family and friends involved, and obtaining certain legal documentation that will protect your joint-property and health-care rights.

IF IT'S NOT LEGAL, WHY DO IT?

There are three major benefits to be gained from having a commitment or marriage ceremony. The first is the mental benefit you derive from solidifying and clarifying your sense of commitment. The second stems from the symbolic and spiritual significance of the ritual. The third benefit relates to the emotional components of a public declaration and celebration, which can be a powerful reinforcement for your relationship. Let's now look at each of these benefits in more detail.

The Mental Benefit of a Ceremony

As I discussed earlier, gay men and lesbian women carry around a myth of marriage based on a heterosexual model, since we have had virtually no homosexual role models. As a result, many of my clients feel they can never have anything like a real "marriage," because "husband and husband" and "wife and wife" just don't sound legitimate.

In truth, homosexual couples can maintain commitment as well as any heterosexual couple. We can, therefore, benefit from publicly declaring our love through a commitment celebration or wedding. Through marriage, we can reclaim the legitimacy of our relationships and demonstrate to other gay and lesbian couples that lasting homosexual love *is* possible.

The Spiritual Benefit of a Ceremony

If spirituality is important to you (that is, if you live by a faith or you recognize a Higher Power or other symbol of spirituality in your life), a religious commitment ceremony can have a profound meaning in your relationship. Generally, spiritually oriented people have more motivation for enterprises they feel are blessed or are otherwise conducted in accordance with divine will. People with a strong spiritual focus may not feel their commitment is "real" unless it is dedicated in a spiritual or religious ceremony.

If you are not members of an organized religion, you may still wish to add a reference in your vows to whatever Higher Power you choose. The sense of blessing can have a strengthening effect on your relationship, helping to build a strong foundation for it. An alternative to having a religious wedding is simply to have your relationship blessed by a clergyperson, as several of my gay client couples have done. Such a ceremony can be very private—just the two of you and the clergyperson—or you can invite friends and family, following the ceremony with a party or reception.

For some people, the idea of a ritual that mentions God, the Bible, or religion may be off-putting and may even produce feelings of anger and resentment. It's important that you don't feel pushed into having a spiritual ceremony against your will. If your partner would like to have such a ceremony but you're uncomfortable about it, talk about your feelings with your partner, friends, and family. If you know a clergyperson who is understanding and supportive (and many are), talk with him or her about your fear, anger, or resistance. Clergypeople with the Metropolitan Community Church (Protestant), Dignity (Roman Catholic), Tikvah (Jewish), and other gay-oriented religious organizations are especially informed and understanding about homosexual religious issues and can help you and your partner to reach a mutually satisfactory solution.

The Emotional Benefit of a Ceremony

Weddings are a celebration of love and of life. Celebration is an essential ingredient of relationship success, because it generates a renewal of energy that keeps us motivated toward furthering our goals. Frequently, couples come to me because the joy and excitement are gone from their relationship. These couples have never celebrated their love. Formal celebration often renews their enthusiasm and motivation to continue. This has been demonstrated so frequently that I have reduced it to an equation I offer couples as a guideline in keeping their love alive: celebration + appreciation = motivation.

Unfortunately, many people have difficulty celebrating. They feel embarrassed and awkward about having any of their accomplishments publicly praised. This, in turn, causes them to focus their attention on mistakes and problems rather than on successes. By not celebrating their love, these people can often wind up perceiving their relationships as being full of problems.

When celebration is part of a gay or lesbian marriage, there can be a greater tendency to develop the enthusiasm and energy needed to stay together on a long-term basis. A wedding or commitment ceremony creates memories that can continually remind you of your love for each other. In addition, a celebration with friends is a strong reminder that you and your lover are part of a community that can help support your relationship during difficult times.

PRECOMMITMENT EVALUATION

If you decide to have a religious ceremony through an organized church, the minister will likely require premarital counseling. I endorse this idea, as such counseling can help you and your partner to clarify the meaning of your marriage. It also has the side benefit of familiarizing the minister with you and your relationship; as a result, he or she can help make the ceremony more meaningful to you. Even if no minister is involved, or yours doesn't counsel you, it can be very helpful to you to do your own precommitment evaluation.

A formal premarital discussion gives you and your partner an opportunity to compare your ideas about marriage. Through such discussion and through your mutual planning of the ceremony, with a focus on expressing your marriage ideals, you can help expose any hidden expectations and thus avoid confusion and hurt later on. The next exercise can help you in conducting your own premarital evaluation.

Premarital-Evaluation Exercise

1. Individually, make a list of marriages or committed relationships (gay or straight) that you admire, and a list of

those you don't admire. You may include people from both the past and the present, fictional or real.

2. Next, compare your lists with your lover, and discuss the reasons for your selections. Be specific about your likes and dislikes. For example:

    "I like that they both work and that they share the financial decisions."

    "They always seem to enjoy each other—they do a lot together."

    "I like the space they have in their relationship. Both of them go out alone with friends, besides doing things together."

    "I hated the awful fights my parents had, and I'm terrified of having fights like that in our marriage."

    "My parents never disagreed in front of my sister and me, so I always felt that the least little argument was awful and wrong. I think I need to learn how to disagree."

    "The love between Albin and George in *La Cage aux Folles* seemed so real, so warm and lasting. It's the only image I have of what a good, long-term gay relationship must be like."

    Allow a few sessions for this phase of the discussion, coming back to it several times. Your first talk will open up new thoughts that you can explore further in the second talk, and so on. Your objective is to understand each other's fantasies and models of marriage. Don't be concerned at this point about any differences of opinion; just find out what they are.

3. Once you have gained an understanding of each other's views and wants concerning marriage, you can begin to discuss how they mesh and where they conflict. Don't be surprised or upset if either your own or your partner's models or fantasies of marriage differ from the reality of your current relationship. That's what this exercise is for! The following guidelines can help you to evaluate any such differences.

    - Do some of your own fantasies of what marriage should be seem unrealistic to you or unsuited to you and your partner? For example, perhaps you've always believed that happily married couples spend all their spare time together, but you know that you or your partner needs lots of time alone.

- Do any of your fantasies indicate that you are dissatisfied with some areas of your relationship? For example, do you dream that being married means having more affection, more time together, and more communication than you have now?
- Are some of your fantasies indicative of things you'd like to bring into reality? For example, do you fantasize about having a business together, buying old houses and renovating them together, or just having more time to take long walks and talk?
- Do you have negative or frightening fantasies? Perhaps you're afraid that getting married means that sex will get boring, or that you'll have to give up your friends or favorite activities, or that you won't be able to spend money the way you want to.

4. By examining your fantasies, you've begun the process of learning your and your partner's definitions of marriage and uncovering any hidden expectations. Now you can begin to design a new definition of marriage for the two of you. Working together, each of you can answer these questions in turn:

   - Is there anything going on now that could turn into a problem once you're married?
   - What do you like most about your time together?
   - What do you like least?
   - In what ways—both good and bad—are you like your parents?
   - In what ways are you different from your parents?
   - Do you feel that anything is missing from your relationship?
   - Does your lover provide you with anything that's better than you had anticipated before entering the relationship?
   - As a couple, how can you mesh your different fantasies of love and marriage?

This discussion may also take a few sessions to complete, and these questions will likely raise others. By the time you're finished with your discussion, you should have a definition of marriage that is unambiguous, mutual, and achievable.

5. Together, write down your objectives for the marriage. For example:

   - We intend to be together permanently.
   - We want our marriage to be about learning and growing together.
   - We want our spiritual values to be important in the marriage, so we will . . .
   - We agree to continue our weekly communication opportunities after we're married. (and so on)

   Keep this list in a safe place so that you can refer to it together in the years to come, perhaps reading it on each anniversary. You will also find this list to be a source of strength during times of relationship difficulty.

THE WEDDING CEREMONY

Many gay and lesbian couples come to me unsure about what type of ceremony would best symbolize and express their commitment. I have come to believe that it's very important for couples who are already breaking old traditions to find new ones of their own. Because the commitment celebration is an important and highly symbolic part of your new traditions together, I encourage you to think about your ceremony carefully, giving consideration to both of your wants. If you have a strong religious affiliation, your clergyperson will most likely have a ceremony to suggest. Still, it's good to be informed and to know what your options are, since many clergy welcome your participation in designing a ceremony. Following is some basic information about weddings and commitment celebrations that can help you to create a personal ceremony.

Parts of the Ceremony

The details of marriage ceremonies vary widely from tradition to tradition. However, most religious marriage ceremonies follow this basic format, which can be adapted to suit your personal needs: opening statement, salutation, declaration of consent, the "giving away" (presentation of the spouse), exchange of vows, exchange of tokens, communion, charge, prayer, proclamation, kiss, blessing, and presentation of the couple. Each of these will be explained in the next few pages.

An important note: since the ceremony itself has no legal status, it does not need to be performed by a licensed clergyperson or judge. (The various legal steps you can take to formalize your commitment will be discussed later in this chapter.) This means that you are free to have anyone who is important to you conduct your celebration. If you work out the whole script carefully, it can be easily followed by a friend or family member. Because you may not have a minister, I will be using the term *presider* to refer to the person conducting the ceremony; I will use *minister* when referring specifically to a representative of any organized religion.

The wedding sequence given here (which can be altered in any way you wish, with additions or deletions made to suit your individual needs) is based on a combination of a Holy Union service provided by the Reverend Frank Muir of the Metropolitan Community Church in Long Beach, California, and several other gay ceremonies I have witnessed. I have included sample wedding excerpts from the 1932 *Methodist Hymnal* (to show a traditional style), from Reverend Muir's service (to show today's MCC style), and from the ceremonies I helped two of my client couples (Nina and Darlene, and Scott and Lewis) write for their own weddings (to show some "do-it-yourself" ideas).

Music can be added anywhere, and there are many options for entering and leaving the celebration.

Opening statement. The opening statement is an introduction. If a scriptural reading is desired, it is usually chosen by the minister. Or, you and your partner could choose a favorite poem or quote that expresses your feelings about the event. You may recite it together, or you may have someone else (the minister, a friend, or a family member) read it. You might also choose to have someone sing an appropriate song.

Salutation. This is the "Dearly beloved, we are gathered here today . . ." part! It begins the formal ceremony with a statement of purpose, explaining your commitment, your decision to formalize it, and the importance of having friends present. It's a very brief history of what you are doing and of what led you here. If you decide to write this yourselves, remember that a few sentences are enough. The salutation is usually given by the minister, but you can also choose to say it yourselves or have a friend read it.

Declaration of consent. This is the part of the ceremony in which the minister asks each partner, "Will you take this person to be your wedded [spouse], forsaking all others?" The traditional response is "I will." The declaration of consent is the couple's formal agreement to continue with the ceremony. Many couples incorporate this part into the vows, a bit later in the ceremony. If you decide to leave the declaration of consent here, the minister or presider asks the question. Here are some examples of wording:

> *Methodist Hymnal:* ________ , wilt thou have this woman to be thy wedded wife, to live together in the holy estate of matrimony? Wilt thou love her, comfort her, honor, and keep her, in sickness and in health, and forsaking all others, keep thee only unto her, so long as ye both shall live?

> *Reverend Muir (MCC):* ________ , will you have this man to live together with you in covenant? Will you take him as a partner in Holy Union? Will you love, comfort, honor, and keep him in sickness and health, and forsaking all others, be faithful to him, nurturing love each day at a time as long as you both shall live?

Giving away. In heterosexual marriages that include a "giving away," the question "Who gives this woman . . . ?" is asked. While this particular wording is obviously sexist and outmoded, this part of the wedding ceremony is useful in that it establishes the couple's relationship to the extended family and acknowledges that a new family unit is being formed. For a gay or lesbian ceremony, the minister or presider could phrase the question this way: "Will you welcome the creation of this new unit within your family?" One person could act as spokesperson for each family and welcome the new member in, or the extended family could respond, pledging support with a chorus of "We will." Or, you could write a simple "Repeat after me . . ." pledge for the family to recite.

Exchange of vows. I consider this to be the heart of the wedding ritual, and I therefore feel that most of your attention needs to be focused here. I'll begin with sample vows from other weddings, and then I'll discuss how to create your own. You can either repeat your vows after the minister or presider or recite them from memory.

Methodist:
I, ________, take thee, ________, to be my wedded [husband or wife], to have and to hold, from this day forward, for better, for worse, for richer, for poorer, in sickness and in health, to love and to cherish, till death us do part, and thereto I plight thee my faith.

Reverend Muir (MCC):
In the name of God, I, ________, take you, ________, to be my partner in Holy Union, to love and remember through prosperity and suffering, from this day forward, for better, for worse, in sickness and in health, to cherish so long as we both shall live.

Scott and Lewis:
I, Scott, give myself to you, Lewis, to be your husband and life partner. In good health, prosperity, and abundance and to the mutual benefit of all, I give you my support, my trust, and my friendship. Together, with patience and a sense of humor, we can accomplish anything.

I, Lewis, give to you, Scott, my trust, support, and friendship. I am your husband and life partner, in good health, prosperity, and abundance and to the mutual benefit of all. Together, our possibilities are endless.

Nina and Darlene:
I, Nina, take you, Darlene, in good health, to the mutual benefit of all, manifesting the creative energy for happiness in the here and now and accomplishment in the proper time and place.

"Couples." This organization designed the following vow for its members. What it says could also be adapted as a declaration.

We, ________ and ________, hereby commit ourselves to sharing our lives and love with one another and joyfully proclaim ourselves a couple. We will venture forth into the sunshine and rainstorms, the lightning and rainbows, in the years ahead with kindness, commitment, compassion, and a sense of humor.

The above examples can give you an idea of the variety of vows possible. You can also ask ministers, friends, and family for examples.

Creating Your Own Marriage Vows

If you have already done the premarital-evaluation exercise, you are well on the way to creating your own vows. The steps that follow provide you with how-to advice.

1. Separately, make a search for quotes, prayers, poems, or song lyrics that seem to best reflect your feelings about your relationship. Books, records, friends (and, of course, your own memory) are all good sources. Take a few days or even a couple of weeks to do this. Alternatively, you can simply write a short statement (a few sentences will suffice) about your feelings.
2. Together, decide which piece or pieces to use (or write two separate short statements). Remember, these will become promises, so keep them within the limits you are willing to live up to.
3. To write your vow, you can begin with the traditional formula ("I, [your name], take you, [partner's name], to be my [spouse, partner, mate, lover, husband, wife]"), or you can make up your own beginning. You can both use the same promise, or you can write two complementary promises.
4. Some time before the ceremony (preferably, at least a day or two), share your completed vows with your presider or minister to ensure that she or he is comfortable with them. If not, discuss any differences and either revise the vows or arrange for a different presider.

Exchange of tokens. Most people believe that weddings require an exchange of rings. Although this is traditionally done, rings aren't legally necessary in any marriage. You may choose to exchange rings, or you may prefer to exchange some other symbolic tokens (for example, the two halves of a two-part pendant, or watches, bracelets, or any other items that can be worn constantly). According to Reverend Muir, "The *mizpah* charm is popular right now. This is a charm that says 'The Lord watch over me and thee while we are absent, one from the other,' and is cut in such a way that half of one charm will fit only its mate." Some people have the tokens inscribed with the wedding date and perhaps with a quote or other words.

If you use tokens, a separate vow usually accompanies their exchange. Here are a few examples of words that may be spoken during the exchange:

> *Methodist:*
> In token and pledge of the vow between us made, with this ring I thee wed: in the Name of the Father, and of the Son, and of the Holy Spirit. Amen.
>
> *Reverend Muir:*
> I give you this ring as a symbol of my vow, with all that I am and all that I have; I honor you, in the name of the Father, Son, and Holy Spirit. Amen.
>
> *Scott and Lewis, Nina and Darlene:*
> I give you this ring as I give you myself, with affection and hope. I offer you love, I offer you strength, I offer you my support and understanding, as long as we both shall love.

Communion. Here, the couple can take traditional communion as prescribed by their faith, or they may simply share a sip of wine or juice. This is also a time during the ceremony when a selected poem or quote may be read or a song performed. Communion is a symbolic sharing of the fruits of life, and it sometimes includes a blessing given by the minister or presider on behalf of a Higher Power. In the Jewish faith, after the wine is shared, a glass (wrapped in cloth for safety) is ceremonially smashed, symbolizing the one-time, unique nature of the event.

Charge. The charge is an empowering statement made by the minister or presider, and it usually begins with the words "I charge you both . . ." The charge is more often found in ordination ceremonies for ministers, but several of my gay clients have incorporated it into their wedding ceremonies in order to feel publicly consecrated to a goal. Here is a sample charge:

> I charge you both with the responsibility to keep alive and grow, to maintain your capacity for wonder, spontaneity, and humor. I charge you to remain pliant, warm, and sensitive, to speak your minds with gentleness and your hearts with openness. I charge you to see the meaning of life through the changing prism of your love for each other, and to live responsibly and creatively. I charge you to live in full awareness of the abundance that has been provided for you, receiving it with respect and gratitude.

Prayer. Traditionally given by the minister, the prayer asks for guidance and help for the couple and for the congregation, whose responsibility it is to support the union. If your orientation is not religious, you can simply ask that everyone join hands to symbolize the solidarity of the community.

Proclamation. The wording of the proclamation, generally given by a minister, is usually something like this: "By the power vested in me, I now pronounce thee partners in life." The couple is thus officially married in the eyes of the church. Since Scott and Lewis did not have a minister officiating, they requested that the presider say the following: "The powers that be in the universe have brought Lewis and Scott together. Let us respect and support their love."

Kiss. Following the proclamation, the minister or presider gives the couple permission to kiss. The kiss is symbolic of the couple's shared love and their newly committed status (and replaces old royal customs in which the closest retainers retired to the bedroom with the couple to witness the consummation!).

Blessing. The minister traditionally gives the couple a blessing. Here's a lovely one written by Reverend Tom Toler:

> And now, may you have love—a love that is new and fresh each hour: as new as the rising of the evening star, as fresh as the coming of each new dawn.
>
> And may you have peace—not the peace of the stagnant

pool, but of deep waters flowing. And may you have poise—not the poise of the sheltered tree, but of the oak: deep rooted, storm strengthened, and free.

And may you have power—not the power of fisted might, but of the seed: quickened, growing toward an infinite and eternal light. Amen. Go in peace.

If you're not connected to a religion, you can ask your presider to express good wishes for you, or you can write a blessing for yourself, to be read by you or by someone of your choosing.

Presentation of the couple. The presentation, which introduces you in your new status together, can be made either at the end of the ceremony or as you enter the reception. The presider says, "Ladies and gentlemen, may I present to you ______," filling in your names, followed by the words "partners in life." While many gay and lesbian couples keep their own names, others choose to hyphenate their surnames or even to adopt an entirely new name together. This choice has the added benefit of letting everyone know how you would like to be addressed from now on.

INVOLVING YOUR FRIENDS AND FAMILY

Friends and family are an extension of your relationship. To encourage their support, especially during this important step in your life, get them involved in your celebration. Of course, in many cases, this may mean coming out to them. As I've discussed before, many gay and lesbian couples who are contemplating moving in together or getting married feel that taking such a step warrants their coming out. Information to help you with this decision is given in chapter 8.

While traditional straight marriage etiquette dictates that the bride's family pay for the wedding expenses, this is obviously not a clear issue in homosexual marriages. Most of my gay and lesbian clients and friends who have had ceremonies have elected to pay the costs themselves. Since most of us cannot afford to have everything professionally provided, friends and family can be of great assistance. This is an excellent opportunity for you to involve others.

Assisting you gives friends and relatives the chance to feel that they are an integral part of your celebration. Wedding clothes can

consult a lawyer in order to have the proper documents created. The descriptions provided here are simply for your information, so you'll know what questions to ask.

If you choose to have a wedding celebration or commitment ceremony, you might wish to consider having your legal documents serve as your "marriage license." You could sign them in full view of your wedding guests, or in private with your marriage witnesses. If you decide to do this, be sure to give your lawyer enough advance notice so that the documents can be drawn up in time.

Durable Power of Attorney for Health Care. This is a document through which you agree to give someone else the power to make health-care decisions for you if you should become unconscious or otherwise incapacitated. (In some states, you need a "designation of preference" instead.) When signed, this document conveys power of attorney (here, the right to make health-care decisions) to whomever you designate. It also allows you to designate someone to make decisions about an autopsy, about disposition of the body, and about the donation of body parts. In California, Durable Power of Attorney for Health Care is effective for seven years.

Many hospitals have visitation restrictions, especially in the case of serious illness, such as AIDS and cancer. Visitors are sometimes limited to members of the patient's immediate family, which legally excludes a gay or lesbian partner—*unless* he or she has a Durable Power of Attorney for Health Care. I strongly recommend that you obtain such a document, as it may be your only chance to allow each other visitation rights and to have your health-care wishes carried out. It is also important for you to know a hospital's regulations *before* you or your partner is admitted. Even if you have Durable Power of Attorney for Health Care, the last thing you need at such a difficult time is a legal battle with the hospital to enforce your rights. Talk to the hospital administration and show them your documentation immediately, before any problems have a chance to arise.

Joint tenancy. When you are purchasing property, joint tenancy is accomplished by means of a contract or deed; when property already purchased in one name is being transferred to joint tenancy, a special procedure is followed. A joint-tenancy deed must read as follows: "[Your name and your partner's name], Joint

Tenants with right of survivorship." Any two competent adults may own property in joint tenancy.

Joint tenancy can also be used for bank accounts, stocks and bonds, and other financial matters. Note that because joint tenancy has tax implications, you should consult an accountant as well as a lawyer when making decisions about property ownership.

If a deed reads "Tenants in Common," it means that you and your partner share ownership (according to whatever percentage is stated), but that upon the death of one partner, the deceased partner's share is to be distributed according to a will or to decisions made in probate (the legal procedure following a death in which a judge distributes the property and determines inheritance tax). The only phrase that conveys the right to inherit is joint tenancy. If a property is owned in joint tenancy, the surviving tenant will retain title regardless of what the will says, unless the court rules that for some reason the will has severed the joint-tenancy agreement.

Wills. Wills are absolutely essential when property or finances are held in common. I have seen many situations in which otherwise reasonable people have done hurtful things to others while under the stress of grief. If you or your partner were to die, the surviving lover might be given little status or consideration by the blood relatives of the deceased. In the long run, having wills is beneficial not only to you and your lover but to your families as well. Proper arrangements in advance can forestall such problems and can also make the probate process easier and less expensive. Be aware that only a competent lawyer can draw up an uncontestable will.

Trusts. If you have considerable property or money, living trusts and other such arrangements can save your lover taxes in the event of your death and will ensure that your wishes are carried out. Besides your lawyer, bankers and financial planners can advise you regarding trusts.

Adoption. Most of us have heard of this option, in which one lover legally adopts the other. In some ways such a step can be useful, because it automatically makes you and your lover "immediate family" in the eyes of the law. However, if your relationship fails, you will very likely be stuck with the adoption anyway. If you decide to adopt, be sure to use a lawyer who is very experienced in this procedure and is therefore familiar with the potential problems.

Contracts. A less complex way to set up legal rights is through a contract. By law, you can make a contract with anyone, about anything that is not illegal; if the contract is properly drawn, it has a good chance of holding up in court.

Contracts are useful in such situations as setting up a business partnership or investing in property together. Discuss what terms you want, and write them down as clearly as you can. Then take your contract to a lawyer, who will translate it into "legalese" and keep it on file. Any contract should contain provisions for voiding it in the event that the agreement changes. I recommend the use of contracts in all legal and financial partnerships (which a committed relationship certainly is), because they cover all the details of an agreement which may not be covered under law, such as time limits, exchanges of information or property, etc. They are especially useful because they are quite simple to change.

Cohabitation contracts. Many heterosexual couples are recognizing the value of prenuptial agreements and marriage contracts in clarifying those areas in which their wants differ from what the law provides. For gay and lesbian couples, such contracts are highly desirable. Your lawyer will probably suggest that you not mention your gay relationship or refer to yourselves as lovers in your cohabitation contract; instead, simply outline your agreements about living together.

Family Announcements and Discussions

I recommend that you discuss not only with your lover but also with your family the arrangements you would like to have made in the event that you become seriously ill or die. This kind of discussion is never easy, but it could save your lover and your family unnecessary distress and heartache later on. Once the issues are out in the open, you will likely feel reassured and more secure. (If you are not "out" to your family, you may wish to discuss these issues with close friends instead.)

Issues to discuss include these:

- any legal arrangements that you and your lover have made
- whether you would want to be on life-support systems if you couldn't sustain your own life
- what funeral/memorial or cremation/burial rites you would want
- whom you would like to name as executor of your estate
- whether you would wish to have body parts donated to science
- what belongings you would like to bequeath to relatives

Before bringing these issues up to your family, you should, of course, be sure that you and your lover are in agreement on them.

If you're planning a wedding or commitment ceremony, you might want to have this family discussion some time before the big day. You could have a small dinner party or other quiet gathering at which you announce your plans. Although the subject matter is serious, handling it in this way can evoke an "engagement announcement" feeling and encourage a pleasant atmosphere. (For various reasons—for instance, if you know that certain relatives don't get along with one another—you may choose to have more than one such gathering, for different groups of people.)

It's a good idea to let those invited know the purpose of the gathering beforehand. If you know the conversation will be difficult for your mother, for example, this forewarning will give her time to adjust to the idea before the discussion.

It's not necessary to discuss the details of your plans at your gathering, but just the general arrangements. You might announce that you and your lover have planned a commitment celebration and so are making certain legal arrangements. You don't need to say how much of your property you're leaving to each other in your wills. It's enough to let your family know that you and your partner are naming each other as executors of your wills, joint tenants, and heirs, and that each of you has filed (or will file) a Durable Power of Attorney for Health Care.

You might want to arrange in advance to have a close friend or relative propose a toast following the discussion of your arrangements. This can lighten the atmosphere and refocus the attention on the coming celebration.

While it's true that heterosexual couples don't discuss these issues at engagement-announcement parties, it's also true that the legal ramifications of heterosexual marriage are spelled out in state and federal law. Homosexual couples need to create their own legal frameworks and make them known, at least to a few key people. Although it's not absolutely necessary to let your family or friends know of your legal plans, I strongly advise gay couples to do this. Making such an announcement lets others know the seriousness of your intent and the importance of your relationship, and it can also help to prevent struggles later on. In addition, by making this announcement, you let family and friends know that you want them to be involved in the plans you and your partner are making to spend your lives together.

The next chapter will give you information to help you in coming out to family and friends and in building a support network for your relationship.

CHAPTER

8

Coming Out, In-Laws, and Support Systems

Most single gay men and women treat the decision to come out haphazardly. Since being openly gay often means incurring social disapproval, it is usually easier and wiser to conceal one's sexual preference. Many single homosexuals tell only a few people and let everyone else assume they're straight.

When you become involved in a significant relationship, however, keeping the secret becomes both much more difficult and very unsatisfying. Going to family gatherings, attending social affairs for business, and just inviting friends over for coffee can all become very stressful. It's uncomfortable to have to make up stories about who your "friend" is, to explain why you don't have a date, or to have to constantly wonder whether guests notice that you and your roommate have only one bedroom.

After years of counseling gay couples, it's evident to me that having a committed relationship is the strongest motivation that homosexuals have for coming out and for building a support network. When my gay clients get to the point of discussing commitment, marriage, and joint legal arrangements, they are usually no longer willing to hide their relationships and to live in constant fear of discovery. Instead, they want to be identified as a couple within the broader context of family, friends, coworkers, and neighbors.

COMING OUT

For most gay men and women, coming out is a complex decision, one that can take years of preparation. Few of us are impervious to the opinions of our friends, associates, and family. The degree of our vulnerability to negative opinion will influence how long it takes us to decide to come out, whom we tell, and how we tell them. Coming out is not necessarily an all-or-nothing proposition. It is not only possible but also often desirable to come out to some people but not to others.

Following are descriptions given by several of my clients about their coming-out circumstances:

> My parents still don't know I'm lesbian. It would upset them too much for me to tell them, and they don't take hints, so I figure they don't want to know. I'm single, so it doesn't matter yet.

> I've been gay since I was a teenager, but my parents never knew. Somehow it was okay for them not to know until I met Brian. Now I want to come out.

> When my mother found out I was gay, she threw herself on my bed and yelled, "Where did I go wrong?" She still prays for my salvation, fifteen years later. Things are fine when I go home, as long as I don't talk about it. If I had a steady lover, I think it would be more of a problem for me.

> I had just taken a weekend workshop. I struggled with my decision, but I decided honesty was important. When I called my mother and told her I was gay, she said, "That's nice, dear. How's the weather out there?" She didn't really understand, but she accepted everything, and her love was clear. When I brought Kevin home, she obviously liked him, she just didn't like the earring he wore.

> I thought my Dad would disown me when he found out. I'm glad I got counseling to help me figure out the best way to tell him. He's not overjoyed, but he says it's my life, and he cares about me. Frank and I go over for Christmas, but it's a little awkward.

> My parents really like Elaine; sometimes I even get jealous! They really treat her like another daughter, and they even let us sleep in the same room when we stay over. I'm really grateful for their understanding.

Considering the range of reactions you can get when you come out, the decision definitely requires forethought and preparation. It can, however, be well worth the effort. Homosexual couples can benefit greatly from having accepting families and a strong social network to compensate for the lack of support and the negative images they encounter in the larger society.

By not coming out to your family and friends, you may be avoiding the pressure of disapproval, but you are creating a new constraint: isolation. Couples in isolation have limited options. If you have only each other to talk to about many important areas of your life, boredom can become a problem. In addition, if you don't have a network of other gay couples around with whom to compare your situation, it can be difficult for you to tell when problems in your relationship need work. Having a support network allows you to observe others with similar issues, to share triumphs and tragedies, and to discuss your problems with understanding friends and family members.

The Pros and Cons of Coming Out

In the end, only you can decide what degree of coming out is right for you, and when, where, and to whom you should make your disclosure. Following are lists of some generalized pros and cons about both coming out and staying closeted. Be aware that you and your partner are likely to have different needs and different attitudes about being open. I suggest that you make your own individualized lists, writing down the specific advantages and disadvantages either decision would have for you. Just getting these down on paper in an organized form will help you to evaluate your choices. (See the sample lists below and on next page.) Begin writing your lists now, adding to them as you continue to read through this chapter.

COMING OUT

Possible Advantages	*Possible Disadvantages*
enhanced self-esteem	abandonment by family and friends
no more hiding your relationship	discrimination on the job
true closeness with those who accept you	hostile reactions from strangers
security of living honestly	

STAYING CLOSETED

Possible Advantages	*Possible Disadvantages*
job security	constant fear of exposure
acceptance from homophobic friends/family	lowered self-esteem
	going alone to family and work gatherings

Preparing to Come Out to Family and Friends

There are times when the decision to disclose our lifestyles is out of our hands—for instance, when discovery or illness makes it clear to others that we're gay. However, we usually have many choices about how and when to come out. Preparation is often the key to how well the announcement is accepted, particularly by family and friends. (Note: There are special considerations that are involved in coming out to your children; these will be covered later in this chapter.)

You can maximize your chances of success by doing the following:

- deciding in advance when and how to tell family members and/or friends, including what you are going to say
- remembering to see the situation from others' point of view as well as your own
- being sure in your own mind of why you're making your disclosure, and of what you would like from those you tell

As preparation, ask yourself the following questions:

1. *Why should I reveal that I'm gay, and what response do I hope to get?* If you know what you want from your family or friends, phrase your objectives as positively as possible when making your disclosure. For example:

   "I would like you to just listen to me, and not tell me how you feel until tomorrow (or next week)."
   "I want to be able to invite you to my house and feel comfortable."
   "I feel distant from you because I've been keeping this secret, but because I love you, I want us to be close."
   "A very important event is about to happen in my life, and I want to share it with you."

"I know this may be hard to understand, but I hope I can help you to see how important it is for me that you do."

Remember that the other person may not be willing or able to grant you the response you wish. However, letting others know what you want can often help encourage the desired reaction.

2. *What have I got to lose?* As close as you may be to your family and friends, there's always the possibility that you'll lose something important when you make your announcement. If you're emotionally or financially dependent on your family, for example, consider carefully whether you would be willing to lose that support.
3. *How can I present the fact that I'm gay in the most positive way?* The best way to do this is to personalize the discussion rather than talking about homosexuality in general. Let your family know about those difficult times in your life when you were depressed, upset, or anxious because you were having trouble understanding your sexual preference. Tell them how relieved you felt once you simply accepted the fact that you're gay. If you refer to specific experiences in your life, your family may recognize those moments of trauma and be more willing to empathize with you and to accept your announcement.
4. *Am I prepared to give family and friends time to deal with my announcement?* Remember how long it took you to accept your own homosexuality? Perhaps you still have occasional trouble with it. The situation will likely be much the same for your family. You're asking them to accept a lifestyle that most of society fears, misunderstands, and doesn't willingly tolerate. Don't be discouraged if they need time to understand what you're telling them. If possible, plan your announcement enough in advance to give them a few months to resolve their discomfort before a major family event, such as Christmas or a wedding.
5. *What do I do if . . . ?* In your imagination, play out a few scenarios of possible reactions, and decide what you would do in each case. For example:

- "If Mom starts to cry, I'll wait until she's recovered her composure, then try to continue the conversation."

- "If Dad yells and says he'll disown me, I'll say I know he's just upset and doesn't really mean it. Then I'll leave, and I'll call the next day. I'll keep calling until he's calmed down."
- "If they really decide to disown me, and I can't change their minds, I'll find a new family of friends to spend holidays with."
- "If they say 'Oh, we knew it all along, we were just waiting for you to tell us,' I'll tell them how wonderful they are and invite them over for a champagne celebration supper."

Imagine both the best and the worst reactions you might get. Playing out such scenarios helps you to let go of a particular expectation and prepare yourself for any reaction. If you feel prepared, you'll be calmer when you approach your family.

6. *Am I willing to make it easy on them?* This discussion is no place for rebelliousness. You're asking your family to handle a potentially difficult subject, so it's counterproductive to ask them to deal with a difficult person, too. The communication and problem-solving techniques you learned earlier can be very helpful here.

   It can also be very helpful for you to talk to gay or lesbian friends who have already come out to their families and friends. You can probably learn a great deal from their experiences—even the bad ones, which will let you know what to avoid!

A special note about coming out to family: There are and can be many personal problems within families. If your relationship with your family is good, however, they can be an excellent support system for you. There is a natural inclination within a family to "take care of its own," and the emotional bonds between you and the members of your family can be a terrific asset to you in the face of the many adverse forces that you and your partner will likely encounter as a homosexual couple.

Preparing to Come Out at Work

Most gay people know how trying it is to remain closeted at work. We cannot invite our lovers to company functions, and we sometimes talk about them as if they were the other sex (even making up names). We don't speak up when colleagues and associates make discriminatory jokes and comments about homosexuals. And we worry about being accidentally discovered.

Keeping your lifestyle secret can make you feel uncomfortable, under stress, and even terrified. Nevertheless, because coming out at work has the potential to make your work situation even *more* stressful, this is one area in which you must very carefully examine all of the pros and cons before making a decision. Following are several questions to ask yourself about coming out at work:

1. *How much do I want this job?* If you very much want to keep the job you're in, and you also feel that it's important for you to come out, be sure to plan your announcement carefully. Good planning can make the difference between success and failure in coming out at work.

   Perry, forty-five, decided to come out when he was offered a partnership in the law firm where he works. He felt that it was unfair to the other partners for him to take the risk having his lifestyle discovered by accident, perhaps causing bad publicity for the firm. He came to me to get assistance in planning a strategy for making his disclosure.

   At my suggestion, Perry first told his mentor, a senior partner at the firm, and asked him for help in deciding what other actions would be appropriate. The executive advised Perry to tell only the partners, making no announcement to the staff. Perry now feels much more secure on the job, and he has had no difficulty with being out. He later told me, "I'm so glad I planned it first. I had no idea how much it would help. The senior partner even thanked me for having confided in him, and he was a big help. And I was much more assured because I had a plan. I think it made a big difference."

   A word of advice: never use coming out as a way to end a job. This will only make life harder for the next gay employee who would like to be open. If you are in a job you don't want, look for another (preferably, one in which you can be open from the start), and then hand in your resignation.

2. *What are the benefits?* The benefits may include enhanced self-esteem, reduced stress, increased awareness of gay

issues among fellow workers, and more openness about bringing your lover to company functions.

3. *What are the costs?* Costs may include hostility, isolation, increased stress, loss of promotions, and even the loss of your job. Although there are laws against discrimination, it is sometimes difficult to prove that you were fired because of your homosexuality. One option you have is to reconsider whether you really want to work in an openly hostile environment. If you are close to retirement or if your job is very important to you, you might feel that the benefits of *not* coming out outweigh any benefits you would gain from doing so. Whatever your situation, consider joining or establishing a support group for other gay people in your profession.
4. *Whom should I tell?* Some professionals (such as doctors, lawyers, and accountants) may need to let only partners and close associates know. If you're an employee, a rule of thumb is to first tell only the highest-level person with whom you have contact. Supervisors have a responsibility to keep things running smoothly, so there is more probability that they will maintain your confidence. You can also ask your boss for his or her opinion on who else should be told. Your boss should *not* find out through office gossip, so it's important that you talk to him or her *before* you talk to your coworkers. Secrets are not easily kept.
5. *Where do I stand with my job?* An employee who does a good job, follows appropriate etiquette, and is a general asset to a company can be difficult to replace. Being valuable to your company gives you the most leverage in coming out. If you have a chip on your shoulder, are difficult to deal with, or have been slacking off, your chances of acceptance dwindle. Evaluate your employment record before making your decision.

Making the Announcement

Once both you and your lover have weighed the above considerations about coming out to family, friends, and coworkers, you'll be ready for the next step: actually making the announcement. Each of you will likely want to come out to your own family alone.

Since people often take their cues from the person presenting an issue, the way in which you present yourself is crucial. The discomfort level of those you tell can thus be a reflection of your own level of discomfort. If you are calm, self-assured, confident, and comfortable with your news, your audience will feel more relaxed, too. The following guidelines can help you to acquire the necessary aplomb before you "drop the bomb." Whether you plan to come out to family, friends, or business associates, the process remains essentially the same.

1. *Do your homework.* You need to be as comfortable with your own life as possible, and you need to present your audience with straightforward, factual information (you may, after all, be their only source of information about homosexuality). It is especially important that you know the facts about AIDS before you make your announcement. Many people are ignorant of how AIDS is transmitted, and some may still think that any contact with a homosexual is dangerous. (Recognize, however, that your first discussion may not be the most appropriate time to talk about sexually transmitted diseases, unless the question comes up naturally.)

   If you're as knowledgeable as possible about homosexuality before coming out, you'll be better prepared to answer such questions as these:

   "Where did we go wrong?"
   "Can you be cured?"
   "Will my children turn out gay if they're around you?"
   "Why don't you just live alone?"
   "What about AIDS?"
   "Can you abstain from sex?"

   You can obtain informational materials from a gay community center, the ACLU, or a gay-rights organization for yourself and for those to whom you'll be coming out (for example, a pamphlet entitled *Our Gay Children,* published by the organization Parents and Friends of Lesbians and Gays, might be very helpful for your family to read).

2. *Choose your time and place carefully.* With family and friends, it's best to organize a quiet gathering with just the essen-

tial people. If you're coming out at work, make a private, formal appointment. It's better not to go out to lunch or dinner unless you are quite certain that your news will not upset anyone.

3. *Choose the people who will be present.* In business situations, make your appointments with one person at a time, from the top of the ladder down. With family and friends, keep the group small. If possible, have someone present who already knows about you and on whom you can count for support—for example, the family doctor or minister, a sibling or other close relative, or anyone else whom the family trusts.
4. *Aim only to have your audience acknowledge that you are gay.* It may take some time to get others to accept your homosexuality. With family and friends, be realistic about your expectations and allow them the opportunity to assimilate the information. At work, however, be alert to discriminatory comments that might prove legally important in the event that you lose your job.
5. *Have a place where you can go for support after you've made your announcement.* Your counselor, minister, gay support group, or gay friends who have themselves come out can help you to regain your composure, if need be, and to analyze the reactions you have gotten.

Kids! How Do They Fit In?

Many gay and lesbian couples have children from previous marriages. Additionally, more and more same-sex couples are choosing to adopt babies or to make other arrangements to have children. While parenting is not the subject of this book, it is essential to state that gay parents must take responsibility for getting proper child-care information. Your child's development, both physical and mental, is dependent on your knowledge of nutrition, psychology, health, and techniques for disciplining and teaching.

If you are a recently divorced gay parent, you need to make a workable arrangement with your former spouse that focuses on the well-being of your children. Coming to a reasonable agreement about visitation rights and child-rearing practices may even require formal arbitration through the legal system. You may also want to consider going to family therapy with your former spouse, your children, and your gay partner.

If your former spouse is homophobic, hostile, or critical about your homosexuality and your relationship, your children will be in conflict, just as they would be if they were to witness any other type of power struggle between their parents. Signs of inner conflict can include sudden emotional, behavioral, or physiological changes. Any child, of course, can undergo changes in mood, eating habits, or activities; the important thing to observe is whether any such change persists for more than a brief time. If it does, seek advice and help from a counselor or pediatrician.

Give your children time to adjust to your gay or lesbian lifestyle and to develop a natural relationship with your partner. Let your children and your lover get to know each other before your lover participates in parenting. Children resent having authority imposed on them by "interlopers," but they respond well when they recognize the authority as coming from an appropriate person. When your child is ready, have your partner take on parenting duties gradually, beginning with small things (such as an afternoon at the zoo or dinner at a restaurant when you're not present).

In my experience, few difficulties that a homosexual parent has with his or her children derive from that parent's being gay. Any problem you have with your child is likely to be a direct result of your interaction with the child, not of your lifestyle. Children usually do fine in a homosexual family environment when it's healthy, loving, and supportive. Following are a few words of advice about coming out to your children:

- It isn't necessary to come out to very young children, who in any case would not fully understand the meaning of your situation. Just give them whatever information they need at the moment.
- Follow current guidelines about explaining sex to children, answering whatever questions your child asks as honestly and comfortably as you can. Use the techniques of active listening and attentive speaking to assess how the child seems to be handling the information. Go to your library or gay (especially feminist) bookstore and get some of the many parent/child books that provide advice on handling discussions of sex and sexual choices.

- If you're very uncomfortable with telling your child about your gay or lesbian lifestyle, or if you have a discussion that goes badly, let the topic go for now. In the latter case, seek to reestablish your ease with your child, and raise the issue again later. Remember, jokes and laughter are okay, and they help to keep the situation from being too dramatic and overpowering for the child.
- Since your children may have known your lover for some time before the subject of sexual preference comes up, you may want to tell them together.

IN-LAWS

You may expect your in-laws to refuse to accept your relationship as real or legitimate. However, keep in mind that in-laws are just people—if your spouse has come out to his or her family and they have accepted it, chances are that they'll accept you, too, and will acknowledge your relationship.

Whatever your situation, avoid getting into struggles with your lover about in-laws. It's not required that your spouse get along with your family, nor you with his or her family. In some instances, it may simply be best for you to see your own families separately. While you may be tempted to step into the middle and act as negotiator if your family and your spouse are at odds, avoid doing this. Instead, you must let them work things out for themselves. If either "side" tries to use you as an intermediary, refuse to do so, requesting that those involved deal with each other directly.

Courtesy will go a long way in helping you and your spouse deal with each other's families. Don't be too vocal with your negative feelings about your lover's relatives. Constant criticism is insulting and will put you at odds with your lover. Be willing to go along to an occasional family gathering, even if it's not your idea of a great time. If you give your in-laws a chance, you may find that you'll begin to accept and even like them.

If one or both of you are from dysfunctional families with serious destructive patterns, you will need to support each other in order to minimize any damaging effects on your own relationship. Here are some guidelines to help you:

- Let your lover know about the problem and the people involved before the two of you spend time with your family. If there are any helpful hints for dealing with certain individuals, give this information to your partner in advance (for example, "My brother [or uncle or grandmother] is homophobic and tries to make me mad. If he starts saying insulting things, it's best to just ignore him.")
- Make "emergency escape" plans. Before you go to a family function, set a signal (a wink, a hand signal, or a nod) that means "Let's go," and stick to your agreement by being willing to leave if your partner gives you the signal.
- Consider attending ACA (Adult Children of Alcoholics), CODA (Co-Dependents Anonymous), or Al-Anon meetings together. All of these groups are designed for the family members of people with addictive problems. In addition, ACA is an excellent source of information and help for adults who grew up in any type of dysfunctional home, whether or not there was a problem of addiction. If dysfunctional or addictive patterns show up in your relationship with your partner, seek professional guidance.

SUPPORT SYSTEMS

If your families will not accept your gay lifestyle, or if they live very far away, it is essential that you establish a support network of friends. I have many gay clients whose lovers are the only people with whom they have true friendships. Often, these couples dropped old friends once they found each other, and they now live isolated even from the gay community around them. If such a relationship were to suddenly end, or if the couple has problems or needs advice, neither partner would have anyone to turn to for support.

The rewards of building a solid support network within which you can nurture your relationship are many. Carol and Renee, both in their mid-twenties, have been lovers for two years. They came to me because they found themselves fighting constantly. After asking them a number of questions about their relationship, I learned that they were quite isolated, having only each other for company and support. They both admitted that the reason they avoided forming other friendships was that they were afraid this would lead to sexual infidelity.

We worked on their insecurities, and I persuaded them to join the gay and lesbian organization Couples (which I mentioned in chapter 1). Within six months, they were very actively involved with a solid network of friends, and their fighting stopped. At that time, Carol said:

> I've learned that when I'm unreasonably irritable with Renee, I probably need a break, so I call up a friend and arrange to do something. Almost every time, my irritation fades as soon as I'm around someone else. When I get back together with Renee, I can enjoy her again. Most of the fights we were having weren't even about anything—they just meant we were too dependent on each other.

The Rewards of Friendship

There are many benefits of friendship for gay couples. As I've said, having trusted friends—homosexual or heterosexual—can relieve the stress of spending all your time with your lover. Friends can add an abundance of love, warmth, and humor to your life. Especially if you are without family, friends can make your holidays and vacations more joyous. Having friends with whom you can learn, grow, and share makes life and love more fun.

A caring, nonjudgmental friend can help you to defuse your anger and regain perspective after you've had an argument with your lover. You could even make a mutual-exchange agreement with a friend through which you could complain to each other about problems in your relationships, secure in the knowledge that your confidences would not be repeated to others. This traditional Arabian poem aptly describes such a pact:

> A friend is one
> To whom one may pour
> Out all the contents
> Of one's heart
> Chaff and grain together
> Knowing that the
> Gentlest of hands
> Will take and sift it,

Keep what is worth keeping
And with a breath of kindness
Blow the rest away.

Homosexual friends can serve as role models and provide reinforcement for your relationship. They can support you when you face problems related to your own or outside homophobia. Their own trials and triumphs can reassure you that your relationship is normal, despite the frustrations and communication difficulties you may occasionally have with your spouse. (This same principle is the basis for therapy groups, because shared experience provides feedback and support.)

Your friends can also help with networking of all kinds. To find a good accountant, doctor, lawyer, tennis coach, or restaurant, whom do you ask? Your friends. Looking for a better job? Friends can supply you with references (and may even be able to help you get hired). In addition, friends can help you out when your spouse is unavailable to assist you with something, or when you and your spouse need an extra hand (for example, if you're moving or repainting).

Finding Friends

Where do you find friends? The answer may seem amazingly simple: *go where other people are involved in doing something, and join in.* Following are some tried-and-true suggestions for finding a wealth of potential friends. (You will likely recognize many of these suggested sources from the discussion earlier in this book on finding a lover. As you'll recall, at that time I told you that even if you didn't find a lover right away by following this advice, you were at the very least likely to make some good friends!) Information on contacting a number of the organizations mentioned here can be found in Appendix A.

- Volunteer for a worthwhile cause. This is the easiest and best way I know of to find a group of involved, energetic people. You might try your church's volunteer services, a political action group, an organization concerned with AIDS (such as the AIDS Project), a local small theater, or a fine-arts organization. Not only will you be doing something socially valuable, but you'll be getting to know the other people involved. Because such organizations also frequently sponsor events and parties, it's possible for you to develop a whole social life through your volunteer connections.

- The gay and lesbian community centers that are all over the country can be your starting point for finding or creating a homosexual couples' social network. The centers are usually clearinghouses for all kinds of social opportunities for gay and lesbian couples, such as dances, tours, and dinner groups. They can also provide referrals to businesses run or staffed by gay people (for example, medical, dental, legal, real estate, and insurance offices).
- The excellent support organization Couples, mentioned earlier, provides an instant and extensive network for gay and lesbian couples. This organization offers raps, outings, workshops, an annual Valentine's Day celebration, and other social and recreational events. Visit your local chapter, or consider forming a chapter of your own.
- Many gay churches are highly organized and offer numerous activities, counseling services, and rap sessions. Find a church that feels good to you and that has the kinds of resources you need. There are several from which to choose, including Metropolitan Community Churches, Christ Chapel (Protestant), Dignity (Roman Catholic), and Tikvah (Jewish). Some meet in gay community centers, and some have their own buildings. Most of the larger ones sponsor gay Alcoholics Anonymous meetings, couples and singles groups, dances, theater groups, choirs and music events, in addition to worship services.
- Although such groups as the Lambda Democratic Club, Lambda Theater Group, and Gay Teachers' Association have specific issues as their primary agendas, they are also excellent places to meet potential friends who share your interests.
- Placing classified ads in gay magazines such as *RFD* can be a useful way to meet friends, particularly for homosexual couples who live in small or rural communities, where it's easy to feel isolated. Because your intent here is to find friends to support you and your relationship, make it very clear in your ad that you're not looking for sexual encoun-

ters. Use a post-office box for receiving replies, and simply ignore inappropriate responses.

As you meet people, use the "squirrel-hunting" techniques you learned in chapter 2 to screen out those who are incompatible with your personal values and lifestyle. As with romantic relationships, don't rush into a friendship until you know the person well enough to feel confident that he or she has something positive to offer you.

With the friends you already have as well as with the new ones you acquire, keep the energy high by frequently sharing informal activities. Have friends over to cook meals together. While formal dinners, cocktail parties, and other "socially correct" events can be fun occasionally, they do not promote the family feeling that is the basis for the strength of a support network.

The next section is intended to help you and your spouse to set up a support network that can expand your friendships and social opportunities.

Building a Relationship-Support Network

The first step in building a support system is to set up a time to discuss networking and friendship with your lover. The two of you need to share your own feelings before reaching out to others. For example, do you believe that having same-sex friends could threaten your relationship in some way? Are you afraid that your lover might be "stolen away," or that friends would encroach on your privacy and time together? Does shyness or a lack of self-esteem prevent one or both of you from forming other friendships?

It takes open conversation about these issues to reassure each other that having personal or mutual friendships does not automatically lead to jealousy, anger, or competition. Use the communication techniques in chapter 4 to foster an honest discussion and to resolve any differences of opinion.

Once you've reached an understanding with your lover, initiate a similar discussion with your friends and begin to establish some guidelines for membership in a support network. The rules can be as formal or informal as you like, but each person in the network must know what behavior is expected.

Being open and willing to talk about sex within the group will foster honesty and mutual support. As I discussed in chapter 5, having sexual relationships with friends is usually destructive not only to the individuals directly involved but also to the group as a whole. If any member of the network has difficulty in trusting that same-sex friends will not turn into rivals, encourage that person and his or her spouse to resolve their own issues of trust before joining the group.

Whenever you meet new people who you think would be an asset to your network, tell them about the group. If they like the idea, arrange an opportunity for them to meet the rest of the group. Remember to review the guidelines and expectations with each new person.

As your network grows, it will change. *The key to managing change is to allow it to happen.* A member may develop new interests, which the group could share. New members can suggest other restaurants or nightclubs to try. As you do in your own relationship, strive for variety, excitement, and challenge in your support network.

Personal Friendships

One of the most prevalent problems I have seen concerning friendship is that of couples who abandon the friends they had when they were single. In such cases, lovers devote all of their time and energy to their new relationship, leaving none for their old friends. Such a couple may believe that being gay makes it impossible for them to maintain same-sex friendships, for reasons of jealousy. As I discussed earlier, the solution to this dilemma is to develop trust and responsibility within your own relationship and to firmly establish the boundaries of your friendships.

Having personal friendships is just as important as having mutual friends and a support network for your relationship. Resist the temptation to spend every second of your time with your new mate, seeing your friends only when your lover is present, too. Instead, honor your previous customs and traditions with old friends whenever possible, and recognize that they deserve time alone with you. If you find it difficult to balance your friendships with your romance, let your friends know that you need some time to develop your new relationship, but that you haven't forgotten them.

On the other hand, if you have friends who are too demanding of your time and attention, your primary relationship can suffer. Knowing how to set limits and to say no when you need to will help prevent not only "friendship burnout" but also friendship-related conflicts with your spouse. You don't need to talk your friend into accepting your limits, nor do you need to justify your decision to yourself or to your friend. If you have trouble saying no, practice saying "I'm sorry, but I can't do that" in the mirror a few times, to develop the habit!

The following advice can help you to develop some techniques for changing unhealthy patterns with old friends.

Setting limits. If you have a friend who needs more than you can supply right now, set up a date to talk with him or her. Arrange for a quiet, uninterrupted time, such as a walk in the park or dinner at your house.

Open the discussion by assertively expressing what you *do* want, rather than what you don't want. For example, instead of saying "I can't spend so much time with you," you might say, "I feel overloaded with all that's going on right now, and I need to reorganize my time. Could we get together just once a week?"

Acknowledge that your request is one-sided, and invite your friend to counteroffer. Don't push for instant agreement, since your friend may need some time to consider your view.

Once the issue has been resolved, tell your friend that you appreciate his or her understanding. If you suspect that your friend is just giving in but may feel resentful, invite further discussion, but don't insist on it. Your friend may be upset, or he or she may simply need more time to process this change. If your friend becomes angry or unreasonable, stay calm and listen. Offer to negotiate or to give both of you a few days to think about the conversation. Remember, it's worth the time and effort it may take to preserve a valuable friendship.

How to Handle Being a "Model" Couple

Gay and lesbian couples in successful long-term relationships often report feeling a sense of pressure from their friends, their support network, and the larger gay community to be a "perfect" couple. Because of the scarcity of gay role models, the pressure on these homosexual couples can be even greater than that on heterosexual couples who stand out in their communities.

Sylvia, a minister in a gay church, and Betty, her spouse, came to see me because they felt tremendous pressure from Sylvia's congregation to be a model couple. Betty said,

I had heard the horror stories about being a minister's wife, but nothing could have prepared me for the reality. I feel like I'm in a fishbowl! If I don't come to church one day, rumors fly. If Sylvia and I actually have words with each other, everyone acts like children whose parents are fighting. If I smile or hug someone, Sylvia is told about it, as though I'd cheated on her.

Sylvia added,

I can't even do pastoral counseling with a female church member without its being reported to Betty. The congregation seems to have appointed itself guardian of our marriage. I feel like leaving the church! I certainly hope you can help us find a different solution.

After a few sessions of counseling, Betty and Sylvia decided to deal with the reality of their public life as a couple by making their limits clear to others. They politely but firmly let church members know that they didn't want to be given reports about each other, and they didn't want to have their relationship discussed publicly. In addition, to help members of the congregation deal with relationship issues in general, they instituted a series of couples seminars and rap sessions at the church. These actions greatly reduced the pressure on Betty and Sylvia's relationship, making their lives in the church pleasant again.

When you are only one of a few, and everyone wants and needs you to succeed, it can be difficult to admit to others and to yourselves that your relationship has problems. However, it's more reassuring to others when you are honest about your problems rather than pretending that everything's perfect. In the long run, you can better serve the function of being a role model for other gay and lesbian couples by demonstrating how you handle your relationship through *both* good and bad times.

A long-term gay relationship can flourish best in a supportive and loving environment. Gay and lesbian couples can gain a great sense of security, belonging, and personal freedom when they have a network of people close to them who accept their lifestyle and honor their relationship. Creating a healthy, supportive family situation and solid friendships is highly rewarding and well worth the effort it may take. To me, it's what life is all about.

CHAPTER 9

Happily Ever After

We have all heard many fables and stories that end ". . . and they lived happily ever after." We have also heard true tales of misery and breakup among many gay and lesbian couples. Is lasting happiness really possible? Can homosexual couples have relationships for life? What happens when gay men and lesbian women spend many years together? Here are two examples:

Eldon and Bill, well known in the gay community in which they live, have been living together since 1977. They celebrated a Holy Union in the Metropolitan Community Church in 1978. As I write this, their relationship is still going strong. Eldon says,

> First, we have a good level of communication . . . . Bill is very sentimental, so I like to surprise him from time to time with flowers, a love note or card, or a small gift. I also try to tell him at least once a day that I love him. Also, we're both religious and attend church regularly, and I believe that God has played an important part in our lives and in our happiness.

Eileen and Mabel, both in their late sixties, have been together for forty years. Mabel says,

> Eileen and I met in school when we were in our twenties. As we got older we became known as "maiden ladies." Eventually, we just decided to share a home. We own our house now, and after all these years together our families just accept us. All our nieces and nephews love to come to our house, and we have Thanksgiving here with both families every year.
>
> I can't imagine life without Eileen. We had some difficulties in the beginning, getting used to each other, but now we get along wonderfully. After all these years, we still talk about everything, and we never run out of things to say to

each other. I love her even more than I did when we were young.

Most homosexual people hear very little about such gay couples. Consequently, many of the gay and lesbian couples I counsel have no idea what to expect in the later years of a devoted relationship. With so few models, some of them believe in a fantasy future in which their romance never changes. Others feel doomed because of their belief that homosexual relationships just can't last. Still others avoid thinking about the issue of relationship longevity at all.

The reality of long-term gay and lesbian relationships is very different from the picture created by these fears and fantasies. Homosexual relationships *can* last. The key is to accept the fact that change is an ongoing aspect of any vital long-term relationship, and to learn to deal with the changes that occur. New issues and questions arise, circumstances change, and both partners learn and grow. Every couple committed to a successful partnership must make the effort to keep up with these changes.

In this chapter we'll look at the issues of long-term relationships, with the goal of helping you to understand the later stages of growth in your relationship and to handle the changes that occur.

THE LATER STAGES OF ROMANCE

As noted, most homosexual people are familiar with only the early stages of gay relationships (meeting, dating, courtship, and making a commitment) and have no clear idea of the later stages: development of intimacy, and settled partnership.

In the phase involving the development of intimacy, the couple's love matures and becomes more realistic. As the magic of the initial romance fades, both partners begin to relax, revealing their innermost, imperfect selves. This can make them feel vulnerable and even awkward with each other. They may argue, struggle for power, and become irritable and distant. As a result, both need lots of reassurance and attention, but they may have trouble providing each other with this.

Many relationships don't make it past this stage, because the lovers often mistakenly think that something is wrong with their romance and decide to break up. Unless either partner has been through a long-term relationship before and so recognizes the issues, it's easy for a couple to become discouraged by problems and give up. (This explains why people often do much better in second or third relationships, when they have both the experience to know what to expect and the skills to get through the trials and tribulations.) If the couple sticks with the relationship, however, they can establish a new style of intimacy, one that is more mature and honest.

The settled-partnership phase presents more new issues. In this phase, the couple learns to handle long-term intimacy, sexuality, and personal growth. Once they have resolved these issues, the partners are able to experience the pleasures of lasting love. At this point, they know how to love each other for who they really are, and they have acquired the wisdom and experience necessary to keep their commitment alive through cooperation and mutual understanding.

It takes several years to achieve the full benefits of these two later stages. Let's look more closely at each of these stages and at the strategies a couple needs in order to pass through them successfully.

The Development of Intimacy

The development-of-intimacy stage is actually somewhat like a replay of the commitment stage, but on a new level. Many of the relationship-dynamic problems are the same but are intensified by time and by the experience of living together.

The two most important strategies you can use in this stage are to continue using your communication and problem-solving skills, and to develop a support network.

With regard to communication and problem solving, it is important to realize that marriage and commitment, in themselves, will not solve your problems. You will still need to deal with arguments, personal-space issues, fears of rejection, and other issues that arise naturally in a relationship. Problem solving and negotiation will foster the increasing intimacy between you.

As I discussed in the previous chapter, having other gay and lesbian couples as part of your support network is very reassuring. Sharing and comparing experiences is especially helpful at this point, because this is a time when trivial disagreements can easily escalate into battles. In particular, talk to other gay couples who have been together longer than you have. More experienced couples can help you to recognize that your situation is "normal," and they can often recommend solutions based on what has worked for them.

Periodic checkups. One specific strategy I recommend for consciously monitoring your relationship is to convert the communication opportunities that you began in the commitment phase into "periodic checkups." Like periodic car checkups, relationship checkups are designed to find minor problems before they have a chance to expand into dramatic ordeals.

Intimacy actually develops more from cooperation and teamwork than from sexual closeness. By keeping the lines of communication open and consulting each other about your daily decisions, you create an atmosphere that encourages honesty and mutuality.

One caveat about periodic checkups: if something is already working, don't fix it! I have seen many cases in which one partner in a gay couple becomes obsessive about the faintest difference of opinion and spends a great deal of energy arguing and problem solving rather than enjoying the romance. This kind of compulsion can be as much of an obstacle to the development of intimacy as ignoring problems. The objective of learning how to solve problems is to avoid being constantly anxious about relationship difficulties. When some aspect of your marriage needs attention, work with your spouse to explore the causes and solutions. Otherwise, relax and let things flow.

Developing transitions. When you are together day in and day out, it becomes necessary to intentionally create opportunities for intimacy. You can't just move from emptying the garbage to feeling romantic; a transition must take place.

When you were dating, there was a built-in transition from living your separate lives to being together. Preparing for a date and driving to meet each other served as an anticipatory period that heightened your sense of excitement and romance. When you have lived together for some time, however, anticipation can easily be preempted by routine. The couple might sense the loss of intimacy, but they may feel that there just isn't enough time in the day for them to be able to set aside time for romance. Couples who don't realize the importance of transitions or who don't know how to develop them can begin to lose the freshness that romantic love needs. It's common for one partner to fear that the other has grown tired of him or her, when the likely truth of the matter is that the couple simply does not know how to move from daily routine to intimacy.

Following are some ideas to help you in developing transitions:

- Suggest or invite instead of complaining or demanding. Saying "I'd love to spend a little time with you tonight—would you like to . . . ?" works far better than "We never spend any time together!" Although offering such invitations was natural when you were dating, it may now feel a little forced. However, it's important that you do it anyway. You'll become more comfortable with practice.
- Transitions that are logical work best. For example, after working in the garden, showering together can be a natural transition to intimacy. After a demanding workday, taking some time to relax together before dinner gives you a chance to "touch base" and tune in to each other.
- Use your commute home from work as preparation time. Consciously try to leave the workday problems behind and anticipate the pleasures of arriving home.
- Program yourself to use mental transitions. For example, when you're driving home or cooking dinner, focus your thinking on your partner and on the good things about your relationship. You'll find that these "transitional" thoughts will come more and more naturally to you and will have a positive impact on the time you spend with your lover.
- Reserve some quiet time together before bed. I suggest the following exercise: Sit quietly and hold hands, and listen to each other's breathing for a few minutes. As you listen, you'll gradually begin to breathe together. Don't force it—just give it enough time to synchronize naturally, bringing the two of you into harmony.
- When doing projects or chores together, take a moment to get in concert about what you are doing. "I'll clean this while you move that" is a simple thing to say and encourages a feeling of teamwork.
- When you finish doing something together, make the transition to separateness deliberately. Saying something as simple as "Thanks for helping me paint this" acknowledges

the togetherness of what you were doing and marks the point of moving apart again. Ending your times of togetherness cleanly allows you to begin fresh with each new time together.

As your intimacy develops, so does one of the most powerful dynamics of long-term relationships—a shared history as a couple. The more good times you share and the more support and help you give each other, the more trust you build. The more thoughtfully you treat each other, the more powerful your bond. When you've built such a strong connection, you have little need to worry about losing the relationship.

SETTLED PARTNERSHIP

Many of my gay and lesbian clients are worried about how to keep love alive throughout a lifetime relationship. They've heard that love fades, or they've watched their parents or other couples grow more distant and more blasé about love over time.

While it's true that for many couples, sexual and emotional intimacy recede into the background of daily pragmatic issues—housework, career, and social obligations—this shift is by no means inevitable. To maintain healthy and satisfying intimacy in a long-term gay relationship, a couple must develop skills in four basic areas:

1. maintaining sexual attraction and generating romance
2. dealing with life changes
3. resolving disappointment when hidden expectations are not met
4. avoiding boredom by learning how to play, to celebrate, and to laugh

At this stage of a relationship, each partner has a substantial investment and is likely to be very reluctant to solve problems by ending the relationship. Handling long-term issues takes patience and maturity—but the reward is a successful relationship based on deep, solid, abiding love. Let's look now at each of these four issues.

Maintaining Sexual Attraction and Generating Romance

Sex is often the issue that brings long-term gay and lesbian couples into my office for counseling. Some are having specific sexual difficulties; others are worried that their sexual excitement is fading.

If you experience sexual disinterest or dysfunction, it's important to find out first of all whether the problem is physical in origin. Diabetes or other physical conditions, certain prescription medicines, or injuries can all diminish your sexual desire and enjoyment.

It's also important to note that sexual problems are *not* inevitable with age. An older gay couple experiencing a sexual problem should not simply resign themselves to it. While there are some sexual changes that occur with aging, most couples can enjoy healthy sex throughout their lives.

Couples can often resolve sudden performance problems (such as impotence or the cessation of orgasms) by learning to be more attentive to transitions and preparatory activities before making love, and by reopening the lines of communication.

Communication problems are at the root of many sexual difficulties, including fading desire. Some long-term couples discuss their degree of sexual satisfaction only rarely, often because the partners are afraid that they might insult each other. You can help to renew your sexual vigor by having more regular and honest discussions about sex.

The greatest damage to intimacy is done by sexual secrets. Being unfaithful or failing to let your partner know if you want to change your sexual contract will lead to the development of inhibiting feelings about sex—guilt, embarrassment, mistrust, and fear of rejection or criticism. If you are in this situation on either side, you may want to reread chapter 5 and use the guidelines there for communicating about sex with your lover. If problems persist, consider seeking professional guidance.

You can help to keep your love life fresh by being willing to change your routines. Try new positions and new times of the day for lovemaking. Don't discount the effect a few simple changes can make: satin sheets, black lights, sexy outfits, explicit movies, and sexual toys and accessories can all help to keep your sexual life together feeling new.

Sex and intimacy are also closely tied to romance. Don't forget to bring home flowers, send cards, create or buy gifts for each other, or write love notes or poems. Develop and maintain the habit of letting each other know the positive things you feel for each other. Celebrate the symbols of the earlier periods of your relationship by periodically revisiting the places that have meaning for you: the gay-pride festival where you met, the restaurant where you had your first date, or the romantic hideaway spot where you had a picnic.

To keep romance and sexuality flourishing, give it a special place in your life. Don't bring up problems, bills, chores, or other potentially distressing issues during your romantic times. Allow yourselves time and space to "get away from it all." Lock the door and don't answer the phone, and just be with each other. This special time is the perfect time for soft music, candles, special foods, perhaps even some provocative clothing. By separating this time and making it special, you are creating the necessary transition and communicating that you are important to each other.

Perhaps the most important thing you can do to keep attraction and romance alive over a long period of time is to remember who you were when your lover originally fell in love with you. Although some physical changes are inevitable over time, good grooming, dressing attractively, and keeping yourself interested in life can be maintained indefinitely. If you become obviously disinterested in yourself, your partner will follow your lead. Conversely, if you maintain your style, your enthusiasm, and your physical fitness, you'll retain your partner's interest and desire. I think this attitude is best expressed by Louise Hay in her book *You Can Heal Your Life:*

> I love myself, therefore I take loving care of my body. I lovingly feed it nourishing foods and beverages, I lovingly groom it and dress it, and my body lovingly responds to me with vibrant health and energy . . . I love myself, therefore I behave and think in a loving way to all people, for I know that that which I give out returns to me multiplied.

Nothing is more boring than being bored, and nothing is more interesting than being interested. The secret to long-lasting sexual satisfaction and to ongoing romance is really as simple as that.

Sex is one of the most reassuring, soothing, and energizing elements of a lasting relationship. By eliminating pressure, keeping sexual communication open, maintaining attractiveness, setting aside special time, and experimenting with new techniques, you can eliminate the sexual stagnation that can poison long-term romance.

Handling Life Changes

As we saw earlier, many gay couples fear change, viewing it as a threat to their relationships. However, change is actually the source of the excitement these couples worry about losing.

Changes can be intentional and voluntary—for example:

coming out
going back to school
changing careers
redecorating or moving
losing weight or getting in shape
developing new interests and hobbies
making new friends
discovering new lovemaking habits
getting a makeover or new look

On the other hand, changes—both pleasant and unpleasant—can also be imposed from the outside. Examples of difficult involuntary changes include:

rejection by family
loss of a job
financial loss
having friends or family move away
the death of a friend or family member

Whatever the nature of the change, having to think about it and accommodate it is what most people find the hardest. To accept change and manage it successfully, you need to be able to recognize the positive results it brings. Even some otherwise undesirable changes can in fact produce excitement and energy in your lives.

Every gay and lesbian couple who comes in to see me must deal with change. Here are the guidelines I give them:

- First, accept the reality that life will keep throwing you curves, and work with your partner to see the positive aspects of change.
- Acknowledge any change that occurs, allow yourself to do any grumbling or complaining you need to do about it to help rid yourself of resentment, and then move on to solving whatever problems the change may have created.
- Explore as many options as you can for dealing with the change, especially if it was imposed from outside. If necessary, discuss your situation with whatever professional is appropriate (for example, a lawyer, counselor, doctor, contractor, or employment counselor).
- Discuss the change and the possible options you've explored with your lover and with anyone else involved (including children). Allow them to air their feelings and to express their wants and needs. Incorporate as many of their ideas as is practical.
- If letting go of your old situation is difficult, consider having some kind of farewell ceremony. This could be a last dinner party in your old house if you're moving, a bon voyage party if someone's leaving, or the packing away of old documents or mementos. In any event, take the time to talk about both what you're losing and what you're gaining.
- Once a positive change is complete, celebrate! Make a toast, hold a celebration party, or have your minister bless a new venture.

Following the above guidelines will allow you to complete your experience of a change and to recognize all of your mixed feelings—sadness and excitement, frustration and elation, anger and joy, loss and gain.

Dealing with Unfulfilled Expectations

A major obstacle to long-term gay and lesbian relationships is the inner turmoil created when a couple's expectations of love meet the reality of life. Because disappointment can be very hard to take, we may have difficulty in letting go of our original goals even after it has become clear that they are inappropriate.

In particular, many gay people have very high expectations about marriage, with little or no actual experience on which to base these expectations. As we saw earlier, many people pattern their ideas of long-term love on the idealized relationships portrayed in movies and books. As a consequence, many gay couples expect their marriages to solve all of their problems, magically transforming them into perfect communicators and superhuman lovers.

In general, I advocate that you live without such expectations about your relationship. I call this "following" the relationship rather than "leading" it. Admittedly, it is not easy to learn to stop struggling with your relationship and allow it to be whatever it is. However, my experience is that when people let go of their expectations and just let things happen naturally, they often get far more than they had hoped for.

Whenever you're feeling dissatisfied with your relationship, consider first whether your expectations might be at the root of the problem. If you're feeling disappointed because your lover has not done something that you'd hoped he or she would do, take the following steps before confronting your lover: Write out your complaints and feelings, uncensored. Without showing the paper to anyone else, put it away for a day or two. Then take it out and reread what you've written. Does it sound unrealistic? Do you think you could achieve what you want with someone else? How important is it to you that your lover be able to fulfill this particular demand?

If you find that your hidden expectations are the problem, take the time to reevaluate them. If necessary, talk things over with an objective friend or a counselor. On the other hand, if you find that you still have concrete, reasonable complaints that can be negotiated, first write down all the ways in which your relationship meets your other needs. Then wait another day or two and reread both lists before discussing the issue with your lover. Reminding yourself of the many positive forces in your relationship will help you to put this particular issue in perspective and will make the negotiation process much smoother. You may be angry, irritated, and impatient, but I believe the waiting period will help you evaluate more rationally, and increase your chance of successful negotiation.

Avoiding Boredom

Boredom seems to be the most feared issue among my clients concerning long-term relationships. However, there's no reason to expect to be bored in your relationship unless you yourself were bored before meeting your partner. Boredom in a relationship is usually the result of avoidance—of each other, of change, of responsibility, or of life.

Boredom is a signal that the two of you have begun to take each other and the relationship for granted. Perhaps your activities have become too routine, or you are avoiding facing a problem. Counter the boredom by taking the necessary risks—for instance, *have* that discussion about sex or your in-laws, or dare to suggest a change in routine. If the cause of the boredom is a too-regular routine, the problem is easily fixed. All you need to do is . . . *anything* different. It doesn't matter what you do, as long as it's different and can be shared.

Use the following three words as your key to avoiding boredom: *celebration, play,* and *laughter.* The next paragraphs will give you some ideas for incorporating these into your relationship.

Celebration. Just as you used celebration as an important ingredient of your marriage or commitment ceremony, you and your spouse need to continue celebrating throughout your lives to keep your energy high and maintain your motivation. Frequent celebrations demonstrate your love and appreciation for each other. Organize festivities with friends, or celebrate alone together. Go away for the weekend to mark a special event or simply to celebrate the fact of your continuing relationship. Plan a special evening at home or at a restaurant; attend a concert or go to an amusement park together.

A celebration need not be expensive. The point is to acknowledge that you're celebrating something. Occasions for celebration are plentiful (a success at work, a project completed or a problem resolved together, a birthday or anniversary, and so on).

Play. Playing together can help you to avoid boredom. It's during play that we re-create and renew our individual and mutual energies. Make recreation, play, and fun a priority in your relationship, setting aside time for play on a regular basis. Filling all of your spare time with overtime work, volunteer work, or other such activities translates into an avoidance of your partner.

If you have difficulty being naturally playful, learn to pay attention to what makes you smile and laugh. What do you enjoy doing, or what would you *like* to do, for the pure fun of it? Remind yourself of the simple pleasures of childhood, and use these as a basis for renewing your ability to play.

Laughter. I believe that after the initial excitement wears off in a long-term relationship, if all goes well, a sense of humor sets in.

Partners in long-term relationships generally have the self-esteem and confidence to laugh at their own and each other's quirks and weaknesses. Laughter can serve as a wonderful way to relieve pressure and to remind ourselves that we're human. A joke, a silly gesture, or a funny greeting card or gift can often heighten intimacy. One gay couple I know has gotten through many trying times together because of a greeting card one partner gave the other some years ago. The front reads, "I love you"; inside, it says, "It's a dirty job, but someone has to do it!"

In my practice, I have seen many couples use conflict as the mainstay of their lives together. Such couples often feel that not having constant dramatic struggles would mean not taking the relationship seriously. Once they learn that constant drama not only does not mean greater love but is in fact unhealthy, these couples are able to relax and substitute the delight of humor for the pain of struggle.

SPLITTING UP

Sometimes all efforts to keep a relationship going fail, and the only possible means of achieving happiness is to split up. When is it necessary to take this step? While no one can really know this except you and your partner, there are certain indicators that let you know a major change of some kind must be made.

If your relationship feels detrimental to your mental, emotional, or physical well-being, it's time for a change. If your lover has or develops severe problems such as addiction, mental illness, or a tendency to be violent, splitting up may be the only way you can protect yourself from physical and emotional harm or financial ruin. If you feel that you may need to take this step, use the following guidelines in making your decision.

- If your partner has a problem with addiction, abuse, or violence, it's important that you seek professional guidance before attempting to confront him or her. Self-help groups, support groups for spouses, and Twelve-Step programs can help you to achieve significant results when they're used in conjunction with couple or family counseling.
- Give it your best shot. Breaking up should be viewed as a last resort, and knowing that you did everything possible to solve the problems of your relationship will help you to avoid being left with feelings of unresolved guilt.
- Don't assume that your spouse knows how you feel. When you discuss the situation, be direct and clear, unless there's a risk of physical harm. Don't say something vague like "I don't think you love me" or "I'm not happy" and just hope that your message gets across. Confronting the issue will not mean destroying the relationship; what *is* deadly to a relationship is hiding from problems or doing nothing to solve them even after you've acknowledged their existence.
- Don't allow long periods of time to pass with little or no communication or sex without trying to find out what's wrong. If you wait until you're so miserable that you simply don't care any more, it may be too late to repair the damage. Sit your partner down, look him or her in the eyes, and say: "This isn't working. If we don't do something to fix it, it's going to end." If necessary, be prepared to leave to let your partner know how serious you consider the situation to be.
- Be willing to admit your role in the problem, and be open to change. The two of you can use your communication and problem-solving skills to take mutual responsibility for changing the dynamics. If you get no response from your partner, or if you are both stuck, consider talking to a professional counselor. I believe that anyone who is considering terminating a long-term relationship should give professional help a chance.

After taking these steps, some couples may realize that what they really need to do is restructure and renew their commitment contract. Your feelings of frustration, confusion, boredom, restlessness, and resentment can become the basis for renegotiation. Renegotiating can help you to identify and resolve the specific issues of conflict so that you don't abandon the entire relationship, "throwing the baby out with the bathwater."

If you are convinced that your problems cannot be settled with further effort and time, let your partner know of your decision immediately, to be fair to him or her and to prevent false hopes from arising.

As I noted in the section earlier in this book on breaking up, I strongly recommend that you end your long-term relationship with a formal ritual (something other than simply dividing up your belongings). An ending ceremony allows both of you to feel closure and opens you up to acknowledging and expressing your emotions. There are many possible rituals you can have. Arrange a good-bye meeting alone or with others present, or tear up a symbolic contract or memento of your relationship.

You will both need to recover from the loss. Even if you feel relieved about cutting your bond, you will experience a period of grief for the hopes and dreams you once had. Recognize that healing takes time, and that you'll probably go through several stages of sadness and depression before you feel ready to begin a new phase of your life.

Even if you decide to remain in each other's lives on some basis, you'll probably need a break from seeing each other. Plan to get together at a future date and talk about the nature of your new bond: distant ex-lovers, close friends, cooperating parents, or continuing members in your old support network. Unless one of you moves away, it's difficult *not* to keep some connection. By focusing on a redefinition of your relationship rather than just on its termination, you can make your breakup less of a struggle.

LOVE AND AGING

I believe that many of you will have relationships that will continue into the later years of your lives. This section will cover the dynamics of growing older together. For this material I solicited help from Dennis Cockrum, director of the Actor's Fund, a division of the Academy of Motion Picture Arts and Sciences that provides care for elderly actors. Here is his very thorough response:

> Gay and lesbian people have the same needs as the general public to love and be loved and to establish intimate relationships. Most such relationships are hidden, probably as a reac-

tion to the world's homophobia, its general prejudice against us. Add to this dynamic the issue of growing old in this youth-oriented culture, and the problems compound. I hope to shed a light of understanding on how growing old in the gay community affects relationships and on how we can guard against some common pitfalls.

Aging is a gradual process that none of us can avoid. It affects one physically, psychologically, and socially. Accepted with grace, growing older can bring wisdom and peace. Feared, it can bring panic and despair. Older people with good health, ample social support, and adequate living conditions feel vigorous, alert, happy, and interested. They have much to contribute.

As people grow older, appearance, internal functioning, and senses change. Some people have good health into their eighties, while others may suffer with severe health problems at a much younger age. There are many theories, but no clearly accepted reason why.

Noticeable cosmetic changes are usually due to hormonal change, loss of calcium, lack of exercise, or improper nutrition. Slumping of shoulders and spinal curvature can cause an elderly person to lose two to three inches of height. As a person becomes less active, muscle is replaced with fat tissue. Because this tissue weighs less, it causes a person to lose weight but gain bulk. Skin becomes drier, and, depending on habits such as smoking and sun exposure, develops wrinkles and blotches. Hair grays and thins, teeth are lost, ears elongate, and the nose flattens. It appears that gay men are much more troubled by these changes than lesbian women. Emotional upset caused by signs of age can profoundly interfere with one's ability to enjoy the later stages of life.

Chronic diseases do occur in old age, but the biggest barrier to treatment seems to be a lack of motivation due to fear or resentment of aging. The four big killers of the elderly are heart disease, cancer, stroke, and Alzheimer's disease. Major treatment breakthroughs are made daily on all these problems. Seeking effective, state-of-the-art medical care is essential to maintaining your quality of life.

Health problems have a significant effect on relationships. Some people may communicate and draw closer; others go into denial, which can push the lovers apart. Embarrassment over changes in appearance and function does far more to damage sexual relations than any real lack of desire or ability.

Fostering good health requires taking a preventive approach, which can include regular medical care, regular exercise and activity, proper nutrition, accident prevention, immunizations, stress management, and elimination of bad health habits, such as smoking.

To reach a satisfying old age, be realistic about limitations, live life as fully as you can, don't waste time on regrets, and constantly look forward.

Gay seniors' needs are very similar to the basic needs for happiness and contentment of people of any other age:

- involvement and growth
- good health and freedom from pain
- social relations
- meaning in life
- enough money to meet one's needs
- a satisfying sex life

Note that most older people are capable of enjoying a full sexual life, which can be comforting and renewing. Only minor adjustments need be made for normal aging, such as the use of lubricants and adjusted frequency and/or energy level.

Living a very long life may mean living with a series of losses: relationships, health, abilities, career, income, and residence and/or possessions. It is very important to learn to let go and to grieve for all of these losses. Doing this allows a person to maintain perspective and to get on with life. Letting losses pile up without dealing with them directly can have serious effects: loss of enthusiasm, sadness, or severe depression, possibly accompanied by substance abuse or suicidal tendencies. A loss is always significant. Its importance can be determined only by the person experiencing it. Spiritual connectedness, individual therapy, and stress management can be of great help in coping with loss.

Retirement is often a difficult time. For many, it signifies the start of "old age." Also, many people are ill prepared for the lack of structure and the reduction in income. Active workers need to become active retirees. Having important personal interests greatly enhances retirement.

Common later-life relationship problems result from:

- *Poor health.* A chronic illness can force one partner into a care-giving role, which can lead to exhaustion and resentment.
- *Money.* The lack of sufficient funds to live comfortably and to pursue interests often causes great stress.
- *Boredom.* Constant time spent in each other's company, with few or no separate interests, can lead to a feeling of boredom with the relationship.

Successful long-term gay relationships seem to share these qualities:

- *Equality.* A fair division of labor and a sense of sharing and cooperation helps couples to maintain their bond.
- *Activity.* A relationship can continue to be vital when both partners are enthusiastic about life and pursue personal interests.
- *Flexibility.* Especially because of changes brought by time, it's important that both partners be willing to try new roles and activities.
- *Support network.* Having a strong support network can be invaluable to an older gay couple, particularly during times of stress.

Aging does affect every aspect of life. It can bring couples closer together or tear them apart. Gay and lesbian lovers are well advised to expand their social connections as far as possible to prevent gradual isolation as life continues. We are, it is hoped, building a future in which homosexuality will not limit our choices.

ALL RELATIONSHIPS MUST END

Sad as it is, even our most solid and happiest relationships must come to an end. I would be doing you a disservice if I were to ignore the issue of dealing with the death of a lover.

In all the grief counseling I do—and, because of AIDS, it's been quite a lot—I find that the people who have the most difficult times are those who did not discuss death with their partners. Losing a lover with whom you have not been able to talk openly about death leaves many wounds that can take a long time to heal.

It is essential in committed relationships to overcome the emotional pain of discussing death. Make your wishes known to each other, and draw up a will. Not doing this can mean forcing your partner to make difficult decisions at a time when his or her grief will likely be overwhelming.

It is equally important to prepare yourself to be a survivor. The primary issue in this preparation is to make sure that you are not so dependent on your lover that you would not be able to live on your own, if need be. Do you have the personal strength and friendships you'd need as the basis for building a new life? Closeness and sharing between life partners are desirable, but helpless dependency will only make the trauma of death even more difficult.

Imagining your partner's death and thinking about what you would do are actually healthy. I occasionally have gay and lesbian clients come to me feeling guilty because they have fantasized or dreamed about the death of a lover. Having such thoughts and dreams does *not* mean that you wish your spouse were dead; rather, these fantasies serve as a way for you to reassure yourself that you could survive alone if you had to. While it is admittedly painful, exploring your dreams and thoughts can help you to prepare to handle your partner's death.

Discussions about death, especially following the death of a friend or family member, are also important in your preparation. In the midst of grief, we are often more willing to be honest and open about our own wishes for burial and about our concerns for our partner's well-being after we are gone. If you attend a funeral or wake, don't shy away from having such discussions.

When you and your partner feel complete in your lives and in harmony with your friends and families, you can acknowledge death as an aspect of life. This attitude will allow you to peacefully prepare for the inevitable. When a death occurs in a relationship where this attitude has been present, there is a sense of miracle and release that the survivors can carry away as inspiration for their own lives.

Handling Grief

Many of the clients who come to me following the death of a spouse are afraid to grieve. Some say, "I'm afraid if I start crying, I won't be able to stop." The truth is that crying will help you and that you *will* stop, naturally. Repressing your grief blocks the emotional release your mind and body need to begin the healing process. If you are suffering a loss, allow yourself to cry as often and for as long as you need to.

The following thoughts about grief can help:

- Grief means that you loved someone. You will grieve in proportion to the importance of that person in your life.
- Grieving takes time, and it happens naturally over time. There is no way to rush it.
- Grief is a combination of feelings: sadness, loss, abandonment, anger, rage, relief, love, helplessness, acceptance, and release.
- Grief is healthy, even if it makes others uncomfortable.
- Grief is organic; it fades gradually. Recognize that the first year is the hardest.
- Allowing yourself to grieve fully will help you to gain greater self-awareness and to feel closer to yourself.
- Expressing your grief helps you to achieve closure.
- Don't be afraid to accept support or to ask for it. You may also want to seek guidance from a professional counselor.

"HAPPILY EVER AFTER" REDEFINED

Many of my gay and lesbian clients are surprised to discover that their relationships improve over the years. Problems that might once have seemed unsolvable are seen as welcome challenges; conflicts disappear or are resolved through negotiation. Intimacy and romance replace struggle and routine.

Those who do the necessary work to create healthy long-term relationships tell me that they gain many things. Among these are:

- an enhanced sense of self-esteem
- pride in being gay or lesbian
- faith in love
- joy in living one's life fully
- better communication skills
- an understanding of true unconditional love
- an improved sense of responsibility

- a sense of humor
- fond memories

The information in this book is just a beginning for gay and lesbian couples. There is no end to the growing and learning you can accomplish in your relationship. How "happily ever after" you live is your choice. I wish you great joy in your life, in your gay or lesbian lifestyle, and in your love.

The following poem, by an unknown author, has been an inspiration to me as well as to my clients. Perhaps it will help you in your journey toward "happily ever after," too.

Together

Every moment that we are together,
I am learning something,
and that knowledge becomes a permanent part of me.

Though my feelings will be different a year from now,
or ten years from now, part of the difference is you.

Because of you, I am a different person,
and the person I will grow to become
will have gotten there partly because of you.

If you were not in my life right now,
I could not be who I am right now,
nor would I be growing in exactly the same way.

I do not worry about our future together,
since we have already touched each other
and affected each other's lives on so many levels
that we can never be totally removed from one another.

A part of me will always be with you,
and a part of you will always be with me.
That much is certain, no matter what else happens.

Appendix A: Resources for Support and Legal Advice

Gay and lesbian relationships are not recognized by law, and many states and counties still have laws on the books that make various homosexual activities illegal. These conditions can affect you

- *on an emotional level:* You and your lover will need to deal with your emotional reactions to both homophobia and prejudice and to inequities under the law, such as the lack of legal recognition of your committed relationship.
- *on a legal level:* You need to know what your rights are and what possible consequences you might face for your actions.
- *with regard to your behavior:* Simple things such as holding hands, dancing together, or kissing in public can become very problematic, depending on the laws of your state, county, or community.
- *in your relationship with your family:* Parents or siblings who can be very understanding about your lifestyle and your relationship may find legal difficulties hard to accept. On the other hand, family members who have trouble accepting your lifestyle may rally to your cause in legal matters.
- *in your relationship with your lover:* If one partner must call the other from jail in the middle of the night, often a great deal of stress is created in the relationship. Whether or not you are innocent, your mate will be shocked and possibly suspicious if you're arrested. In addition to the facts,

frank, open discussion about feelings on both sides is needed. If you are unable to resolve the issues, professional counseling is essential. Otherwise you and your partner—like many of my clients—may find yourselves discussing your feelings of betrayal and anger in a lawyer's office. This is not only a sad situation, but a very expensive way to fight. Lily, a client who came to me for help after her relationship ended, says,

> After I was arrested, it was never the same at home. Pam was so angry! I didn't know what to do. I guess the relationship just couldn't stand the stress. We broke up as soon as my court case ended. I have to hand it to Pam, though—she did hang in there until I was okay. Still, I wish I had thought of getting relationship counseling while it was all going on. I was so scared that all I thought about was lawyers until it was too late.

Because gay and lesbian relationships are more likely to have to face legal issues than heterosexual marriages are, it makes sense to be prepared. It's important to be informed about the laws in your state, county, and city and to have a lawyer you can trust. Consider introducing yourself to an attorney who volunteers time at your local gay community center, so you'll have the reassurance of knowing an attorney experienced in homosexual legal issues *before* anything happens.

At my request, Los Angeles attorney Shelly M. Mandell asked several of her colleagues to list common mistakes made by clients who have been unexpectedly arrested or taken in for questioning. Based on their answers, I offer the following advice in the event that you come into contact with law-enforcement authorities:

Most gay and lesbian people consider themselves to be law-abiding citizens, and so they often believe that any situation can be resolved through reasonable discussion and full sharing of information. However, whether you are homosexual or straight, this thinking can create trouble for you if you are stopped or detained by police. The attorneys polled reported that clients who had given full statements to the police prior to speaking with their lawyers gave one or more of the following reasons for having done so:

1. They felt that anything less than full disclosure would make the officers think they were guilty or had something to hide.
2. They thought that if they didn't give a full statement, the police officers would be angry and would make things worse for them.
3. They believed that they were legally required to answer all questions and would get in trouble if they did not make a full confession.
4. They felt that giving a full explanation was the moral and proper thing for a citizen to do.

Many people who have made statements to police based on such reasoning have later had their words used against them in court to convict them of crimes they did not commit. Attorneys agree on the following guidelines (check with your own attorney about the specific laws of your state or county):

- The *only* information you are required to give a police officer if you are arrested or read your rights is your name and address. Your next statement should be that you want to call your attorney.
- Usually, you are allowed one or two *completed* phone calls. It is suggested that you use the first to call a lawyer, and the second to call family, friends, or a bail bondsman. If you are out of your home state, you can either call your own lawyer (probably collect) and have him or her make the necessary arrangements, or you can call a local county or state bar attorney-referral service (most major cities have these) and ask for the name of an attorney who specializes in criminal law. *Check with the police officer to make sure that a call made to a referral service will not use up your only call.* If it will, and if you know someone in the area, use the call to contact that person and have him or her call the referral service and the attorney for you. Otherwise, use the State Bar referral service or ask for an attorney to be appointed to you.
- While the details of criminal procedure vary from state to state, the U.S. Constitution guarantees a person the right to have an attorney present at every critical stage of criminal

proceedings. Questioning by police officers is considered to be a very critical stage. If you do not have the funds for a private attorney, you are entitled to request a public defender.

- If you or your lover has full or part-time custody of minor children, speak with an attorney to be sure that you do not unwittingly open yourself up to any possible accusations. If an ex-spouse harbors ill feelings about the breakup or about your lifestyle, or if he or she sometimes misinterprets things the children say, *be especially careful.* Once you are informed about the laws in your state, there is no reason why you can't have a wonderful and full relationship with your children or your partner's children.
- If you wish to commit civil disobedience as a formal protest for gay rights, do it within the context of an organized group that can help you to make an effective statement and that has the resources to help you handle any legal issues.
- It is possible for you to be arrested without actually breaking the law. This is called entrapment, and several of my gay male clients have experienced it. One such client, Greg, described his experience this way:

> I was in a public rest room, and I went into a stall and closed the door. There was some commotion in the bathroom. I didn't know exactly what was happening, but when I came out, there were two cops there who said I'd been masturbating and arrested me.
>
> In the first place, I wasn't—but even if I were, they wouldn't have known, because the door to my stall was closed. But they arrested everyone in the bathroom, and I had to go to court. It was my word against theirs. My lawyer suggested that I take a reduced fine for "disturbing the peace" and not risk getting a sexual-offender conviction, so I did. But I'm still not sure I should have.

Men in "gay areas" of town are often harassed and questioned without cause. Arrests are commonplace among the gay male population and are becoming more frequent among the lesbian population. It's smart to be informed about the law.

Resources

PERSONAL AND RELATIONSHIP DEVELOPMENT

Newsletters

Partners: The Newsletter for Gay & Lesbian Couples (Box 9685, Seattle, WA 98109).

Books

Berzon, Betty. *Positively Gay.* Los Angeles: Mediamix, 1979.

Bradshaw, John. *Bradshaw On: The Family—A Revolutionary Way of Self-Discovery.* Deerfield Beach, Fla.: Health Communications, 1988.

Clark, Don. *Loving Someone Gay.* New York: Signet, 1977.

Cowan, Thomas. *Gay Men and Women Who Enriched the World.* Chicago: Mulvey, 1989.

Keyes, Ken. *A Conscious Person's Guide to Relationships.* Coos Bay, Ore.: Cornucopia Books, 1979.

Perry, Troy. *The Lord Is My Shepherd and He Knows I'm Gay.* Los Angeles: Nash.

Roberts, Denton I., with Frances Thronson. *Able and Equal: A Gentle Path to Peace.* Culver City, Calif.: Human Esteem Publishing, 1984.

Smith, Riley K., and Tina B. Tessina. *How to Be a Couple and Still Be Free.* North Hollywood, Calif.: Newcastle, 1980.

Tessina, Tina B. *Lovestyles: How to Celebrate Your Differences.* North Hollywood, Calif.: Newcastle, 1987.

Woods, Richard. *Another Kind of Love.* Fort Wayne, Ind.: Knoll, 1988.

Gay book catalogs are available from these bookstores:

A Different Light (4014 Santa Monica Blvd., Los Angeles, CA 90029)

Lambda Rising (1724 20th Street, N.W., Washington, D.C. 20009)

Oscar Wilde Memorial Bookshop (15 Christopher Street, New York, NY 10014)

Giovanni's Room (1426 Spruce Street, Philadelphia, PA 19102)

Organizations

Couples National Network, Inc. (Box 813212, Smyrna, GA 30081; 404/333-0937)

Federation of Parents and Friends of Lesbians and Gays (Parents' FLAG) (Box 24565, Los Angeles, CA 90024; 213/472-8952)

National Association of Black and White Men Together (584 Castro Street, San Francisco, CA 94114; 414/431-1976)

A current listing of gay and lesbian organizations in the United States can be obtained from the National Gay Task Force, 80 Fifth Avenue, New York, NY 10011; 212/741-5800.
Also see:

The Gay Yellow Pages (Renaissance House, Box 292, Village Station, New York, NY 10014)

GENERAL LEGAL ASSISTANCE

Books

Clair, Bernard F., and Anthony R. Daniele. *Love Pact: A Layman's Complete Guide to Legal Living-Together Agreements.* Houston: Grove Press, 1980.

Curry, Hayden, and Denis Clifford. *A Legal Guide for Lesbian and Gay Couples.* Berkeley, Calif.: Nolo Press, 1986.

Gay Rights Organizations

American Civil Liberties Union, Lesbian and Gay Rights Project (132 West 43rd Street, New York, NY 10036; 212/944-9800)

Center for Personal Rights Advocacy (Thomas F. Coleman, Attorney, Box 65756, Los Angeles, CA 90065)

National Gay Rights Advocates (540 Castro Street, San Francisco, CA 94114; 415/863-3624)

Couples' Rights Information

Domestic Partnership Committee, Mayor's Lesbian and Gay Task Force (Office for Women's Rights, 400 Yesler Building, 5th Floor, Seattle, WA 98104)

GAY PARENTING

Books

Pies, Cheri. *Considering Parenthood: A Handbook for Lesbians.* San Francisco, Calif.: Spinsters/Aunt Lute Book Co., 1985.

Schulenburg, Joy. *Gay Parenting.* Garden City, N.Y.: Anchor Press/Doubleday, 1985.

ORGANIZATIONS

Gay and Lesbian Parents' Coalition (Box 50360, Washington, D.C. 20004-0360; 703/548-3238)

Legal Help on Parenting

Custody Action for Lesbian Mothers (CALM) (Box 281, Narberth, PA 19072; 215/667-7508)

Lesbian Mothers' National Defense Fund (Box 21567, Seattle, WA 98111; 206/325-2643)

Lesbian Rights Project, Adoption and Foster Parenting Program (1370 Mission Street, 4th Floor, San Francisco, CA 94103; 415/621-0674) (also serves gay men)

ADDICTION AND VIOLENCE

Books

Beattie, Melody. *Codependent No More: How to Stop Controlling Others and Start Caring for Yourself.* New York: Harper/Hazelden, 1987.

Cermak, Timmen L. *A Time to Heal: The Road to Recovery for Adult Children of Alcoholics.* Los Angeles: Jeremy P. Tarcher, Inc., 1988.

Johnson Institute. *Intervention: How to Help Someone Who Doesn't Want Help.* Minneapolis: Johnson Institute Books, 1986.

Sonkin, Daniel Jay, and Michael Durphy. *Learning to Live without Violence: A Handbook for Men.* San Francisco, Calif.: Volcano, 1982. (heterosexually oriented, but good information and exercises)

Organizations

Al-Anon Family Groups (P.O. Box 182, Madison Square Station, New York, NY 10159)

Alcoholics Anonymous World Services, Inc. (468 Park Avenue South, New York, NY 10016)

Narcotics Anonymous World Service Office (P.O. Box 9999, Van Nuys, CA 91409; 818/780-3951)

National Association of Children of Alcoholics (31582 Coast Highway, Suite B, South Laguna, CA 92677-3044; 714/499-3889)

National Association of Lesbian/Gay Alcoholism Professionals (NALGAP) (So. Calif. Chapter, Jean Reynolds, M.F.C.C., 9033 Wilshire Blvd. #406, Beverly Hills, CA 90211)

You can find listings for local chapters of these organizations in your phone book, or write to the above addresses.

AIDS AND ILLNESS

Books

Living with AIDS: A Self-Care Manual. Los Angeles: AIDS Project/Los Angeles, Inc., 1986.

Moffatt, Betty Clare. *When Someone You Love Has AIDS: A Book of Hope for Family and Friends.* New York: NAI/Penguin, 1986.

Segal, Jeanne. *Living beyond Fear: A Tool for Transformation.* North Hollywood, Calif.: Newcastle, 1984.

Organizations

AIDS Project/Los Angeles, Inc. (7362 Santa Monica Blvd., Los Angeles, CA 90046; 213/876-8951)

Shanti Foundation (6855 Santa Monica Blvd., Suite 408, Los Angeles, CA 90038; 213/962-8197)

Appendix B: Safe-Sex Information

Even though we've all been aware of AIDS for several years now, and most gay people are well informed about safe-sex practices, I'm going to list the guidelines yet again—it is, after all, a life-and-death issue.

Safe-sex practices are also effective against other sexually transmitted diseases (STDs). Although lesbians are at a lower risk of contracting AIDS than are gay men, they are as likely to contract gonorrhea, syphilis, herpes, chlamydia, and condyloma. Although these STDs are more treatable than AIDS, many researchers believe that a person with recurring exposure to them has an increased vulnerability to AIDS.

Appearing in a television special called "AIDS: A Town Meeting," playwright Harvey Fierstein made the point that being gay and promiscuous created little risk of AIDS, *if* one's sexual activity were limited to mutual masturbation. How true that is, and how courageous of him to say it on national TV! In the midst of this current crisis, being gay or bisexual suddenly feels dangerous. Actually, it's homophobic to believe that one gets diseases *because* one is gay or lesbian. Further, the fear of the disease can itself be dangerous, because it can lead to hopelessness and failure to take preventive measures. The guidelines in Appendix C ("Advice for Dealing with Homophobia") can help you to overcome the fear and, consequently, to think more clearly, which makes taking simple precautions much easier.

PRACTICING SAFE SEX

You have many more options than you may think you have. Many gay people have been enjoying open, active sex lives for years without ever contracting any major sexually transmitted diseases. Safe practices make the difference.

AIDS is contracted through blood/blood or semen/blood contact. Venereal warts are contracted through coming into contact with someone's existing warts. Herpes is contracted through contact with an open herpes sore on a partner's mouth or genitals. Because certain other diseases can possibly be passed through the contact of semen or blood with mucous membranes, such exchange and/or contact should be avoided.

Mutual masturbation, hugging, stroking, massage, erotic talk, role-playing, and other sexual activities that do not involve the above exchanges are quite safe. There is a lot of choice available to all of us, regardless of preference, and being creative makes staying healthy fun. Trying new ways to have sex can actually be more fun than following the old, familiar ways. Here are some guidelines for smart sex:

- Since your sex practices are more limited, create more options. For example, try out all your unused fantasies (see chapter 5). Use costumes, props, and toys. Learn sensual massage, and use touch more often.
- Keep your immune system healthy. Because stress has been implicated in weakening the immune system, try to reduce stress as much as possible (note that laughter and play have been shown to be effective in reducing stress and promoting healing). Get sufficient rest, exercise, and nourishment. Giving up smoking, alcohol, and drugs may be the most important health steps you can take. Don't take antibiotics without full medical supervision; let your doctor know that you're worried about the immunosuppression effects, and ask about alternatives.
- If you don't have a monogamous agreement with your lover, or you're not sure of your partner's practices, limit your activities to what is safe (this will reduce both your stress and your chances of exposure). If your partner is a user, be extra careful.
- Know whom you're dealing with. Before becoming sexually involved with someone, take the time to talk and ask questions. Be sure, too, that you really *look* at your partner's body and lifestyle.

Special Advice for Gay Men and Bisexual Women

Have you learned to use condoms effectively? Your local gay community center has knowledgeable people who can tell you how to do this (so do Planned Parenthood and your county's department of health). While condoms do not provide 100 percent safety against disease, they do reduce the risks substantially. If you're taking any risks (anal or vaginal sex with a nonmonogamous partner, or oral sex, especially with ejaculation), *use condoms.* (If you don't feel skilled at using them, practice by putting condoms on a peeled banana!)

Special Advice for Gay Men Only

Parks, baths, and "tea rooms " (public bathrooms) have long been used by gay men as places to meet others for casual, anonymous sex. Although the atmosphere has changed considerably since the gay community became aware of AIDS, all of these options still make casual, anonymous sex freely available. Therefore, I feel that a discussion of the risks involved is important.

Sex with unknown partners is risky because of the possibility of contracting not only AIDS but also other STDs, infections, and parasites. In addition, cruising at parks, beaches, and public bathrooms is especially risky, as there is the ever-present danger of being arrested by a plainclothes policeman simply for being in a suspicious location (see Appendix A). Arrest is embarrassing, possibly physically dangerous, and expensive, and it can endanger your career. While many people are excited by the danger of clandestine sex, risking arrest or disease is more than exciting—it's irrational. If you are risking your livelihood, your health, or your life, I strongly urge you to get therapy or to attend meetings of the Sexual Compulsives Anonymous organization (see your phone book for listings of local chapters).

You are not as likely to be mugged or arrested at the baths as you are in a park or public bathroom. At the baths—spa-like, men-only clubs that are open all night—the main issue is safe sex. Until recently, bathhouses were numerous and unsupervised. Since the onset of AIDS, however, many bathhouses have closed, and others now offer safe-sex education and free condoms and have rules against anal intercourse. Some allow masturbation only. I have heard many men talk fondly of the baths as places to relax and to be with other gay men. As long as you follow safe-sex practices, there's no reason to give up the baths completely.

Following are some rules for safe cruising at parks and beaches:

- Stay in your car; do not walk around or use the bathrooms (muggers and vice-squad officers abound in known cruising areas).
- If you see someone who looks interesting, stop and talk—but stay in your car. If you don't connect, or if you feel suspicious, say a cheerful "good night" and move on. If the initial talk goes well and you feel good about the other person, invite him into your car (keeping an eye out for police) or to a restaurant for coffee.
- Talk openly about safe sex, AIDS, and general responsibility. Be very clear about what you expect, and be willing to go home without "scoring."

While the guidelines in this appendix do not, of course, offer perfect safety, they can help you to reduce your risk. The choices are up to you.

Appendix C: Advice for Dealing with Homophobia

As I discussed in the introduction, homophobia is an offshoot of xenophobia, which is an exaggerated fear of anything different. As long as homosexuality is seen as being "strange" or "different" by portions of the society, we will encounter homophobia.

There are two major types of homophobia that gay and lesbian people need to confront: external and internal. External homophobia is the fear that others have about homosexuals. This fear is sometimes attached to latent homosexual tendencies or to the fear of becoming homosexual. Internal homophobia is one's own fear of being homosexual. It's the fear that you can't have a healthy, happy, productive life if you're gay. It may be an issue for you or for a friend or lover, and it frequently gets in the way of successful relationships.

EXTERNAL HOMOPHOBIA

Like xenophobia, homophobia results from ignorance and is based on frightening fantasies. Homophobic people often don't believe that they personally know anyone who is gay, since their idea of a homosexual person is usually very exaggerated. The most effective cure for homophobia is education. As homophobic people get to know more about homosexual people and lifestyles and begin to see that gay men and lesbian women are ordinary people, and that straights are not in danger of being "attacked" or "converted," their fear fades. One reason that gay educators and gay political groups encourage us to come out is that publicity about successful homosexuals educates the general public and helps dispel such fears.

Following are some suggestions to help you in dealing with external homophobia:

- If you encounter a hostile, homophobic person at work, among your social circle, or within your own family, keep in mind that the hostility usually masks fear.
- Do what you can to find out what the person's misconceptions are and to reassure him or her. Ask sincere questions, such as these: "What upsets you about homosexuality?" "Have you ever known anyone who was homosexual?" Don't try to argue with someone who is homophobic; becoming defensive and angry doesn't work and will only have a negative effect. You'll get a lot farther by being open, relaxed, and secure—a reassuring example of a gay person—than by trying to change the other person's mind.
- If you must deal with a lot of external homophobia, it's very important that you have a strong support network (see chapter 8).
- If you are still closeted, reread chapter 8 for information and advice on coming out. Even if you don't think that coming out is right for you, find out what your options are, perhaps by taking a workshop that deals with this issue.

INTERNAL HOMOPHOBIA

Internal homophobia is much more subtle than external homophobia. Even among gay people who feel they have overcome their homophobic fears, unresolved issues can sometimes pop up unexpectedly. If you find yourself feeling irrationally guilty, angry, or uneasy about your own or your partner's behavior, internal homophobia may be operating.

Homophobia-related relationship problems are often handled quite simply, especially if you keep in mind that neither you nor your lover is to blame for homophobic issues. It is society that creates the problem. *Do not blame each other for closet issues!* Be gentle with yourselves and with each other. Learn to talk openly about homophobic issues, and treat them as problems that the two of you need to solve together.

To help yourself deal with internal homophobia, ask yourself the following questions (you may want to write down your answers):

1. *What is the problem?* While this question may sound simplistic, if you're upset, you may not be thinking clearly, and so you may not be seeing the issue clearly. Are you having trouble with sex because you feel it's "wrong"? Are you afraid that your relationship can't succeed because "gay relationships don't work"? Think it through, so that when you present the issue to your lover you'll be understood.
2. *What do I wish would happen?* Don't censor yourself here or try to be practical—this is a time to be totally honest with yourself about your gut-level feelings and fantasies however "crazy" they may seem to you. For instance:

   I wish I were straight.
   I wish I could take you to the office party as my lover and spouse.
   I wish we lived in the magical land of Darkover, where we could join the lesbian Sisterhood, and our love would be accepted.
   I wish I could believe that God loves me even though I'm gay—and even *because* I'm gay.

3. *What am I afraid will happen?* This is the category for "horror stories": here, write down all of your worst fears about being gay—for example, that your boss will find out you're gay and fire you, or that you'll be run out of town on a rail. Again, don't consider whether it makes sense or could really happen; just acknowledge your fears as they are. For example:

   I'm afraid I'll go to hell when I die.
   I'm afraid my straight friends would never speak to me again if they found out I was gay.
   I'm afraid I'll never have anything but short, painful relationships because I'm gay.

4. *What solutions have I considered?* This is where possibility and rational thinking come in. You don't have to have a final solution on your list, or even one you like yet. Just record what you have already considered. For instance:

   I could take a straight "date" with me to the office party.
   I could find a gay minister who would reexplain sin to me.
   I could join a coming-out support group to help me understand my feelings about being gay.

Share your answers to the above questions with your partner. Ask your lover if she or he would like to answer the same questions and then discuss the answers with you. If the issue is very difficult or complex, you may want to discuss it with an uninvolved, objective friend or a counselor. Talking honestly with others about your homophobia-related problems will help you to put them into perspective; just knowing that other people have had the same feelings of fear and confusion can help a great deal.

When you and your partner are willing to have open discussions about homophobic issues and to work together to solve the problems they may cause, you're on your way to finding real resolution of these issues in your lives.